Internet and Computer Slang Dictionary

First Edition

James Kittell II

Reviewed and edited by Kevin Anderson and All Ivy Writing
Services, Inc.—http://www.aiwriting.com

Copyright ©2012 James S. Kittell II
All rights reserved.
ISBN-10: 1468013211
ISBN-13: 9781468013214
Library of Congress Control Number: 2011961945
CreateSpace, North Charleston, South Carolina

UPPERCASE	LOWERCASE	MEANING
!	!	I have a comment.
#	#	twitter hashtag, number
#1	#1	number one
#·o	#·o	Duh!
$#!+	$#!+	shit
$$	$$	money
$_$	$_$	has money, greedy
$H!T	$h!t	shit
$XY	$xy	sexy
%)	%)	drunk, giddy
(!)	(!)	sarcasm
(&)	(&)	dog face (MSN)
()	()	football
(*)	(*)	star (MSN)
(*V*)	(*v*)	bird
(.V.)	(.v.)	alien
(:	(:	happy
(·:	(·:	left-handed smiley face
(:|	(:|	tired
(@)	(@)	cat face (MSN)
(^)	(^)	birthday cake (MSN)
(^^^)	(^^^)	shark
(_8^(I)	(_8^(i)	Homer Simpson
({)	({)	left hug (MSN)
(||)	(||)	bowl (MSN)
(})	(})	right hug (MSN)
(·)(·)	(·)(·)	kissing
(~)	(~)	filmstrip (MSN)
(A)	(a)	angel (MSN)
(ap)	(ap)	airplane (MSN)
(AU)	(au)	auto (MSN)
(B)	(b)	beer mug (MSN)
(bah)	(bah)	black sheep (MSN)
(C)	(c)	coffee cup (MSN)
(CO)	(co)	computer (MSN)
(D)	(d)	martini glass (MSN)
(E)	(e)	e-mail (MSN)
(F)	(f)	red rose (MSN)
(G)	(g)	gift with a bow (MSN)
(H)	(h)	cool dude emoticon (MSN)
(I)	(i)	light bulb (MSN)
(IP)	(ip)	island with a palm tree (MSN)

UPPERCASE	LOWERCASE	MEANING
(K)	(k)	kiss (MSN)
(L)	(l)	love heart (MSN)
(LI)	(li)	lightning (MSN)
(M)	(m)	MSN messenger icon (MSN)
(MO)	(mo)	money (MSN)
(MP)	(mp)	mobile phone (MSN)
(N)	(n)	thumbs-down (MSN)
(O)	(o)	clock (MSN)
(P)	(p)	camera (MSN)
(PI)	(pi)	pizza (MSN)
(PL)	(pl)	plate (MSN)
(S)	(s)	seriously
(S)	(s)	sleeping half-moon (MSN)
(SN)	(sn)	snail (MSN)
(SO)	(so)	soccer ball (MSN)
(ST)	(st)	stormy cloud (MSN)
(T)	(t)	telephone receiver (MSN)
(U)	(u)	heartbroken (MSN)
(UM)	(um)	umbrella (MSN)
(W)	(w)	wilted rose (MSN)
(X)	(x)	girl (MSN)
(Y)	(y)	thumbs-up (MSN)
(YN)	(yn)	fingers crossed (MSN)
(Z)	(z)	boy (MSN)
)-:	)-:	left-handed sad face
*	*	indicating a spelling correction
*$	*$	Starbucks
*$$	*$$	Starbucks
*-)	*-)	thinking (MSN)
*)	*)	wink
*-)	*-)	wink
.	*.*	dazed
**==	**==	United States flag
.	*.*	every file on a computer
_	*_*	in love, dazed
*<:-)	*<:-)	clown
*<:o)	*<:o)	clown
*4U	*4u	kiss for you
*67	*67	unknown
EG	*eg*	evil grin
G	*g*	grin
O	*o*	confused, surprised, shocked

UPPERCASE	LOWERCASE	MEANING
S	*s*	salute
S	*s*	smile
* TREK	* trek	*Star Trek*
W	*w*	wink
* WARS	* wars	*Star Wars*
,!!!!	,!!!!	talk to the hand
·.·	·.·	annoyance
.·.	.·.	sad, unhappy
.02	.02	my (or your) two cents worth
.CO	.co	alternative to .com
.COM	.com	top-level domain for commerce
.EDU	.edu	top-level domain for education
.GOV	.gov	top-level domain for governments
.MIL	.mil	top-level domain for the military
.NET	.net	top-level domain originally for network providers
.ORG	.org	top-level domain for nonprofit organizations
/.	/.	slashdot
//	//	love, I love you
//_^	//_^	Emo
/B/	/b/	4chan's random image board
/O/	/o/	happy, arms in the air
/O\	/o\	frustrated, hands on head
/R/	/r/	requesting
/S	/s	sarcasm
/THREAD	/thread	end of a thread on a forum
/W	/w	whisper
:#	:#	sealed lips, embarrassed
:-#	:-#	don't tell anyone (MSN)
:$	:$	embarrassed (MSN)
:-$	:-$	embarrassed (MSN)
:&	:&	tongue-tied, speechless
:-&	:-&	tongue-tied
:(	:(	unhappy, sad, frown
:'(	:'(	crying
:-(	:-(	sad, frown
:(:)	:(:)	pig
:(|)	:(|)	monkey
:)	:)	happy
:')	:')	crying with joy
:-)	:-)	smile
:-)(-:	:-)(-:	married
:-)*	:-)*	kiss me

UPPERCASE	LOWERCASE	MEANING
:)~	:)~	drooling
:-)>....	:-)>....	drooling
:)BOOK	:)book	Facebook
:*	:*	kiss
:-*	:-*	secret telling (MSN)
:*)	:*)	drunk
:/	:/	sarcasm
:-/	:-/	perplexed
::POOF::	::poof::	I'm gone
:?	:?	confused
:@	:@	angry
:-@	:-@	screaming
:[	:[	sad, frown
:[	:[	vampire bat (MSN)
:-[	:-[	sad, frown, vampire bat (MSN)
:-\	:-\	undecided
:]	:]	happy
:^)	:^)	happy
:_(	:_(	crying
:{	:{	sad, frown
:()	:()	happy with a moustache
:|	:|	disgust, disapproval, not funny
:-|	:-|	disgust, disapproval, not funny
:}	:}	sticking tongue out, happy
:<	:<	sad, frown
:-<	:-<	sad, frown
:>	:>	mischievous smile, happy
:->	:->	grin
:0	:0	surprised, shocked
:3	:3	cute/goofy face
:-7	:-7	sarcastic
:9	:9	yum, licking
:B	:b	buckteeth
:-B		nerd
:C	:c	very sad
:-C	:-c	very sad
:C)	:c)	happy
:D		happy, laughing, big grin
:-D		open-mouthed (MSN)
:DD	:DD	very happy
:-E		vampire
:F	:f	drooling

UPPERCASE	LOWERCASE	MEANING
:J	:j	smirk
:·J	:·J	tongue in cheek
:K	:k	vampire teeth, snake's tongue
:L	:l	laughing
:O	:o	surprised
:·O	:·o	shocked
:O)	:o)	clown nose smiley face
:O3	:o3	dog
:P	:p	tongue out (MSN)
:Q	:q	smoking
:·Q		smoking
:S	:s	confused
:·S		confused
:T	:t	side smile
:X	:x	zipped lips
:·X		zipped lips
;(	;(	crying
;·)	;·)	wink
;)	;)	wink
;*(	;*(	crying
;]	;]	wink
;·]	;·]	wink
;D	;d	wink
;O	;o	joking
;P	;p	winking and sticking tongue out
?	?	I have a question.
?	?	What?
?	?	I don't understand what you mean.
??	??	What?
?^	?^	Hook up? What's up?
?_?	?_?	confused, lost
?4U	?4u	question for you
?U@	?u@	Where are you?
?UP	?up	What's up?
@	@	at
@$$	@$$	ass
@$$ #013	@$$ #013	asshole
@$$HOLE	@$$hole	asshole
@@@	@@@	warning of parents nearby
@_@	@_@	hypnotized, dazed
@}···>····	@}···>····	a rose
@~)~~~~	@~)~~~~	a rose

UPPERCASE	LOWERCASE	MEANING
@BBIE	@bbie	Abbie (Jewish male · ethnic slur/derogatory)
@BBO	@bbo	Abbo (Australian Aboriginal person · ethnic slur/derogatory)
@BE	@be	Abe (Jewish male · ethnic slur/derogatory)
@BIE	@bie	Abie (Jewish male · ethnic slur/derogatory)
@BO	@bo	Abbo (Australian Aboriginal person · ethnic slur/derogatory)
@H	@h	asshole
@PE	@pe	Ape (African American person · ethnic slur/derogatory)
@TEOTD	@teotd	at the end of the day
\%%%/	\%%%/	queen
\&&&/	\&&&/	princess
\,,/	\,,/	Rock on.
\\//	\\//	peace, Vulcan salute
\M/	\m/	horns, rock on
\O	\o	waving
\O/	\o/	happy, arms in the air
\VVV/	\VVV/	king
^	^	up
^.^	^.^	happy
^.~	^.~	wink
^^	^^	happy, read line or "message above"
^^&>	^^&>	up, up, and away
^^^	^^^	reference to line above
^_^	^_^	happiness, satisfied, overjoyed
^10	^10	high ten
^5	^5	high five
^o)	^o)	sarcastic (MSN)
^O^	^o^	hurrah
^RUP^	^rup^	read up, please
^URS	^urs	up yours
^W^	^w^	happy
·_·	·_·	annoyed, tired
	_n|m	fuck you (right hand)
	_n|m m|n_	fuck you (both hands)
{ }	{ }	hug
|-)	|·)	sleepy (MSN)
|_P	|_P	cup of coffee
|·O	|·O	yawn
|O|	|o|	same as LOL
}:-)	}:·)	devilish smile
~,~	~,~	napping
~:0	~:0	baby

UPPERCASE	LOWERCASE	MEANING
+_+	+_+	dead man
+REP	+rep	boost reputation on Xbox live
<#	<#	misspelling of
<.<	<.<	frown
</3	</3	brokenhearted
<:3)~	<:3)~	mouse
<:O)	<:o)	party (MSN)
<_<	<_<	sarcasm, look left
<>	<>	not equal, no comment
<><	<><	fish
<2	<2	not quite love
<3	<3	love (heart shape)
<333	<333	multiple hearts
<3U	<3u	love you
<4	<4	more than love
<B	<b	hate
<G>	<g>	grin
<l:0		partying
<PENIS	<penis	big penis
=(	=(	sad
=)	=)	happy
=.=	=.=	tired
=/	=/	mad
=/=	=/=	not equal to
=[	=[	sad
=]	=]	happy
=^.^=	=^.^=	cat
=+o()	=+o()	sick (MSN)
=8)	=8)	pig
=D		happy, laughing, big grin
=·D		laughing, big grin
=F		vampire, drooling
=I		indifference
=O	=o	shocked
=·O	=·o	uh-oh
=P		sticking tongue out
=S		confused
=W=	=w=	*Weezer* (band)
=X		no comment
>,<	>,<	angry, annoyed
>.<	>.<	frustrated, angry, upset, in pain
>.>	>.>	suspicious, wary

UPPERCASE	LOWERCASE	MEANING
>//<	>//<	embarrassed, blushing
>:(	>:(	angry
>:·)	>:·)	devilish smile
>:)	>:)	devilish smile
>:[	>:[	frown
>:]	>:]	happy
>:D		laughing, big grin
>:D<	>:d<	hug
>:O	>:o	angry
>:X		sealed lips, embarrassed
>;)	>;)	devilish smile
>;]	>;]	wink
>_<	>_<	frustrated
>_>	>_>	looking left, shifty look
><	><	frustration
>3	>3	evil but happy, hate (opposite of love)
>B]		shades
>O<	>o<	yelling
>PENIS	>penis	small penis
·8	·8	musical note (MSN)
·6	·6	devil (MSN)
0	0	surprised, shocked
1	1	one, won, partner
2	2	to, too
3	3	Cute, goofy face, the letter *e*
4	4	for
5	5	LOL (5=101 in binary)
8	8	ate, hate, oral sex
8	8	oral sex
9	9	parent is watching
10	10	perfect-looking woman
11	11	one louder than ten
12	12	Forever, the police
20	20	location
22	22	a .22 caliber handgun
39	39	thank you
44	44	.44 magnum
46	46	money for sex
50	50	police (from *Hawaii Five-0*)
72	72	seventy-two hours, three days
73	73	best regards (amateur radio)
81	81	Hells Angels (h=8th letter of alphabet, a=1st letter of alphabet)

UPPERCASE	LOWERCASE	MEANING
86	86	over, get rid of something
88	88	bye-bye (Mandarin Chinese), hail Hitler (*h* is 8th letter), hugs and kisses
93	93	rough suburb of Paris
99	99	parent stopped watching, parent has left
101	101	basic introduction
111	111	excited
112	112	European emergency number
120	120	LOL! (101! = 5! = 120)
121	121	one-to-one (private chat initiation)
123	123	I agree
143	143	I love you. (letters in each word)
153	153	I adore you. (letters in each word)
180	180	turn around, 180 degrees
182	182	I hate you.
187	187	police code for murder or death
211	211	police code for robbery
220	220	second to none
224	224	today, tomorrow, forever
241	241	two for one
250	250	stupid person (Chinese)
304	304	hoe
313	313	area code for Detroit
333	333	half evil
360	360	complete circle
360	360	Xbox 360
381	381	I love you. (3 words, 8 letters, 1 meaning)
404	404	I don't know.
404	404	page not found, error
411	411	information
419	419	Nigerian e-mail scam
420	420	weed, pot, marijuana , let's get high
459	459	I love you (ILY is 459 using keypad numbers)
511	511	too much information (more than 411)
520	520	I love you. (Chinese)
555	555	sobbing, crying (Mandarin Chinese), hahaha (Thai)
637	637	always and forever (letters in each word)
666	666	the number of the beast
730	730	crazy
808	808	police code for disturbing the peace
823	823	thinking of you
831	831	I love you. (8 letters, 3 words, 1 meaning)
881	881	bye-bye (from Chinese pronunciation)

UPPERCASE	LOWERCASE	MEANING
886	886	bye-bye (Hong Kong Cantonese)
888	888	ate, ate, ate
911	911	US emergency number
999	999	UK emergency number
1234	1234	one thing to say three words for you (I love you)
1314	1314	forever (Chinese)
1337	1337	elite
1432	1432	I love you too.
1437	1437	I love you forever.
4221	4221	forever together to love one another
4311	4311	hell
5150	5150	police code for crazy person on the loose
7734	7734	hell
8008	8008	boob
14344	14344	I love you very much. (letters in each word)
31337	31337	elite
40000	40000	forever
40653	40653	April 20, weed smoking day
40817	40817	radio code for "receiving poorly"
40818	40818	radio code for "receiving well"
40820	40820	understood, OK
55555	55555	crying your eyes out (Mandarin Chinese), laughing (Thai)
80085	80085	boobs
313373	313373	elite
8008135	8008135	boobies
88888888	88888888	clapping
0.0	0.o	raised eyebrow, WTF
0/	0/	waving
0:-3	0:-3	angel, innocent
0_0	0_0	shocked
0DAY	0day	software illegally obtained before it was released
0NOE	0noe	oh no
10CHAR	10char	padding where at least ten characters are required
10Q	10q	thank you
10TACLE	10tacle	tentacle
10X	10x	thanks
12B	12b	wannabe
133T	133t	elite
13ITCH	13itch	bitch
14AA41	14aa41	one for all, and all for one
1AAT	1aat	one at a time
1AB	1ab	wannabe

UPPERCASE	LOWERCASE	MEANING
1CE	1ce	once
1DAFUL	1daful	wonderful
1DERING	1dering	wondering
1DR	1dr	I wonder
1NAM	1nam	one in a million
1NCE	1nce	once
1SEC	1sec	one second
1TG	1tg	number of balls needed for win (online gaming/bingo)
1UP	1up	extra life in a game
24/7	24/7	twenty-four hours a day, seven days a week
2B	2b	to be
2B4U	2b4u	too bad for you
2BAD4U2	2bad4u2	too bad for you too
2BH	2bh	to be honest
2BZ4UQT	2bz4uqt	too busy for you, cutey
2DA	2da	to the
2DAE	2dae	today
2DAY	2day	today
2DITD	2ditd	today is the day
2EZ	2ez	too easy
2G	2g	too good
2G2B4G	2g2b4g	too good to be forgotten
2G2BT	2g2bt	too good to be true
2GE4	2ge4	together
2GETHA	2getha	together
2GETHER	2gether	together
2GETHR	2gethr	together
2GETR	2getr	together
2H2H	2h2h	too hot to handle
2H4U	2h4u	too hot for you
2K0	2k0	2000
2K1	2k1	2001
2K10	2k10	2010
2K4	2k4	2004
2K4U	2k4u	to cool for you
2K6	2k6	2006
2K7	2k7	2007
2K8	2k8	2008
2K9	2k9	2009
2L8	2l8	too late
2M	2m	tomorrow
2M2H	2m2h	too much too handle

UPPERCASE	LOWERCASE	MEANING
2M4U	2m4u	too much for you
2MA	2ma	tomorrow
2MARO	2maro	tomorrow
2MI	2mi	too much information
2MMRW	2mmrw	tomorrow
2MO	2mo	tomorrow
2MOR	2mor	tomorrow
2MORA	2mora	tomorrow
2MORO	2moro	tomorrow
2MOROW	2morow	tomorrow
2MORRO	2morro	tomorrow
2MORROW	2morrow	tomorrow
2MOZ	2moz	tomorrow
2MOZZ	2mozz	tomorrow
2MRO	2mro	tomorrow
2MRW	2mrw	tomorrow
2MW	2mw	tomorrow
2MZ	2mz	tomorrow
2NIGHT	2night	tonight
2NITE	2nite	tonight
2NYT	2nyt	tonight
2O4S	2o4s	too old for sex
2QT	2qt	too cute
2SDAY	2sday	Tuesday
2TALI	2tali	totally
2TG	2tg	number of balls needed for win (online gaming/bingo)
2TM	2tm	to the max
2TRD	2trd	too tired
2U	2u	to you
2U2	2u2	to you too
3 WHEELIN	3 wheelin	driving with one wheel off the ground
3>	3>	hate (opposite of love)
301ING	301ing	referring traffic to another site
30STM	30stm	*30 Seconds to Mars* (band)
31EE7	31ee7	elite
3ARC	3arc	Treyarch
3DG	3dg	*Three Days Grace* (band)
3G	3g	third-generation mobile phone network
3Q	3q	thank you
3U	3u	thank you
3VI1	3vi1	evil
3Y3 Y4M	3y3 y4m	I am

UPPERCASE	LOWERCASE	MEANING
401K	401k	retirement investment plan
420 FRIENDLY	420 friendly	person who likes smoking pot
42N8	42n8	fortunate
4AO	4ao	for adults only
4CHAN	4chan	Internet message/image board
4COL	4col	for crying out loud
4E&E	4e&e	forever and ever
4EAE	4eae	forever and ever
4EVA	4eva	forever
4EVER	4ever	forever
4EVR	4evr	forever
4EVS	4evs	forever
4FS	4fs	for fuck's sake
4GAI	4gai	forget about it
4GEIT	4geit	forget it
4GET	4get	forget
4GETU	4getu	forget you
4GIVE	4give	forgive
4GM	4gm	forgive me
4GOT	4got	forgot
4GV	4gv	forgive
4HEAD	4head	forehead
4KER	4ker	fucker
4KING	4king	fucking
4LYF3	4lyf3	for life
4LYFE	4lyfe	for life
4M	4m	forum, form
4N	4n	phone
4NR	4nr	foreigner
4Q	4q	fuck you
4R3AL	4r3al	for real
4RL?	4rl?	For real?
4RM	4rm	from
4SHO	4sho	for sure
4SRS	4srs	For serious?
4TLOG	4tlog	for the love of god
4TW	4tw	for the win
4U	4u	for you
4UMB	4umb	for you maybe
4US	4us	for us
4WARD	4ward	forward
4WD	4wd	forward

UPPERCASE	LOWERCASE	MEANING
4X4	4x4	four-wheel drive vehicle
4YEO	4yeo	for your eyes only
5 BY 5	5 by 5	loud and clear, fine
5 HOLE	5 hole	gap between goalie's legs in hockey
5!	5!	LOL!
53X	53x	sex
5FS	5fs	five-finger salute
5H17	5h17	shit
5N	5n	fine
5O	5o	police
5-OH	5-oh	cop
5X5	5x5	loud and clear
6_6	6_6	looking down, suspicious
6FLX	6flx	X-rated movie (sex flick)
6UP	6up	cops in area
6Y	6y	sexy
7DAW	7daw	seven days a week
7K	7k	sick
7UCK	7uck	fuck
8)	8)	cool, happy
8·)	8·)	cool (sunglasses)
8·)	8·)	eye-rolling (MSN)
8·)	8·)	shades
8)	8)	shades
8*	8*	kiss
8·|	8·|	nerd (MSN)
80S	80s	the eighties, 1980s
81TC#	81tc#	bitch
8D		laughing, big grin
8·D		laughing, big grin
8o|	8o|	baring teeth (MSN)
9_9	9_9	rolling the eyes
9009L3	900913	Google
911SC	911sc	emergency, let's stop chatting
9JA	9ja	Nigeria
9T	9t	night
A$$	a$$	ass
A$$_/\_	a$$_/_	ass-hat (idiot)
A$$BG	a$$bg	assbag (idiot)
A$$BG	a$$bg	assbandit (homosexual slur/derogatory)
A$$BGR	a$$bgr	assbanger (homosexual slur/derogatory)
A$$BT	a$$bt	assbite (idiot)

UPPERCASE	LOWERCASE	MEANING
A$$CK	a$$ck	asscock (idiot)
A$$CKR	a$$ckr	asssucker (idiot)
A$$CLWN	a$$clwn	assclown (butt)
A$$CRCKR	a$$crckr	asscracker (butt)
A$$FACE	a$$face	assface (butt)
A$$FK	a$$fk	assfuck (rear-loving)
A$$FKR	a$$fkr	assfucker (homosexual slur/derogatory)
A$$GBLN	a$$gbln	assgoblin (homosexual slur/derogatory)
A$$HD	a$$hd	asshead (idiot)
A$$HPPR	a$$hppr	asshopper (homosexual slur/derogatory)
A$$HT	a$$ht	asshat (butt)
A$$JBBR	a$$jbbr	ass-jabber (homosexual slur/derogatory)
A$$JCKR	a$$jckr	assjacker (homosexual slur/derogatory)
A$$LK	a$$lk	asslick (idiot)
A$$LKR	a$$lkr	asslicker (buttlicker)
A$$MNCH	a$$mnch	assmunch (idiot)
A$$MNCHR	a$$mnchr	assmuncher (butt)
A$$MNKY	a$$mnky	assmonkey (idiot)
A$$NGGR	a$$nggr	assnigger (African American - ethnic slur/derogatory)
A$$PRT	a$$prt	ass-pirate (homosexual slur/derogatory)
A$$PRTE	a$$prte	ass-pirate (homosexual slur/derogatory)
A$$SHT	a$$sht	assshit (idiot)
A$$WD	a$$wd	asswad (butt)
A$$WP	a$$wp	asswipe (butt)
A&F	a&f	Abercrombie & Fitch
A&F	a&f	always and forever
A&R	a&r	artists and repertoire
A/L	a/l	age and location
A/M	a/m	away message
A/N	a/n	author's note
A/S/L	a/s/l	age/sex/location
A/S/L/P	a/s/l/p	age/sex/location/picture
A/S/L/R	a/s/l/r	age/sex/location/race
A/W	a/w	anyway
A'IGHT	a'ight	all right
A1	a1	top quality
A1T	a1t	anyone there
A3	a3	anywhere, anytime, any place
A7A	a7a	frustration, anger (Arabic)
A7X	a7x	*Avenged Sevenfold* (band)
AA	aa	African American
AA	aa	Alcoholics Anonymous

UPPERCASE	LOWERCASE	MEANING
AA	aa	as above
AA	aa	ask about
AA	aa	automobile association
AAA	aaa	American Automobile Association
AAA	aaa	battery size
AAAAA	aaaaa	American Association Against Acronym Abuse
AAB	aab	average at best
AABF	aabf	as a best friend
AAF	aaf	always and forever
AAF	aaf	as a friend
AAF	aaf	as a matter of fact
AAK	aak	alive and kicking
AAK	aak	asleep at keyboard
AAMOF	aamof	as a matter of fact
AAMOI	aamoi	as a matter of interest
AAP	aap	always a pleasure
AAR	aar	at any rate
AARP	aarp	American Association of Retired Persons
AAS	aas	alive and smiling
AASHTA	aashta	as always, Sheldon has the answer
AAT	aat	and another thing
AAT	aat	at all times
AATF	aatf	always and totally forever
AATK	aatk	always at the keyboard
AAWY	aawy	and also with you
AAYF	aayf	as always, your friend
ABA	aba	Another Bloody Australian, used in Canadian ski resorts (ethnic slur/derogatory)
ABBR	abbr	abbreviation
ABC	abc	already been chewed
ABC	abc	American-born Chinese person (ethnic slur/derogatory)
ABCD	abcd	American-born confused Desi (ethnic slur/derogatory)
ABD	abd	already been done
ABDC	abdc	*America's Best Dance Crew* (TV show)
ABEND	abend	absent by enforced Net deprivation
ABF	abf	all but face
ABFT	abft	about fucking time
ABG	abg	Asian baby girl
ABH	abh	actual bodily harm
ABO	abo	Australian aboriginal (ethnic slur/derogatory)
ABOOT	aboot	about
ABP	abp	already been posted

UPPERCASE	LOWERCASE	MEANING
ABPH	abph	a big poohead
ABS	abs	absolutely
ABSNT	absnt	absent
ABT	abt	about
ABT2	abt2	about to
ABTA	abta	good-bye (sign off)
ABU	abu	all bugged up
ABU	abu	anyone but (Manchester) United
ABWT	abwt	about
AC	ac	acceptable content
AC	ac	air-conditioning
AC	ac	alternating current
AC/DC	ac/dc	rock band
ACAPELLA	acapella	vocal music without instruments
ACC	acc	account
ACC	acc	actually
ACC	acc	anyone can come
ACCT	acct	account
ACD	acd	ALT/CONTROL/DELETE
ACDNT	acdnt	accident
ACE	ace	excellent, great
ACE	ace	marijuana cigarette
ACGAF	acgaf	absolutely couldn't give a fuck
ACK	ack	acknowledgment, acknowledged, acknowledge
ACK	ack	disgust, frustration
ACL	acl	Access Control List
ACLU	aclu	American Civil Liberties Union
ACME	acme	a company that makes everything
ACP	acp	automatic colt pistol
ACPT	acpt	accept
ACQSTN	acqstn	acquisition
ACT	act	SAT-type test
ACU	acu	army combat uniform
AD	ad	anno Domini (in the year of our Lord)
AD HOC	ad hoc	for the specific purpose
AD HOC	ad hoc	improvised, impromptu
ADAD	adad	another day, another dollar
ADBB	adbb	all done, bye-bye
ADC	adc	Analog-to-Digital Converter
ADD	add	address
ADD	add	advanced dumbass disorder
ADD	add	attention deficit disorder
ADDY	addy	address

UPPERCASE	LOWERCASE	MEANING
ADF	adf	automatic document feeder
ADGTH	adgth	*All Dogs Go to Heaven*
ADHD	adhd	attention deficit hyperactivity disorder
ADIH	adih	another day in hell
ADIP	adip	another day in paradise
ADL	adl	all day long
ADM	adm	*¡ay dios mío!* (Spanish for "oh my god!")
ADMIN	admin	administrator
ADMINR	adminr	administrator
ADN	adn	any day now
ADOLF	adolf	Germans, referring to Adolf Hitler (ethnic slur/derogatory)
ADR	adr	address
ADS	ads	aim(ing) down sights
ADSL	adsl	asymmetric digital subscriber line
ADTR	adtr	*A Day to Remember* (band)
AE	ae	American Eagle (clothing)
AEAE	aeae	and ever and ever
AEAP	aeap	as early as possible
AF	af	April Fool's
AF	af	assface
AFAIAA	afaiaa	as far as I am aware
AFAIAC	afaiac	as far as I am concerned
AFAIC	afaic	as far as I'm concerned
AFAICR	afaicr	as far as I can remember
AFAICS	afaics	as far as I can see
AFAICT	afaict	as far as I can tell
AFAIK	afaik	as far as I know
AFAIR	afair	as far as I recall
AFAIR	afair	as far as I remember
AFAIU	afaiu	as far as I understand
AFAIUI	afaiui	as far as I understand it
AFAP	afap	as far as possible
AFC	afc	away from computer
AFCPMGO	afcpmgo	away from computer parents; may go on
AFF	aff	affirmative
AFFA	affa	Angels Forever, Forever Angels
AFG	afg	away from game
AFI	afi	*A Fire Inside* (band)
AFJ	afj	April Fool's joke
AFK	afk	away from keyboard
AFKB	afkb	away from keyboard
AFL	afl	Australian Football League

UPPERCASE	LOWERCASE	MEANING
AFN	afn	all for now
AFP	afp	away from phone
AFPOE	afpoe	a fresh pair of eyes
AFS	afs	always, forever, and seriously
AFT	aft	about fucking time
AFZ	afz	acronym-free zone
AG	ag	aggressive
AGC	agc	automatic gain control
AGGY	aggy	agitated
AGH	agh	ain't gonna happen
AGM	agm	annual general meeting
AGN	agn	again
AGP	agp	Accelerated Graphics Port
AGRO	agro	hostile, angry
AGT	agt	*America's Got Talent* (TV show)
AGW	agw	all going well
AH	ah	asshole
AH	ah	at home
AHA	aha	expression of discovery or realization
AHAB	ahab	an Arab, from the novelty song "Ahab the Arab" (ethnic slur/derogatory)
AHEM	ahem	throat-clearing sound
AHOLE	ahole	asshole
AHT	aht	out
AI	ai	"American Ignorance" used for US citizens (ethnic slur/derogatory)
AI	ai	artificial intelligence
AI	ai	as if
AIADW	aiadw	all in a day's work
AIAMU	aiamu	and I'm a monkey's uncle
AIB	aib	Am I bored?
AICMFP	aicmfp	and I claim my five pounds
AIDS	aids	acquired immune deficiency syndrome
AIFF	aiff	Audio Interchange File Format
AIGF	aigf	all in good fun
AIGHT	aight	all right
AIGHTZ	aightz	all right
AII	aii	all right
AIIC	aiic	as if I care
AIID	aiid	and if I did
AIIGHT	aiight	all right
AIIT	aiit	all right
AIKRN	aikrn	all I know right now

UPPERCASE	LOWERCASE	MEANING
AIM	aim	AOL Instant Messenger
AIMBOT	aimbot	targeting script in games
AIMO	aimo	idiot
AINEC	ainec	and it's not even close
AINT	aint	am not/are not/is not
AIO	aio	all in one
AIR	air	as I remember
AIR	air	blanked, ignored
AIRHEAD	airhead	stupid person
AISB	aisb	as I said before
AISB	aisb	as it should be
AISI	aisi	as I see it
AIT	ait	all right
AITE	aite	all right
AITR	aitr	adult in the room
AITYD	aityd	and I think you do
AIUI	aiui	as I understand it
AIWS	aiws	as I was saying
AIX	aix	Advanced Interactive Executive
AIYA	aiya	Cantonese expression of exasperation
AJ	aj	apple juice
AJAX	ajax	asynchronous JavaScript and XML
AK	ak	AK-47 assault rifle
AK	ak	Alaska
AK47	ak47	assault rifle
AKA	aka	also known as
AKI	aki	autumn, fall
AKS	aks	ask
AKTF	aktf	Always keep the faith.
AL	al	alcohol
ALA	ala	in the style of (French)
ALAP	alap	as late/long/little as possible
ALAS	alas	expression of regret, sorrow
ALAYTM	alaytm	as long as you tell me
ALBO	albo	Albanians (ethnic slur/derogatory)
ALCON	alcon	all concerned
ALF	alf	animal liberation front
ALG	alg	ain't life grand
ALI	ali	best friend
ALIE	alie	init
ALIHAL	alihal	At least I have a life.
ALKQN	alkqn	almighty Latin king and queen nation

UPPERCASE	LOWERCASE	MEANING
ALLOW	allow	let it be, forget it
ALOL	alol	actually laughing out loud
ALOT	alot	a lot
ALOTBSOL	alotbsol	always look on the bright side of life
ALPHA	alpha	head person of a group
ALRATO	alrato	later
ALRIGHT	alright	all right
ALRITE	alrite	all right
ALRT	alrt	all right
ALRYT	alryt	all right
ALT	alt	alternative character in RPG
ALU	alu	Arithmetic Logic Unit
AM	am	amplitude modulation (radio signal)
AM	am	ante meridiem (before midday)
AMA	ama	against medical advice
AMA	ama	ask me anything
AMAP	amap	as much/many as possible
AMBW	ambw	all my best wishes
AMC	amc	American Motors Corporation
AMD	amd	Advanced Micro Devices
AMEX	amex	American Express
AMF	amf	adios, motherfucker
AMG	amg	ah, my god
AMIGO	amigo	friend
AMIIC	amiic	Ask me if I care.
AMIIGAF	amiigaf	Ask me if I give a fuck.
AMIRITE	amirite	Am I right?
AML	aml	all my love
AMO	amo	Amish (ethnic slur/derogatory)
AMOF	amof	as a matter of fact
AMOG	amog	alpha male of group
AMP	amp	amplifier
AMPED	amped	excited, fired up
AMSP	amsp	Ask me something personal.
AMT	amt	alpha-methyltryptamine
AMTRAK	amtrak	National Railroad Passenger Corporation
AMV	amv	Anime Music Video
AMW	amw	*America's Most Wanted* (TV show)
AMZ	amz	amazing
ANC	anc	African National Congress
ANF	anf	Abercrombie & Fitch
ANFAWFOS	anfawfos	and now for a word from our sponsor

UPPERCASE	LOWERCASE	MEANING
ANFSCD	anfscd	and now for something completely different
ANIM8	anim8	animate
ANIME	anime	Japanese-style animation
ANL	anl	all night long
ANLSX	anlsx	anal sex
ANON	anon	unknown person, anonymous
ANS	ans	answer
ANSI	ansi	American National Standards Institute
ANTI	anti	against
ANTM	antm	*America's Next Top Model*
ANUDA	anuda	another
ANW	anw	anyways
ANWWI	anwwi	All right now, where was I?
ANY1	any1	anyone
ANYWAZ	anywaz	anyways
ANYWHO	anywho	anyhow
AO	ao	adults only
AOB	aob	any other business
AOC	aoc	age of consent
AOC	aoc	available on cell
AOE	aoe	Age of Empires
AOE	aoe	area of effect
AOK	aok	*Age of Kings* (game)
AOK	aok	all OK
AOL	aol	America Online
AOM	aom	*Age of Mythology* (game)
AON	aon	all or nothing
AON	aon	as of now
AOS	aos	adult over shoulder
AOS	aos	ahead of schedule
AOT	aot	among other things
AOT	aot	as opposed to
AOTA	aota	all of the above
AOTO	aoto	amen on that one
AOTS	aots	*Attack of the Show* (TV show)
AOW	aow	all-out war
AOYP	aoyp	angel on your pillow
AOYS	aoys	angel on your shoulder
AP	ap	Associated Press
APAC	apac	all praise and credit
APB	apb	all-points bulletin
APC	apc	armored personnel carrier

UPPERCASE	LOWERCASE	MEANING
APE	ape	mad, crazy
API	api	application programming interface
APM	apm	actions per minute
APO	apo	authorized personnel only
APOD	apod	another point of discussion
APP	app	application
APPROX	approx	approximately
APPS	apps	applications (software)
APPT	appt	appointment
APR	apr	annual percentage rate
APRECE8	aprece8	appreciate
APRECI8	apreci8	appreciate
APU	apu	as per usual
AQ	aq	*Adventure Quest* (game)
AQAP	aqap	as quickly as possible
AQAP	aqap	as quiet as possible
AQF	aqf	ay, que funny, LOL
AR	ar	are
AR	ar	assault rifle
ARC	arc	archive (compressed files)
ARD	ard	all right
ARE	are	acronym-rich environment
ARE	are	misspelling of "our"
AREA 51	area 51	top secret military base in Nevada
ARG	arg	alternate reality gaming
ARG	arg	argument
ARGH	argh	expression of frustration or anger
ARIGATO	arigato	thank you (Japanese)
ARK	ark	act of random kindness
ARND	arnd	around
ARP	arp	address resolution protocol
ARPA	arpa	advanced research projects agency (made early Internet)
ARPANET	arpanet	advanced research projects agency network (early Internet)
ARS	ars	arse (butt)
ARS0	ars0	arsehole (butt)
ARSE	arse	ass
ARSED	arsed	bothered
ART	art	all right
ARVO	arvo	afternoon
AS	as	another subject
AS	as	ape shit

UPPERCASE	LOWERCASE	MEANING
ASA	asa	and so on
ASAFP	asafp	as soon as fucking possible
ASAIC	asaic	as soon as I can
ASAIK	asaik	as soon as I know
ASAP	asap	as soon as possible
ASAS	asas	as soon as sensible
ASBO	asbo	antisocial behavior order
ASCII	ascii	American Standard Code for Information Interchange
ASD	asd	sequence of letters on many keyboards
ASDFGHJKL;	asdfghjkl;	I'm bored
ASE	ase	age, sex, ethnicity
ASF	asf	and so forth
ASHL	ashl	asshole
ASHOLE	ashole	asshole
ASIAN NGGR	asian nggr	Asian nigger (Filipino person - ethnic slur/derogatory)
ASIC	asic	application-specific integrated circuit
ASIG	asig	and so it goes
ASL	asl	age/sex/location
ASL	asl	American Sign Language
ASLA	asla	age/sex/location/availability
ASLMH	aslmh	age/sex/location/music/hobbies
ASLO	aslo	age/sex/location/orientation
ASLOP	aslop	age/sex/location/orientation/picture
ASLP	aslp	age/sex/location/picture
ASLR	aslr	age /sex/location/race
ASLRP	aslrp	age /sex/location/race/picture
ASN	asn	any second now
ASO	aso	I see
ASP	asp	active server page or application service provider
ASP	asp	at some point
ASR	asr	age/sex/race
ASS_/_	ass_/_	ass-hat (idiot)
ASSBG	assbg	assbag (idiot)
ASSBG	assbg	assbandit (homosexual slur/derogatory)
ASSBGR	assbgr	assbanger (homosexual slur/derogatory)
ASSBT	assbt	assbite (idiot)
ASSCK	assck	asscock (idiot)
ASSCKR	assckr	asssucker (idiot)
ASSCLWN	assclwn	assclown (butt)
ASSCRCKR	asscrckr	asscracker (butt)
ASSFACE	assface	assface (butt)
ASSFK	assfk	assfuck (rear-loving)

UPPERCASE	LOWERCASE	MEANING
ASSFKR	assfkr	assfucker (homosexual slur/derogatory)
ASSGBLN	assgbln	assgoblin (homosexual slur/derogatory)
ASSHD	asshd	asshead (idiot)
ASSHLE	asshle	asshole
ASSHPPR	asshppr	asshopper (homosexual slur/derogatory)
ASSHT	assht	asshat (butt)
ASSJBBR	assjbbr	ass-jabber (homosexual slur/derogatory)
ASSJCKR	assjckr	assjacker (homosexual slur/derogatory)
ASSLK	asslk	asslick (idiot)
ASSLKR	asslkr	asslicker (buttlicker)
ASSMNCH	assmnch	assmunch (idiot)
ASSMNCHR	assmnchr	assmuncher (butt)
ASSMNKY	assmnky	assmonkey (idiot)
ASSNGGR	assnggr	assnigger (ethnic slur/derogatory)
ASSPRT	assprt	ass-pirate (homosexual slur/derogatory)
ASSPRTE	assprte	ass-pirate (homosexual slur/derogatory)
ASSSHT	asssht	assshit (idiot)
ASSWD	asswd	asswad (butt)
ASSWP	asswp	asswipe (butt)
AT	at	at your terminal
ATA	ata	actual time of arrival
ATA	ata	advanced technology attachment
ATA	ata	air to air
ATAB	atab	ain't that a bitch
ATB	atb	all the best
ATC	atc	air traffic control
ATD	atd	attention to detail
ATDIYR	atdiyr	a thousand dicks in your religion
ATEOTD	ateotd	at the end of the day
ATF	atf	all-time favorite
ATFP	atfp	Answer the fucking phone.
ATGATT	atgatt	all the gear all the time (motorcycling)
ATI	ati	Array Technology Inc. (graphics card maker)
ATK	atk	attack
ATL	atl	Atlanta, Georgia
ATM	atm	asynchronous transfer mode
ATM	atm	at the moment
ATM	atm	automated teller machine (cash machine)
ATMO	atmo	according to my opinion
ATN	atn	any time now
ATO	ato	against the odds
ATOP	atop	at time of posting

UPPERCASE	LOWERCASE	MEANING
ATP	atp	Answer the phone.
ATQ	atq	Answer the question.
ATSITS	atsits	all the stars in the sky
ATSL	atsl	along the same line (or lines)
ATST	atst	at the same time
ATT	att	all the time, at this time
ATTN	attn	attention
ATTOTP	attotp	at the time of this post
ATTT	attt	ain't that the truth
ATV	atv	all-terrain vehicle
ATVB	atvb	all the very best
ATW	atw	all the way
ATWA	atwa	air, trees, water, animals
ATWA	atwa	all the way alive
ATX	atx	Austin, Texas
ATY	aty	according to you
ATYS	atys	anything you say
AU	au	alternate universe
AU	au	gold
AUDY	audy	Are you done yet?
AUFM	aufm	Are you fucking mental?
AUFS	aufs	Are you fucking serious?
AUFSM	aufsm	Are you fucking shitting me?
AUO	auo	I don't know
AUP	aup	acceptable use policy
AUP	aup	another useless post
AV	av	adult video
AV	av	antivirus
AV	av	audio/video
AV7X	av7x	*Avenged Sevenfold* (band)
AVA	ava	*Angels and Airwaves* (band)
AVGN	avgn	angry video game nerd
AVI	avi	audio video interleaved (media format)
AVIE	avie	avatar
AVO	avo	afternoon
AVPM	avpm	*A Very Potter Musical*
AVSB	avsb	a very special boy
AVTR	avtr	avatar
AVVIE	avvie	avatar
AVY	avy	avatar
AWA	awa	as well as

UPPERCASE	LOWERCASE	MEANING
AWES	awes	awesome
AWESO	aweso	awesome
AWESOME	awesome	amazing, wonderful, cool
AWHFY	awhfy	Are we having fun yet?
AWK	awk	awkward
AWNP	awnp	all work, no play
AWOL	awol	absent without leave
AWP	awp	arctic warfare police sniper rifle
AWS	aws	as we speak
AWSIC	awsic	And why should I care?
AWSM	awsm	awesome
AWSOME	awsome	awesome
AWW	aww	any which way
AX	ax	ask
AYAGOB	ayagob	Are you a girl or boy?
AYB	ayb	all your base
AYBAB2M	aybab2m	all your base are belong to me
AYBAB2U	aybab2u	all your base are belong to us
AYBABTG	aybabtg	all your base are belong to Google
AYBABTU	aybabtu	all your base are belong to us
AYBRB2U	aybrb2u	all your base are belong to us
AYC	ayc	awaiting your comments
AYCS	aycs	as you can see
AYD	ayd	Are you done?
AYDY	aydy	Are you done yet?
AYE	aye	yes
AYEC	ayec	at your earliest convenience
AYFK	ayfk	Are you fucking kidding?
AYFKM	ayfkm	Are you fucking kidding me?
AYFR	ayfr	Are you for real?
AYFS	ayfs	Are you fucking serious?
AYFT	ayft	Are you free today?
AYK	ayk	Are you kidding?
AYK	ayk	as you know
AYKM	aykm	Are you kidding me?
AYL	ayl	Are you listening?
AYMF	aymf	Are you my friends?
AYO	ayo	Hey, you.
AYOK	ayok	Are you OK?
AYOR	ayor	at your own risk
AYPI	aypi	And your point is?

UPPERCASE	LOWERCASE	MEANING
AYS	ays	Are you serious?
AYSM	aysm	Are you shitting me?
AYSOS	aysos	Are you stupid or something?
AYST	ayst	Are you still there?
AYT	ayt	Are you there?
AYTE	ayte	all right
AYTF	aytf	Are you there, fucker?
AYTMTB	aytmtb	and you're telling me this because
AYTY	ayty	Are you there yet?
AYV	ayv	Are you vertical?
AYW	ayw	as you were
AYW	ayw	as you wish
AZHOL	azhol	asshole
AZN	azn	Asian
AZZ	azz	ass
AZZBG	azzbg	assbag (idiot)
AZZBG	azzbg	assbandit (homosexual slur/derogatory)
AZZBGR	azzbgr	assbanger (homosexual slur/derogatory)
AZZBT	azzbt	assbite (idiot)
AZZCK	azzck	asscock (idiot)
AZZCKR	azzckr	asssucker (idiot)
AZZCLWN	azzclwn	assclown (butt)
AZZCRCKR	azzcrckr	asscracker (butt)
AZZFACE	azzface	assface (butt)
AZZFK	azzfk	assfuck (rear-loving)
AZZFKR	azzfkr	assfucker (homosexual slur/derogatory)
AZZGBLN	azzgbln	assgoblin (homosexual slur/derogatory)
AZZHD	azzhd	asshead (idiot)
AZZHPPR	azzhppr	asshopper (homosexual slur/derogatory)
AZZJBBR	azzjbbr	ass-jabber (homosexual slur/derogatory)
AZZJCKR	azzjckr	assjacker (homosexual slur/derogatory)
AZZLK	azzlk	asslick (idiot)
AZZLKR	azzlkr	asslicker (buttlicker)
AZZMNCH	azzmnch	assmunch (idiot)
AZZMNCHR	azzmnchr	assmuncher (butt)
AZZMNKY	azzmnky	assmonkey (idiot)
AZZNGGR	azznggr	assnigger (ethnic slur/derogatory)
AZZPRT	azzprt	ass-pirate (homosexual slur/derogatory)
AZZPRTE	azzprte	ass-pirate (homosexual slur/derogatory)
AZZSHT	azzsht	assshit (idiot)
AZZWD	azzwd	asswad (butt)
AZZWP	azzwp	asswipe (butt)

UPPERCASE	LOWERCASE	MEANING
B	b	back
B	b	be
B	b	bro
B&	b&	band
B&	b&	banned
B&B	b&b	bed and breakfast
B&E	b&e	breaking and entering
B&M	b&m	bricks and mortar
B&W	b&w	black and white
B)	b)	smiley with sunglasses
B-)		cool
B/C	b/c	because
B/COS	b/cos	because
B/F	b/f	boyfriend
B/G	b/g	background
B/S/L	b/s/l	bisexual/straight/lesbian
B/T	b/t	between
B/W	b/w	between
B/W	b/w	black and white
B@	b@	banned
B'DAY	b'day	birthday
B00N	b00n	new person
B00T	b00t	boot
B0RKED	b0rked	broken
B1TCH	b1tch	bitch
B2B	b2b	back to back
B2B	b2b	business to business
B2C	b2c	business to consumer
B2S	b2s	back to school
B2U	b2u	back to you
B2W	b2w	back to work
B3	b3	be
B4	b4	before
B4MV	b4mv	*Bullet for My Valentine* (band)
B4N	b4n	bye for now
B4U	b4u	before you
B7	b7	banned (b7=b&=band)
B8	b8	bait
B82REZ	b82rez	batteries
B8REZ	b8rez	batteries
B9	b9	boss is watching
BA	ba	badass
BAAS	baas	boss
BAB	bab	big ass boobs
BABI	babi	baby
BABYSITTING	babysitting	holding the weed too long
BAC	bac	back at computer
BAC	bac	blood alcohol content
BAC	bac	by any chance
BAD	bad	good
BADASS	badass	cool, confident person
BADMAN	badman	gangster
BAE	bae	baby

UPPERCASE	LOWERCASE	MEANING
BAF	baf	bring a friend
BAG	bag	busting a gut
BAG	bag	get
BAGGKYKO	baggkyko	be a good girl, keep your knickers on
BAGL	bagl	bust a gut laughing
BAH	bah	bored as hell
BAH	bah	I don't really care
BAHAHA	bahaha	evil laugh
BAI	bai	bye
BAIL	bail	leave
BAIRN	bairn	child, baby
BAIT	bait	blatant, obvious
BAK	bak	back
BAK	bak	back at keyboard
BAKA	baka	fool, idiot
BAKED	baked	stoned, wasted
BAKK	bakk	back
BALLER	baller	successful ball player
BALLIN	ballin	living the good life
BALLIN	ballin	playing basketball
BALZ	balz	balls
BAM	bam	below average mentality
BAM	bam	exclamation of happiness
BAMA	bama	person lacking style
BAMF	bamf	badass motherfucker
BAMN	bamn	by any means necessary
BAMOFO	bamofo	bitch-ass motherfucker
BANANA	banana	code word for penis
BANDWIDTH	bandwidth	amount of data through an interface over time
BANGING	banging	very beautiful, sexy
BANGTIDY	bangtidy	sexy, fit
BANJAX	banjax	break, destroy
BANTER	banter	playful, witty chat
BAO	bao	be aware of
BAP	bap	Black American Princess (ethnic slur/derogatory)
BARBIE	barbie	barbecue
BARE	bare	lots of, very
BASER	baser	drug user
BASIC	basic	Beginner's All-purpose Symbolic Instruction Code
BASIC	basic	uncool, boring
BASOR	basor	breathing a sigh of relief
BATE	bate	obvious
BAU	bau	back at you
BAU	bau	business as usual
BAY	bay	baby
BAY	bay	back at ya
BB	bb	be back
BB	bb	*bebi*/baby (Spanish SMS)
BB	bb	big brother
BB	bb	bye-bye
BB4H	bb4h	bros before hoes
BB4N	bb4n	bye-bye for now
BBAM	bbam	be back after meal
BBB	bbb	bugging beyond belief

UPPERCASE	LOWERCASE	MEANING
BBBJ	bbbj	bareback blow job
BBBW	bbbw	big beautiful black woman
BBC	bbc	big bad challenge
BBC	bbc	British Broadcasting Corporation
BBE	bbe	babe/baby
BBEG	bbeg	big bad evil guy
BBF	bbf	best boyfriend
BBFL	bbfl	best buds for life
BBFN	bbfn	bye-bye for now
BBFS	bbfs	best boyfriends
BBFU	bbfu	be back for you
BBG	bbg	best be going
BBI	bbi	baby
BBIAB	bbiab	be back in a bit
BBIAF	bbiaf	be back in a few
BBIAM	bbiam	be back in a minute
BBIAS	bbias	be back in a sec/second
BBIAW	bbiaw	be back in a while
BBIFS	bbifs	be back in a few seconds
BBILB	bbilb	be back in a little bit
BBILFM	bbilfm	be back in like five minutes
BBIM	bbim	be back in minute
BBK	bbk	Be back, OK?
BBK	bbk	boy better know
BBL	bbl	be back later
BBL8A	bbl8a	be back later
BBLIG	bblig	be back later...I guess
BBM	bbm	BlackBerry messenger
BBMFIC	bbmfic	big badass motherfucker in charge
BBML	bbml	be back much later
BBN	bbn	be back never
BBN	bbn	bye-bye now
BBOL	bbol	be back online later
BBP	bbp	banned by parents
BBQ	bbq	barbecue
BBQ	bbq	be back quick
BBQ	bbq	better be quick
BBR	bbr	blonde, brunette, redhead
BBS	bbs	be back soon
BBS	bbs	bulletin board system
BBSTS	bbsts	be back sometime soon
BBT	bbt	be back tomorrow
BBTN	bbtn	be back tonight
BBVL	bbvl	be back very later
BBW	bbw	be back whenever
BBW	bbw	big beautiful woman
BBWB	bbwb	best buddy with boobs
BBWE	bbwe	be back whenever
BBWL	bbwl	be back way later
BBY	bby	baby
BBZ	bbz	babes
BC	bc	be cool
BC	bc	because
BC	bc	before Christ

UPPERCASE	LOWERCASE	MEANING
BCBTB	bcbtb	boobs can't be too big
BCBTB	bcbtb	breasts can't be too big
BCBW	bcbw	bow, chica, bowwow
BCC	bcc	blind carbon copy
BCD	bcd	behind closed doors
BCE	bce	before the Christian Era (like BC)
BCF	bcf	best cousin forever
BCG	bcg	birth control glasses
BCH	bch	bitch
BCK	bck	back
BCNU	bcnu	be seeing you
BCNUL8R	bcnul8r	be seeing you later
BCO	bco	big crush on
BCOS	bcos	because
BCOY	bcoy	big crush on you
BCOZ	bcoz	because
BCURL8	bcurl8	because you're late
BCUZ	bcuz	because
B-CUZ	b-cuz	because
BD	bd	big deal
BD	bd	birthday
BDAY	bday	birthday
B-DAY	b-day	birthday
BDFL	bdfl	benevolent dictator for life
BDN	bdn	big darn number
BDOML	bdoml	best day of my life
BDONG	bdong	bad and wrong
BE4	be4	before
BEANS	beans	ecstasy
BEAR	bear	large man with body hair
BEAST	beast	person/thing that is good, awesome
BEASTLY	beastly	being good at something, cool
BEATCH	beatch	bitch
BEB	beb	babe
BEBE	bebe	babe
BECUSE	becuse	because
BECUZ	becuz	because
BEECH	beech	bitch
BEEF	beef	problem, fight, argument
BEEOCH	beeoch	bitch
BEEZY	beezy	bitch
BEF	bef	best e-mail friend
BEF	bef	best enemies forever
BEG	beg	big evil grin
BELF	belf	*blood elf* (WOW)
BELLIG	bellig	belligerent (when drunk)
BENJAMIN	benjamin	$100 bill
BENZ	benz	£10 bag of marijuana
BEOTCH	beotch	bitch
BER	ber	beyond economical repair
BESITOS	besitos	little kisses (Spanish)
BESO	beso	kiss (Spanish)
BESOS	besos	kisses (Spanish)
BEST	best	best regards

UPPERCASE	LOWERCASE	MEANING
BESTIE	bestie	best friend
BESTY	besty	best friend
BET	bet	Black Entertainment Television
BETA	beta	better
BETA	beta	prerelease version
BETCH	betch	bitch
BETCHA	betcha	bet you
BETTR	bettr	better
BEWB	bewb	boob
BEWBS	bewbs	boobs
BEWBZ	bewbz	boobs
BEWT	bewt	boot
BEYATCH	beyatch	bitch
BEYOTCH	beyotch	bitch
BEZZIE	bezzie	best friend
BF	bf	bad fucker
BF	bf	best friend
BF	bf	boyfriend
BF	bf	brain fart
BF'S	bf's	boyfriend's
BF+GF	bf+gf	boyfriend and girlfriend
BF2	bf2	*Battlefield 2* (game)
BF4E	bf4e	best friends forever
BF4EVA	bf4eva	best friends forever
BF4L	bf4l	best friends for life
BFA	bfa	best friends always
BFAM	bfam	brother from another mother
BFAW	bfaw	best friend at work
BFB	bfb	better from behind
BFD	bfd	big fucking deal/big freaking deal
BFE	bfe	bumfuck Egypt
BFF	bff	best friend forever
BFF	bff	big fat friend/female
BFF4L	bff4l	best friend forever for life
BFFA	bffa	best friends for always
BFFAA	bffaa	best friends forever and always
BFFAE	bffae	best friends for all eternity
BFFAE	bffae	best friends forever and ever
BFFAW	bffaw	best friends for a while
BFFE	bffe	best friends forever
BFFEAE	bffeae	best friend for ever and ever
BFFENE	bffene	best friends for ever and ever
BFFL	bffl	best friend for life
BFFLE	bffle	best friends for like ever
BFFLNMW	bfflnmw	best friends for life, no matter what
BFFLTDDUP	bffltddup	best friends for life till death do us part
BFFN	bffn	best friends for now
BFFTDDUP	bfftddup	best friends forever till death do us part
BFFWB	bffwb	best friend forever with benefits
BFG	bfg	big fucking gun
BFH	bfh	bitch from hell
BFHD	bfhd	big fat hairy deal
BFITWW	bfitww	best friend in the whole world
BFK	bfk	big fat kiss

UPPERCASE	LOWERCASE	MEANING
BFL	bfl	big fat liar
BFMV	bfmv	*Bullet for My Valentine* (band)
BFN	bfn	bye for now
BFP	bfp	bad for pics
BFP	bfp	big fat positive, i.e., pregnant
BFR	bfr	big fucking rock
BFS	bfs	boyfriends
BFT	bft	big fucking tits
BFTP	bftp	blast from the past
BFUT	bfut	best friends until tomorrow
BFWB	bfwb	best friend with benefits
BG	bg	baby gangster
BG	bg	background
BG	bg	bad game
BG	bg	big grin
BGD	bgd	black gangster disciples
BGF	bgf	best girl/guy friend
BGL	bgl	big game license, likes fat people
BGM	bgm	background music
BGT	bgt	*Britain's Got Talent* (TV show)
BGWM	bgwm	be gentle with me
BH	bh	be happy
BH	bh	big head
BH	bh	bloody hell
BHD	bhd	bad hair day
BHH	bhh	bless his/her heart
BHL8	bhl8	be home late
BHM	bhm	big handsome man
BHO	bho	Barack Hussein Obama
BHUM	bhum	sexy, fit
BHWU	bhwu	back home with you
BI	bi	bye
BIAB	biab	back in a bit
BIACH	biach	bitch
BIAF	biaf	back in a few
BIATCH	biatch	bitch
BIB	bib	boss is back
BIBI	bibi	bye-bye
BIBIFN	bibifn	bye-bye for now
BIBO	bibo	beer in, beer out
BIC	bic	believe it, comrade
BIC	bic	butt in chair
BICBW	bicbw	but I could be wrong
BICH	bich	bitch
BIDDIE	biddie	good-looking girl
BIDDY	biddy	girl, woman
BIEH	bieh	best I ever had
BIF	bif	before I forget
BIFF	biff	best friend, bff
BIFFL	biffl	best Internet friend for life
BIFFLE	biffle	(same as "bffl")
BIG	big	great, really good
BIG TIME	big time	more than usual
BIG UP	big up	expression of respect

UPPERCASE	LOWERCASE	MEANING
BIGD	bigd	big deal
BIH	bih	burn in hell
BII	bii	bye
BIL	bil	brother-in-law
BILF	bilf	brother I'd like to fuck
BILU	bilu	baby, I love you
BIM	bim	Barbados
BIN	bin	buy it now
BING	bing	but it's not Google
BIO	bio	biological (toilet) break
BIOIYA	bioiya	break it off in your ass
BION	bion	believe it or not
BIOS	bios	Basic Input/Output System
BIOTCH	biotch	bitch
BIOYA	bioya	blow it out your ass
BIOYA	bioya	blow it out your asshole
BIOYN	bioyn	blow it out your nose
BIRD	bird	cocaine
BIRD	bird	young woman
BIS	bis	best in slot
BISCUIT	biscuit	attractive person
BISCUIT	biscuit	cookie
BISFLATM	bisflatm	Boy, I sure feel like a turquoise monkey!
BISH	bish	bitch
BISLY	bisly	but I still love you
BISOU	bisou	kiss (French)
BIT	bit	binary digit – 1 or 0
BITCH	bitch	basically in the clear, homey
BITFOB	bitfob	bring it the fuck on, bitch
BITMT	bitmt	but in the meantime
BITTIE	bittie	girl
BIW	biw	boss is watching
BIWM	biwm	bisexual white male
BIZ	biz	business
BIZATCH	bizatch	bitch
BIZI	bizi	busy
BIZNATCH	biznatch	bitch
BIZNITCH	biznitch	bitch
BIZZLE	bizzle	bitch
BJ	bj	bad job
BJ	bj	blowjob
BK	bk	back
BK	bk	Burger King
BKA	bka	better known as
BL	bl	bad luck
BL	bl	belly laugh
BL	bl	bottom line
BLAD	blad	brother/friend (from "blood")
BLAH	blah	nothing to say
BLANK	blank	ignore
BLAR	blar	expression of boredom, blah
BLARG	blarg	expression of boredom
BLAST	blast	damn
BLAST	blast	good time

UPPERCASE	LOWERCASE	MEANING
BLATES	blates	blatantly
BLAZE	blaze	smoke weed
BLAZED	blazed	stoned
BLAZING	blazing	smoking weed
BLD	bld	bad life decision
BLEH	bleh	expression of boredom
BLEM	blem	high on marijuana
BLEME	bleme	blog me
BLEVE	bleve	believe
BLG	blg	blog
BLG	blg	*Boys Like Girls* (band)
BLH	blh	bored like hell
BLICK	blick	a very black person
BLIND	blind	in love
BLING	bling	flashy jewelry
BLING-BLING	bling-bling	jewelry
BLINK	blink	*Blink 182* (band)
BLJ	blj	blowjob
BLJB	bljb	blowjob
BLK	blk	black
BLKM	blkm	black male
BLLKS	bllks	bollocks (male genitalia)
BLLX	bllx	bollox (male genitalia)
BLNT	blnt	better luck next time
BLOB	blob	binary large object
BLOG	blog	Weblog, online diary
BLOGGER	blogger	Weblogger
BLOKE	bloke	guy, man
BLOL	blol	big laugh out loud
BLOOD	blood	close friend
BLOOD	blood	gang member
BLOOPER	blooper	mistake, embarrassing moment
BLOTTO	blotto	drunk
BLOW	blow	cocaine
BLOWN	blown	high
BLT	blt	bacon, lettuce, and tomato sandwich
BLTN	bltn	better late than never
BLU	blu	blue
BLUD	blud	mate (from blood brother)
BLUE	blue	sad
BLUE CHIP	blue chip	high-quality, low-risk
BLUEBERRY	blueberry	form of marijuana
BLUF	bluf	bottom line up front
BLUNT	blunt	marijuana cigar
BM	bm	bite me
BM	bm	black man
BM	bm	BMW
BM	bm	bowel movement
BM&Y	bm&y	between me and you
BM4L	bm4l	best mates for life
BMA	bma	best mates always
BMAY	bmay	between me and you
BMB	bmb	be my bitch, be my buddy, boy meets boy, bring more beer

UPPERCASE	LOWERCASE	MEANING
BMBLFK	bmblfk	bumblefuck (homosexual slur/derogatory)
BMBO	bmbo	blow my brains out
BME	bme	based on my experience
BME	bme	body modification e-zine
BMF	bmf	bad motherfucker
BMF	bmf	be my friend
BMFE	bmfe	best mates forever
BMFL	bmfl	best mates for life
BMG	bmg	be my guest
BMHA	bmha	bite my hairy ass
BMI	bmi	body mass index
BML	bml	bless my life
BMOC	bmoc	big man on campus
BMP	bmp	bitmap
BMPT	bmpt	bampot (idiot)
BMT	bmt	basic military training
BMT	bmt	before my time
BMTH	bmth	*Bring Me the Horizon* (band)
BMTTVE	bmttve	best mates 'til the very end
BMTTVEOT	bmttveot	best mates till the very end of time
BMUS	bmus	beam me up, Scotty
BMVP	bmvp	be my valentine, please
BMW	bmw	Bavarian Motor Works (car manufacturer)
BMX	bmx	bicycle motocross
BN	bn	bad news
BN	bn	been
BNB	bnb	*Bad News Bears* (movie)
BNB	bnb	bed and breakfast
BNB	bnb	bread and butter
BNDM3OVR	bndm3ovr	bend me over
BNF	bnf	big name fan
BNG	bng	blow and go
BNI	bni	batteries not included
BNIB	bnib	brand new in box
BNOL	bnol	be nice or leave
BNP	bnp	British National Party
BNR	bnr	banner
BNR	bnr	beaner (Mexican person - ethnic slur/derogatory)
BNR	bnr	boner (erection)
BNR	bnr	but not really
BNWOT	bnwot	brand new without tags
BNWT	bnwt	brand new with tags
BO	bo	body odor
BOATI	boati	bend over and take it
BOB	bob	back off, bastard/bitch
BOBBA	bobba	replacement swear word
BOBFOC	bobfoc	body off *Baywatch*, face off crime watch
BOBW	bobw	best of both worlds
BOE	boe	*Bind on Equip* (online gaming)
BOED	boed	*Book of Exalted Deeds* (MMORPG)
BOF	bof	whatever
BOFFIN	boffin	technical expert
BOFFUM	boffum	both of them
BOFH	bofh	bastard operator from hell

UPPERCASE	LOWERCASE	MEANING
BOG	bog	toilet
BOGAN	bogan	poorly educated, vulgar person (Australian)
BOGO	bogo	buy one get one
BOGOF	bogof	buy one get one free
BOGSAT	bogsat	bunch of guys sitting around talking
BOGSATT	bogsatt	bunch of guys sitting around the table
BOH	boh	gunshot sound
BOHIC	bohic	bend over, here it comes
BOHICA	bohica	bend over, here it comes again
BOI	boi	boy
BOILER	boiler	ugly woman
BOKE	boke	gag, almost vomit
BOL	bol	barking out loud
BOL	bol	best of luck
BOLO	bolo	be on the lookout
BOLSHY	bolshy	argumentative
BOLSHY	bolshy	Bolshevik, communist
BOLTOP	boltop	better on lips than on paper
BOM	bom	bitch of mine
BOM	bom	bro, dude, friend
BOMB	bomb	something really bad/good
BOMBSHELL	bombshell	very attractive woman
BOMM	bomm	(same as "boom")
BONE UP	bone up	learn about, revise
BONG	bong	water pipe for smoking dope
BONKERS	bonkers	crazy
BONR	bonr	boner
BONZA	bonza	brilliant, excellent
BOO	boo	boyfriend/girlfriend
BOOGER	booger	dried nose mucus
BOOHOO	boohoo	crying
BOOK	book	cool (predictive text)
BOOM	boom	great, amazing
BOOMERS	boomers	psilocybin (magic) mushrooms
BOOMM	boomm	bored out of my mind
BOOMS	booms	(same as "boomers")
BOOMS	booms	bored out of my skull
BOOMTING	boomting	good-looking girl
BOON	boon	someone who has been a noob for ages
BOOT	boot	inexperienced person
BOOT	boot	vomit
BOOZE	booze	alcoholic beverages
BORD	bord	bored
BOS	bos	boss over shoulder
BOS	bos	boyfriend over shoulder
BOSMKL	bosmkl	bending over smacking my knee laughing
BOSS	boss	cool, awesome
BOT	bot	back on topic
BOT	bot	be on that
BOTCH	botch	mess up
BOTDF	botdf	*Blood on the Dance Floor* (band)
BOTOH	botoh	but on the other hand
BOTS	bots	robots, automated processes
BOTTS	botts	back on to the subject

UPPERCASE	LOWERCASE	MEANING
BOUL	boul	bull
BOUT	bout	about
BOVERED	bovered	bothered
BOWL	bowl	part of a marijuana pipe
BOWS	bows	elbows
BOWT	bowt	about
BOXOR	boxor	box
BOXORZ	boxorz	boxers
BOYF	boyf	boyfriend
BPENIS	bpenis	big penis
BPLM	bplm	big person, little mind
BPLUG	bplug	butt plug (cork)
BPOT	bpot	big pair of tits
BPS	bps	bits/bytes per second
BQ	bq	be quiet
BR	br	bathroom
BR	br	best regards
BRAH	brah	bro, friend
BRAT	brat	annoying, spoiled child
BRAVO	bravo	well done
BRB	brb	be right back
BRBB	brbb	be right back, babe/baby
BRBBRB	brbbrb	be right back, bathroom break
BRBF	brbf	be right back, fucker
BRBG2P	brbg2p	be right back, got to pee
BRBIGTP	brbigtp	be right back, I got to pee
BRBL	brbl	be right back later
BRBMF	brbmf	be right back, motherfucker
BRBN2GBR	brbn2gbr	be right back, I need to go to the bathroom
BRBS	brbs	be right back soon
BRBTS	brbts	be right back, taking shit
BRD	brd	*Blackrock Depths* (WOW)
BRD	brd	bored
BRE	bre	sexy girl
BREAD	bread	money
BREDRIN	bredrin	friend
BREDRINS	bredrins	close friends, brothers
BREH	breh	brethren, brothers
BREW	brew	beer
BREW	brew	brother
BREW	brew	tea
BRFB	brfb	be right fucking back
BRGDS	brgds	best regards
BRH	brh	be right here
BRICKS	bricks	drugs, dope
BRITCHES	britches	pants, trousers
BRNC	brnc	be right back, nature calls
BRO	bro	brother, buddy, friend
BROAD	broad	woman
BROCHACHO	brochacho	(same as "bro")
BROFKR	brofkr	brotherfucker (homosexual slur/derogatory)
BROHAN	brohan	(same as "bro")
BROLLY	brolly	umbrella
BROS	bros	brothers

UPPERCASE	LOWERCASE	MEANING
BROSEPH	broseph	brother
BROSKI	broski	bro
BROVER	brover	brother
BROWN	brown	heroin
BROWN BREAD	brown bread	dead
BRT	brt	be right there
BRU	bru	(same as "bro")
BRUDDA	brudda	brother
BRUH	bruh	(same as "bro")
BRUH BRUH	bruh bruh	brother, friend
BRUHH	bruhh	brother
BRUK	bruk	broken
BRUV	bruv	brother/mate
BRUVA	bruva	brother
BRUZ	bruz	brothers
BS	bs	big smile
BS	bs	bullshit
BSB	bsb	*Backstreet Boys* (band)
BSC	bsc	bachelor of science (university degree)
BSER	bser	backstabber
BSF	bsf	but seriously, folks
BSG	bsg	*Battlestar Galactica* (TV show)
BSMFH	bsmfh	bastard system manager from hell
BSNS	bsns	business
BSOD	bsod	Blue Screen of Death (Windows)
BSOF	bsof	big smile on face
BSOFN	bsofn	big smile on face now
BSOMN	bsomn	blowing stuff out my nose
BST	bst	but seriously though
BSTFU	bstfu	bitch, shut the fuck up
BSTRD	bstrd	bastard
BSTS	bsts	better safe than sorry
BSU	bsu	boring status update
BSX	bsx	bisexual
BSXC	bsxc	be sexy
BT	bt	between technologies
BT	bt	bite this
BT	bt	BitTorrent (communications protocol)
BT	bt	British Telecom
BT DUBS	bt dubs	(same as "btw")
BTA	bta	but then again...
BTAIM	btaim	be that as it may
BTB	btb	by the by
BTBAM	btbam	*Between the Buried and Me* (band)
BTCH	btch	bitch
BTCHASS	btchass	bitchass (idiot)
BTCHAZZ	btchazz	bitchass (idiot)
BTCHTTS	btchtts	bitchtits (homosexual slur/derogatory)
BTCHY	btchy	bitchy (mean)
BTCN	btcn	better than Chuck Norris
BTD	btd	bored to death
BTDT	btdt	been there done that
BTDTGTTS	btdtgtts	been there, done that, got the T-shirt

UPPERCASE LOWERCASE MEANING

BTDTGTTSAWIO	btdtgttsawio	been there, done that, got the T-shirt, and wore it out
BTDUBS	btdubs	(same as "btw")
BTE	bte	best time ever
BTFL	btfl	beautiful
BTFO	btfo	back the fuck off
BTFO	btfo	bend the fuck over
BTFW	btfw	by the fucking way
BTGOG	btgog	by the grace of God
BTHO	btho	beat the hell outta
BTHOM	bthom	beats the hell outta me
BTIAS	btias	be there in a second
BTL	btl	between the lines
BTM	btm	be there moment
BTNGR	Btngr	boat nigger (Cuban or anyone from the Caribbean - ethnic slur/derogatory)
BTR	btr	better
BTS	bts	be there soon
BTSOOM	btsoom	beats the shit out of me
BTT	btt	bump to top (forum posts)
BTTF	bttf	back to the future
BTTT	bttt	back to the top
BTTT	bttt	been there, tried that
BTTYL	bttyl	be talking to you later
BTU	btu	British thermal unit
BTW	btw	by the way
BTWILU	btwilu	by the way, I love you
BTWITIAILWU	btwitiailwu	By the way, I think I am in love with you
BTWN	btwn	between
BTY	bty	back to you
BTYCL	btycl	booty call
BU	bu	backup
BU2M	bu2m	Been up too much?
BUB	bub	buddy, friend
BUB	bub	champagne
BUBAR	bubar	bushed up beyond all recognition
BUBI	bubi	bye
BUBS	bubs	babe
BUBZ	bubz	pet name for bf or gf
BUCK	buck	fight
BUCK	buck	money
BUCKS	bucks	dollars, money
BUD	bud	marijuana
BUDDY	buddy	friend
BUDZECKS	budzecks	butt sex
BUEY	buey	similar to dude
BUFF	buff	big ugly fat fuck
BUFF	buff	good-looking
BUG	bug	bother, annoy
BUGLE	bugle	cocaine
BUH	buh	expression of dismay, disgust
BUHBI	buhbi	bye-bye
BUKKET	bukket	bucket
BUMMED	bummed	disappointed, upset
BUMMER	bummer	bad luck

UPPERCASE	LOWERCASE	MEANING
BUMP	bump	bring up my post
BUN	bun	smoke marijuana
BUN	bun	ugly
BUR	bur	(same as "LOL")
BUR	bur	pussy
BURD	burd	bird, girlfriend
BURK	burk	idiot, fool
BURMA	burma	be undressed ready, my angel
BURMA	burma	be upstairs ready, my angel
BURNED	burned	insulted
BURNT	burnt	out of it, having smoked too much pot
BURR	burr	cold
BUSKING	busking	playing music in public for money
BUSTED	busted	caught
BUSTED	busted	very ugly
BUSZAY	buszay	busy
BUT6	but6	butt sex
BUTCH	butch	masculine
BUTSECKS	butsecks	butt sex
BUTT DIAL	butt dial	accidental call from a phone in your pocket
BUTT HURT	butt hurt	offended, upset
BUTTER FACE	butter face	girl who is good-looking except for her face
BUTTERFACE	butterface	everything is hot but her face
BUTTERS	butters	ugly
BUTTERZ	butterz	ugly
BUTTFCKA	buttfcka	buttfucka (homosexual slur/derogatory)
BUTTFCKR	buttfckr	buttfucker (homosexual slur/derogatory)
BUWU	buwu	breaking up with you
BUZZ	buzz	excitement
BUZZ	buzz	feeling when high
BUZZ KILL	buzz kill	ruin a special moment
BUZZED	buzzed	tipsy, slightly drunk
BV	bv	bad vibe
BVB	bvb	*Black Veil Brides* (band)
BW	bw	beautiful woman
BW	bw	black and white
BW3	bw3	Buffalo Wild Wings
BWC	bwc	But who cares?
BWIM	bwim	by which I mean
BWL	bwl	bursting with laughter
BWOC	bwoc	big woman on campus
BWPWAP	bwpwap	back when Pluto was a planet
BWT	bwt	but when though
BWT	bwt	misspelling of btw
BWTH	bwth	but what the hell
BY&M	by&m	between you and me
BYAK	byak	blowing you a kiss
BYAM	byam	between you and me
BYEAS	byeas	good-bye
BYES	byes	bye-bye
BYKI	byki	before you know it
BYKT	bykt	but you knew that
BYO	byo	bring your own
BYOH	byoh	bat you on (the) head

UPPERCASE	LOWERCASE	MEANING
BYOA	byoa	bring your own Advil
BYOB	byob	bring your own beer
BYOB	byob	bring your own boy
BYOC	byoc	bring your own chick
BYOC	byoc	bring your own computer
BYOC	byoc	bring your own condoms
BYOF	byof	bring your own fucker
BYOG	byog	bring your own girl
BYOI	byoi	bring your own idiot
BYOL	byol	bring your own laptop
BYOM	byom	bring your own man
BYOM	byom	bring your own meat
BYOM	byom	bring your own music
BYOP	byop	bring your own paint (paintball)
BYOS	byos	bring your own soda
BYOW	byow	bring your own Web site
BYOW	byow	bring your own whore
BYOW	byow	bring your own woman
BYSELF	byself	by myself
BYT	byt	before your time
BYT	byt	bright young thing
BYTABM	bytabm	beat you to a bloody mess
BYTCH	bytch	bitch
BYTM	bytm	better you than me
BZ	bz	busy
BZNS	bzns	business
BZY	bzy	busy
BZZY	bzzy	busy
C	c	computer language
C	c	see
C	c	speed of light
C 2 C	c 2 c	cam to cam (Webcams)
C#	c#	Microsoft programming language
C&C	c&c	*Command and Conquer* (game)
C&G	c&g	chuckle and grin
C&P	c&p	copy and paste
C.Y.A	c.y.a	cover your ass
C/B	c/b	comment back
C/D	c/d	confirm/deny
C/O	c/o	class of...
C/P	c/p	cross post
C/T	c/t	can't talk
C:	c:	very happy
C@	c@	cat
C@@CHIE	c@@chie	coochie (female genitalia)
C@@CHY	c@@chy	coochy (female genitalia)
C@@L	c@@l	cool
C@@N	c@@n	coon (African American · ethnic slur/derogatory)
C@@TER	c@@ter	cooter (vagina)
C@CK	c@ck	cock (penis)
C|N>K	c|n>k	coffee through nose into keyboard
C'MON	c'mon	come on
C1	c1	affirmative, roger that
C14N	c14n	canonicalization

UPPERCASE	LOWERCASE	MEANING
C2	c2	come to
C2C	c2c	cam to cam
C2C	c2c	Care to chat?
C2C	c2c	consumer to consumer
C2TC	c2tc	cut to the chase
C4	c4	plastic explosive
C4ASHG	c4ashg	care for a shag
C4C	c4c	cam for cam
C4C	c4c	comment for comment
C4N	c4n	ciao for now
CA	ca	congratulations, asshole
CACHAI	cachai	Do you understand?
CACHE	cache	store for temporary computer files
CACTUS	cactus	broken, dead
CAD	cad	Computer-Aided Design
CAD	cad	Control + Alt + Delete
CAD	cad	short for Canada/Canadian
CADDY	caddy	Cadillac
CAKE	cake	kilo of cocaine
CAKING	caking	flirting
CAM	cam	camera
CAMEL	camel	brand of cigarettes
CAMPER	camper	player who lies in wait for a target
CANCER STICK	cancer stick	cigarette
CANON	canon	original, official
CANTO	canto	Cantonese
CAPISH	capish	Do you understand?
CAPS	caps	bullets
CAPS	caps	mushrooms
CAPTCHA	captcha	Completely Automated Public Turing Test to Tell Computers and Humans Apart
CARD	card	amusing, eccentric person
CARE	care	I don't care
CARRIED	carried	told off, dissed
CASJ	casj	casual
CAT	cat	computerized axial tomography
CAT	cat	cool person
CATWOT	catwot	complete and total waste of time
CAUSE	cause	because
CAVE	cave	give up, give in
CAWK	cawk	cock
CAZ	caz	crazy in a nice way
CB	cb	chat break
CB	cb	coffee break
CB	cb	come back
CB	cb	crazy bitch/bastard
CBA	cba	can't be arsed
CBB	cbb	can't be bothered
CBBC	cbbc	Children's BBC
CBC	cbc	Canadian Broadcasting Corporation
CBCD	cbcd	Canadian-born confused Desi (ethnic slur/derogatory)
CBF	cbf	can't be fucked
CBFA	cbfa	can't be fucking arsed

UPPERCASE	LOWERCASE	MEANING
CBFED	cbfed	can't be fucked
CBI	cbi	California Bureau of Investigation
CBI	cbi	can't believe it
CBI	cbi	Confederation of British Industry
CBS	cbs	can't be stuffed
CBT	cbt	cognitive behavioral therapy
CC	cc	carbon copy
CC	cc	country code
CC	cc	credit card
CC	cc	crowd control
CCC	ccc	Coricidin cough and cold (dextromethorphan or DXM)
CCD	ccd	charged-coupled device
CCL	ccl	couldn't care less
CCNA	ccna	Cisco Certified Network Associate
CCTV	cctv	closed-circuit television
CD	cd	compact disc
CD	cd	cross-dresser
CD9	cd9	code 9, "parents are around"
CDC	cdc	crudely drawn cock
CDC	cdc	*Cult of the Dead Cow* (the most infamous group of hackers)
CDFS	cdfs	Compact Disc File System
CDMA	cdma	code division multiple access (voice/data transmission)
CDN	cdn	Canadian
CDP	cdp	calm down, please
CDR	cdr	compact disc recordable
CD-R	cd-r	compact disc recordable
CD-ROM	cd-rom	compact disc read-only memory
CD-RW	cd-rw	compact disc re-writable
CEEB	ceeb	(same as "CBB")
CEEBS	ceebs	(same as "CBB")
CEEBZ	ceebz	(same as "CBB")
CELL	cell	cell phone
CELLY	celly	cell phone
CEO	ceo	chief executive officer
CEPT	cept	except
CEREAL	cereal	serious
CES	ces	consumer electronics show
CET	cet	Central European Time
CEWL	cewl	cool
CEX	cex	sex
CEXY	cexy	sexy
CFAS	cfas	Care for a secret?
CFC	cfc	chlorofluorocarbon
CFID	cfid	check for identification
CFL	cfl	Canadian Football League
CFM	cfm	come fuck me
CFN	cfn	ciao for now
CFO	cfo	chief financial officer
CFS	cfs	Care for secret?
CFV	cfv	call for votes
CFY	cfy	calling for you
CG	cg	computer graphics

UPPERCASE	LOWERCASE	MEANING
CG	cg	congratulations
CGAD	cgad	couldn't give a damn
CGAF	cgaf	couldn't give a fuck
CGF	cgf	cute guy friend
CGI	cgi	Common Gateway Interface
CH@	ch@	chat
CHA	cha	yes
CHADROOL	chadrool	stupid person
CHAMP	champ	uncool
CHAMPION	champion	good, great
CHAO	chao	good-bye (Spanish)
CHAP	chap	man
CHAR	char	character
CHAV	chav	poorly educated, vulgar youth
CHAW	chaw	chewing tobacco
CHEA	chea	yeah
CHEAPSKATE	cheapskate	mean/stingy person
CHEDDA	chedda	cash, money
CHEDDAR	cheddar	money
CHEERIO	cheerio	good-bye
CHEERS	cheers	good-bye / thanks
CHEESE	cheese	drug, starter heroin
CHEESE	cheese	money
CHEESY	cheesy	corny, lame
CHEEZ	cheez	cheese
CHEEZBURGER	cheezburger	cheeseburger
CHGGR	chggr	Chigger, a person of mixed African/Asian ancestry (ethnic slur/derogatory)
CHI	chi	Chicago
CHI	chi	life force, energy
CHICK	chick	girl
CHICKEN	chicken	kilogram of cocaine
CHIK	chik	chick
CHILAX	chilax	chill and relax in one word
CHILAXING	chilaxing	chilling and relaxing
CHILL	chill	relax, hang out
CHILL OUT	chill out	(same as "chill")
CHILLAX	chillax	chill and relax
CHILLIN	chillin	relaxing
CHINK	chink	an Asian or Chinese person (ethnic slur/derogatory)
CHINWAG	chinwag	chat
CHIO	chio	sexy, good-looking, girl
CHIPOTLE	chipotle	Mexican-style restaurant
CHIRP	chirp	insult
CHIRPSE	chirpse	flirt
CHIZ	chiz	swiz, swindle
CHIZZ	chizz	chill out, relax
CHK	chk	check
CHNC	chnc	chinc (Chinese person - ethnic slur/derogatory)
CHNK	chnk	chink (Asian person - ethnic slur/derogatory)
CHOLO	cholo	Mexican gangster
CHOO	choo	you
CHOOB	choob	high-level player who acts like a noob
CHOONG	choong	good-looking, buff

UPPERCASE	LOWERCASE	MEANING
CHOP IT UP	chop it up	talk
CHOPPER	chopper	AK-47 assault rifle
CHOUT	chout	chill out/watch out
CHOW	chow	bye
CHOW	chow	food
CHP	chp	California Highway Patrol
CHR	chr	character
CHRONIC	chronic	marijuana
CHSWM	chswm	Come have sex with me.
CHSWMRN	chswmrn	Come have sex with me right now.
CHU	chu	you
CHULA	chula	cute, sexy
CHUNDER	chunder	be sick, vomit
CHUNG	chung	good-looking, buff
CHUT	chut	pussy
CHUTIYA	chutiya	mild Indian expletive
CHYA	chya	yes, yeah
CI	ci	confidential informant
CIA	cia	Central Intelligence Agency
CIAO	ciao	Italian for "hi" or "bye"
CICO	cico	coffee in, coffee out
CID	cid	acid, LSD
CID	cid	consider it done
CID	cid	crying in disgrace
CIG	cig	cigarette
CIGGY	ciggy	cigarette
CIGS	cigs	cigarettes
CIHSWU	cihswu	Can I have sex with you?
CIHY	cihy	Can I help you?
CILF	cilf	child I'd like to fuck
CING	cing	seeing
CINI	cini	cinema
CIO	cio	check it out
CIR	cir	committed information rate (minimum bandwidth)
CIS	cis	computer information system
CISC	cisc	Complex Instruction Set Computing
CITA	cita	caught in the act
CIWWAF	ciwwaf	cute is what we aim for
CK	ck	crip killa
CKASS	ckass	cockass (jerk)
CKAZZ	ckazz	cockass (jerk)
CKBITE	ckbite	cockbite (idiot)
CKBURGER	ckburger	cockburger (idiot)
CKFACE	ckface	cockface (idiot)
CKFCKR	ckfckr	cockfucker (idiot)
CKHEAD	ckhead	cockhead (idiot)
CKJKY	ckjky	cockjockey (homosexual slur/derogatory)
CKKNKR	ckknkr	cockknoker (homosexual slur/derogatory)
CKMNCHR	ckmnchr	cockmuncher (homosexual slur/derogatory)
CKMNKY	ckmnky	cockmonkey (idiot)
CKMSTR	ckmstr	cockmaster (homosexual slur/derogatory)
CKSHT	cksht	cockshit (idiot)
CKSKR	ckskr	cocksucker (homosexual slur/derogatory)
CKSNFFR	cksnffr	cocksniffer (homosexual slur/derogatory)

UPPERCASE	LOWERCASE	MEANING
CL	cl	chain letter
CL	cl	Craigslist
CLAB	clab	crying like a baby
CLAPPED	clapped	shot
CLARET	claret	blood
CLASS	class	cool, excellent
CLEO	cleo	chief law enforcement officer
CLESS	cless	clanless
CLI	cli	command-line interface
CLICK	click	kilometer
CLIQUE	clique	group of friends
CLM	clm	career-limiting move
CLM	clm	cool like me
CLOB	clob	Character Large Object
CLOCK	clock	hit
CLOCK	clock	look at
CLOUD	cloud	the Internet (nonlocal storage, software, etc.)
CLOUD 9	cloud 9	feeling of euphoria, high
CLT	clt	clit (female genitals)
CLT	clt	cool like that
CLTFACE	cltface	clitface (idiot)
CLTFK	cltfk	clitfuck (sexual act)
CLUBBING	clubbing	visiting nightclubs
CLUBHEAD	clubhead	person who goes to clubs a lot
CLUEBIE	cluebie	clueless newbie
CLUT	clut	clumsy person
CLUTCH	clutch	perform under pressure
CM	cm	call me
CMA	cma	cover my ass
CMAO	cmao	crying my ass off
CMAR	cmar	cry me a river
CMB	cmb	call me back/comment me back
CMBO	cmbo	combo
CMC	cmc	*casi me cago* (Spanish LOL)
CMCP	cmcp	call my cell phone
CMD	cmd	command
CMEO	cmeo	crying my eyes out
CMH	cmh	call my house
CMI	cmi	count me in
CMIIW	cmiiw	correct me if I'm wrong
CMITM	cmitm	call me in the morning
CML	cml	call me later
CML8R	cml8r	call me later
CMLIUW2	cmliuw2	call me later if you want to
CMNT	cmnt	comment
CMO	cmo	count me out
CMOMC	cmomc	call me on my cell
CMON	cmon	come on
CMOS	cmos	Complementary Metal-Oxide Semiconductor
CMPLCDD	cmplcdd	complicated
CMPLTE	cmplte	complete
CMS	cms	content management system
CMT	cmt	comment
CMU	cmu	cracks me up

UPPERCASE	LOWERCASE	MEANING
CMW	cmw	cutting my wrists
CMYK	cmyk	cyan, magenta, yellow, and key or black
CN	cn	can
CNC	cnc	*Command and Conquer*
CNN	cnn	Cable News Network
CNP	cnp	continued (in) next post
CNT	cnt	can't
CNT	cnt	cunt (vagina)
CNTAZZ	cntazz	cuntass (idiot)
CO	co	commanding officer
CO	co	company
CO	co	corrections officer
CO	co	counteroffer
COA	coa	certificate of authenticity
COALBURNER	coalburner	white woman that dates black men
COB	cob	close of business
COCK UP	cock up	mistake, mess
COCKY	cocky	thinking too highly of yourself
COD	cod	*Call of Duty* (game)
COD	cod	cash on delivery
COD4	cod4	*Call of Duty 4* (game)
CODE 29	code 29	moderator is watching
CODE 8	code 8	parents are watching
CODE 9	code 9	parents are watching
CODE9	code9	other people nearby
COED	coed	coeducational (men and women together)
COF	cof	crying on the floor
COG	cog	*Coalition of Gears* (game)
COH	coh	*City of Heroes* (online gaming)
COIWTA	coiwta	come on, I won't tell anyone
COKE	coke	Coca-Cola/cocaine
COL	col	crying out loud
COLA	cola	top bud of a marijuana plant
COMIN'	comin'	coming
COMNT	comnt	comment
COMP	comp	computer
COMPY	compy	computer
CONDO	condo	apartment
CONGRATS	congrats	congratulations
CONTRIB	contrib	contribution
CONTRIBS	contribs	contributions
CONVO	convo	conversation
COO	coo	cool
COOD	cood	could
COOKIE	cookie	small file relating to a Web site
COOL	cool	awesome, great
COOL BEANS	cool beans	cool, awesome, great
COOLIN	coolin	same as chilling
COP	cop	close of play
COP	cop	officer of the law
COPACETIC	copacetic	cool, OK, excellent
COPY THAT	copy that	I understand
COPYCAT	copycat	someone who copies someone else
COPYPASTA	copypasta	post that has been copied and pasted

UPPERCASE	LOWERCASE	MEANING
COPYVIO	copyvio	copyright violation
CORNY	corny	uncool, overused
COS	cos	because
COSPLAY	cosplay	costume play
COTCH	cotch	relax, chill
COTF	cotf	crying on the floor
COTM	cotm	check out this Myspace
COUCH POTATO	couch potato	lazy person who sits all day watching TV
COUGAR	cougar	older woman looking for a younger man
COUGER	couger	older woman looking for a younger man
COUPLE	couple	two people in a relationship
COURSE	course	of course, certainly
COW	cow	offensive term for a woman
COWBOY CHOKER	cowboy choker	cigarette
COYB	coyb	come on, you blues
COYOTE	coyote	person who smuggles immigrants
COYS	coys	come on, you spurs
COZ	coz	because
CP	cp	chat post
CP	cp	child porn
C-P	c-p	sleepy
CPA	cpa	cost per action
CPC	cpc	cost per click
CPL	cpl	cost per lead
CPL	cpl	*Cyberathlete Professional League* (game)
CPM	cpm	cost per thousand
CPP	cpp	(cee plus plus) C++ (programming language)
CPR	cpr	cardiopulmonary resuscitation
CPS	cps	classroom performance system
CPT	cpt	colored people's time
CPTN	cptn	captain
CPU	cpu	central processing unit
CPY	cpy	copy
CQB	cqb	close quarters battle
CQTMS	cqtms	chuckle quietly to myself
CR	cr	can't remember
CR	cr	carriage return
CR	cr	copyright
CR	cr	credit
CR@CKER	cr@cker	cracker (white person · ethnic slur/derogatory)
CR8	cr8	crate
CR8	cr8	create
CRAB	crab	derogatory word for a crippled person
CRACK	crack	a form of cocaine
CRAFT	craft	can't remember a fucking thing
CRAIC	craic	good times/gossip/music/drinking (Irish)
CRAKALAKIN	crakalakin	happening
CRAWS	craws	can't remember anything worth a shit
CRAY CRAY	cray cray	really crazy
CRAZN	crazn	crazy Asian
CRB	crb	come right back
CRBT	crbt	crying real big tears

UPPERCASE	LOWERCASE	MEANING
CRC	crc	chat room chuckle
CRC	crc	cyclic redundancy check
CRCKR	crckr	cracker (white person - ethnic slur/derogatory)
CRE8OR	cre8or	creator
CREASING	creasing	laughing
CREEP	creep	weird, undesirable person
CREEPER	creeper	someone who views your profile but doesn't make contact
CREPS	creps	trainers
CRIB	crib	house, residence
CRICKETS	crickets	said after a lame joke to break the silence
CRIMBO	crimbo	Christmas
CRIP	crip	Community Restoration in Progress (gang)
CRIP	crip	gang member
CRM	crm	customer relationship management
CROW	crow	marijuana
CRP	crp	crap
CRS	crs	can't remember shit
CRT	crt	cathode-ray tube
CRUNK	crunk	combination of crazy and drunk
CRUSH	crush	infatuation, attraction
CRUSTY	crusty	dirty, unwashed person
CRZ	crz	craze
CRZY	crzy	crazy
CS	cs	cocksucker
CS	cs	Counter-Strike
CS:S	cs:s	Counter-Strike: Source
CSA	csa	cheap-shot artist
CSB	csb	cool story, bro (sarcastic)
CSG	csg	chuckle, snicker, grin
CSI	csi	*Crime Scene Investigation* (TV show)
CSKR	cskr	cocksucker
CSL	csl	can't stop laughing
CSS	css	Cascading Style Sheet
CSS	css	Counter-Strike: Source
CST	cst	Central Standard Time
CSV	csv	comma-separated values
CT	ct	camel toe (female genitalia)
CT	ct	can't talk
CTC	ctc	call the cell
CTC	ctc	Care to chat?
CTD	ctd	crash to desktop
CTF	ctf	capture the flag
CTF	ctf	claim to fame
CTFD	ctfd	calm the fuck down
CTFO	ctfo	chill the fuck out
CTFO	ctfo	come the fuck on
CTFU	ctfu	cracking the fuck up
CTHU	cthu	cracking the heck up
CTM	ctm	chuckle to myself/chuckling to myself
CTN	ctn	can't talk now
CTNBOS	ctnbos	can't talk now, boss over shoulder
CTNCL	ctncl	can't talk now, call later
CTO	cto	check this out

UPPERCASE	LOWERCASE	MEANING
CTP	ctp	Composite Theoretical Performance
CTPC	ctpc	can't talk parent(s) coming
CTPOS	ctpos	can't talk, parent over shoulder
CTR	ctr	Click-Through Rate
CTRL	ctrl	control (key)
CTRN	ctrn	can't talk right now
CTS	cts	change the subject
CTS	cts	chuckles to self
CTT	ctt	change the topic
CU	cu	see you/good-bye
CU2	cu2	see you too/good-bye too
CU2NIT	cu2nit	see you tonight
CU46	cu46	see you for sex
CUA	cua	see you around
CUATU	cuatu	see you around the universe
CUBI	cubi	Can you believe it?
CUCKOO	cuckoo	mad, bonkers, crazy
CUD	cud	could
CUDDY	cuddy	buddy, friend
CUFF	cuff	overprotect, smother
CUFFED	cuffed	taken, has a bf or gf
CUH	cuh	cousin, homie, bro
CUIAB	cuiab	see you in a bit
CUIC	cuic	see you in class
CUL	cul	see you later
CUL83R	cul83r	see you later
CUL8ER	cul8er	see you later
CUL8R	cul8r	see you later
CUL8TR	cul8tr	see you later
CULA	cula	see you later, alligator
CULB	culb	see you later, babe
CULD	culd	could
CUMBBBLE	cumbbble	cumbubble (idiot)
CUMDMPSTR	cumdmpstr	cumdumpster (prostitute)
CUMGZZLR	cumgzzlr	cumguzzler (homosexual slur/derogatory)
CUMID	cumid	see you in my dreams
CUMJCKY	cumjcky	cumjockey (homosexual slur/derogatory)
CUMSLT	cumslt	cumslut (dirty girl)
CUNT	cunt	vagina
CUOL	cuol	see you on line
CUOM	cuom	see you on Monday
CUPCAKE	cupcake	soft, loving person
CUPLE	cuple	couple
CUPPA	cuppa	cup of (usually) tea
CURLO	curlo	see you around like a donut
CURN	curn	calling you right now
CUS	cus	friend
CUSH	cush	high-grade marijuana
CUSHTI	cushti	good, great
CUSS	cuss	curse, swear
CUT	cut	see you there/see you tomorrow
CUT3	cut3	cute
CUTCH	cutch	snuggle up
CUTE	cute	someone/thing that is attractive in an innocent way

UPPERCASE	LOWERCASE	MEANING
CUTIE	cutie	cute, attractive person
CUTY	cuty	cutie
CUWUL	cuwul	catch up with you later
CUZ	cuz	because
CUZZ	cuzz	because
CUZZ	cuzz	friend, cousin
CUZZO	cuzzo	friend
CV	cv	curriculum vitae, resume
CVQ	cvq	chucking very quietly
CW	cw	continuous wave, Morse code
CW2CU	cw2cu	can`t wait to see you
CWM	cwm	come with me
CWMAOS	cwmaos	coffee with milk and one sugar
CWOT	cwot	complete waste of time
CWTCU	cwtcu	can't wait to see you
CWTGYPO	cwtgypo	can't wait to get your panties off
CWTSY	cwtsy	can't wait to see you
CWYL	cwyl	chat with you later
CYA	cya	cover your ass
CYA	cya	see ya/see you/good-bye
CYAL	cyal	see you later
CYAL8R	cyal8r	see you later
CYAS	cyas	see you soon
CYB	cyb	count your blessings
CYB	cyb	cyber
CYBI	cybi	Can you believe it?
CYBL	cybl	call you back later
CYBR	cybr	cyber
CYBSECKZ	cybseckz	cyber sex
CYE	cye	check your e-mail
CYE	cye	close your eyes
CYFF	cyff	change your font, fucker
CYL	cyl	catch you later/see you later
CYL,A	cyl,a	catch you later, alligator/see ya later, alligator
CYL8	cyl8	see you later
CYL8ER	cyl8er	see you later
CYL8R	cyl8r	see you later
CYLBD	cylbd	catch ya later, baby doll
CYLOR	cylor	check your local orthodox rabbi
CYM	cym	check your mail
CYO	cyo	see you online
CYT	cyt	see you tomorrow
CYU	cyu	see you
CZ	cz	*Condition Zero* (game)
D BO	d bo	steal
D&C	d&c	divide and conquer
D&D	d&d	*Dungeons & Dragons* (game)
D&DF	d&df	drug and disease free
D&M	d&m	deep and meaningful
D.W	d.w	don't worry
D/C	d/c	disconnected
D/L	d/l	download
D/M	d/m	doesn't matter
D/W	d/w	don't worry

UPPERCASE	LOWERCASE	MEANING
D-':	D-':	horror, disgust, sadness
D:	D:	horror, disgust, sadness
D:<	D:<	horror, disgust, sadness
D;	D;	horror, disgust, sadness
D=	D=	horror, disgust, sadness
D00D	d00d	dude
D1CK	d1ck	dick
D2	d2	*dedos* / fingers (Spanish SMS)
D2	d2	*Diablo 2* (game)
D2F	d2f	(same as "DTF")
D2M	d2m	dead to me
D46?	d46?	Down for sex?
D8	d8	date
D8	D8	horror, disgust, sadness
DA	da	dad
DA	da	district attorney
DA	da	the
DAB	dab	Digital Audio Broadcasting
DAC	dac	Digital-to-Analog Converter
DADA	dada	Defence Against the Dark Arts (*Harry Potter*)
DADT	dadt	don't ask, don't tell
DAE	dae	Does anybody else?
DAFS	dafs	do a fucking search
DAFUQ	dafuq	(same as "WTF")
DAG	dag	damn
DAG	dag	unfashionable person
DAGO	dago	offensive term for an Italian
DAH	dah	dumb as hell
DAII	daii	day
DAM	dam	don't ask me
DAMAGE	damage	cost of something
DAMHIK	damhik	don't ask me how I know
DAMHIKIJK	damhikijk	don't ask me how I know, I just know
DAMHIKT	damhikt	don't ask me how I know that/this
DAMHIKT	damhikt	don't ask me how I know this
DANG	dang	damn
DANK	dank	incredibly good, awesome
DANK	dank	very potent marijuana
DAOC	daoc	*Dark Age of Camelot* (online gaming)
DAP	dap	touching-of-fists greeting
DAQ	daq	don't ask questions
DARE	dare	Drug Abuse Resistance Education
DARL	darl	darling
DARN	darn	damn
DARPA	darpa	Defense Advanced Research Projects Agency
DASS	dass	dumbass
DAT	dat	that
DATO	dato	dining at the orifice
DATS	dats	that's
DAVID	david	cool guy
DAW	daw	digital audio workstation
DAWG	dawg	close friend
DAWG	dawg	friend
DAYUM	dayum	damn

UPPERCASE	LOWERCASE	MEANING
DAYUMM	dayumm	damn
DB	db	database
DB	db	dear brother
DB	db	douche bag
DB4L	db4l	drinking buddy for life
DBAB	dbab	don't be a bitch
DBABAI	dbabai	don't be a bitch about it
DBAFWTT	dbafwtt	don't be a fool wrap the tool
DBAG	dbag	douchebag
DBAU	dbau	doing business as usual
DBEYR	dbeyr	don't believe everything you read
DBF	dbf	darling boyfriend
DBG	dbg	don't be gay
DBH	dbh	don't be hating
DBI	dbi	don't beg it
DBI	dbi	douche bag index
DBM	dbm	don't bother me
DBMS	dbms	database management system
DBNT	dbnt	don't bother next time
DBR	dbr	damaged beyond repair
DBZ	dbz	*Dragon Ball Z* (game)
DC	dc	disconnect
DC	dc	don't care
DC'D	dc'd	disconnected
DCF	dcf	department of children and families
DCHBG	dchbg	douche bag (idiot)
DCHE	dche	douche (female hygene product)
DCHEBAG	dchebag	douchebag (female hygene accessory)
DCHEFG	dchefg	douche-fag (idiot)
DCHWAFFLE	dchwaffle	douchewaffle (homosexual slur/derogatory)
DCIM	dcim	digital camera images
DCKBAG	dckbag	dickbag (idiot)
DCKBTR	dckbtr	dickbeaters (hands)
DCKFACE	dckface	dickface (idiot)
DCKFK	dckfk	dickfuck (idiot)
DCKFKR	dckfkr	dickfucker (homosexual slur/derogatory)
DCKHD	dckhd	dickhead (phallace face)
DCKHOLE	dckhole	dickhole (male genitalia)
DCKJUICE	dckjuice	dickjuice (semen)
DCKMILK	dckmilk	dickmilk (sperm)
DCKMNGR	dckmngr	dickmonger (homosexual slur/derogatory)
DCKO	dcko	dickhole (male genitalia)
DCKS	dcks	dicks (penises)
DCKSCKING	dckscking	dicksucking (sexual act)
DCKSCKR	dcksckr	dicksucker (homosexual slur/derogatory)
DCKSLP	dckslp	dickslap (sexual act)
DCKSNZZ	dcksnzz	dick-sneeze (orgasm)
DCKTCKLR	dcktcklr	dicktickler (homosexual slur/derogatory)
DCKWD	dckwd	dickwad (idiot)
DCKWD	dckwd	dickweed (idiot)
DCKWOD	dckwod	dickwod (idiot)
DCKWSL	dckwsl	dickweasel (idiot)
DCOI	dcoi	don't count on it
DCTNRY	dctnry	dictionary

UPPERCASE	LOWERCASE	MEANING
DCW	dcw	doing classwork
DD	dd	dear daughter
DD	dd	don't die
DD	dd	due diligence
D-DAY	d-day	16229
D-DAY	d-day	designated day when operations are due to commence
DDB	ddb	deaf, dumb, blind (disability slur/derogatory)
DDF	ddf	drug and disease free
DDG	ddg	drop-dead gorgeous
DDI	ddi	don't do it
DDL	ddl	data definition language
DDL	ddl	direct download
DDMMYY	ddmmyy	day month year
DDOS	ddos	distributed denial of service (network attack)
DDR	ddr	*Dance Dance Revolution* (game)
DDR	ddr	double data rate
DDR2	ddr2	double data rate 2
DDSOS	ddsos	different day, same old shit
DDT	ddt	don't do that
DE	de	the
DEA	dea	Drug Enforcement Administration
DEAD ASS	dead ass	serious
DEALING	dealing	acting like boyfriend/girlfriend
DEALING	dealing	selling drugs
DEAR	dear	drop everything and read
DEB	deb	don't even bother
DEC	dec	decent
DECENT	decent	good, awesome
DED	ded	dead from joy, hilarity, etc.
DEECE	deece	decent, cool, great
DEETS	deets	details
DEEZ	deez	these
DEF	def	cool, great, excellent, definitely
DEFFO	deffo	definitely
DEFO	defo	definitely
DEFS	defs	definitely
DEGMT	degmt	Don't even give me that.
DEGT	degt	Don't even go there. (i.e., I don't want to talk about it)
DEKE	deke	avoid, fake, decoy
DELISH	delish	delicious
DEM	dem	them
DEN	den	private room
DEN	den	then
DEPT	dept	department
DER	der	Duh!
DER	der	there
DERE	dere	there
DERNOE	dernoe	I don't know.
DERO	dero	derelict, loser
DEROB	derob	very bored
DERP	derp	reply to stupid comment or action
DERR	derr	(same as "duh")
DESI	desi	someone from the Indian (ethnic slur/derogatory)

UPPERCASE	LOWERCASE	MEANING
DET	det	Don't even trip.
DETAI	detai	Don't even think about it.
DEUCES	deuces	peace
DEVO	devo	devastated
DEWD	dewd	dude
DEY	dey	they
DF	df	Don't even go there.
DF	df	dumb fuck
DF	df	dumb-ass Frankenstein
DF	df	WTF
DFC	dfc	don't fucking care
DFE	dfe	dead fish experience
DFO	dfo	dumb fucking operator
DFS	dfs	dating for sport
DFTBA	dftba	Don't forget to be awesome.
DFTC	dftc	down for the count
DFTT	dftt	Don't feed the troll.
DFU	dfu	Don't fuck up.
DFW	dfw	Don't fucking worry.
DFW	dfw	down for whatever
DFW/M	dfw/m	Don't fuck with me.
DFWH	dfwh	Don't fuck with her/him.
DFWM	dfwm	Don't fuck with me.
DFWT	dfwt	Don't fuck with them.
DFWU	dfwu	Don't fuck with us.
DG	dg	Dago (Italian person - ethnic slur/derogatory)
DG	dg	Don't go.
DGA	dga	Don't go anywhere.
DGAC	dgac	don't give a crap
DGAF	dgaf	don't give a fuck
DGARA	dgara	don't give a rat's ass
DGAS	dgas	don't give a shit
DGF	dgf	darling girlfriend
DGGO	dggo	deggo (Italian person - ethnic slur/derogatory)
DGK	dgk	dirty ghetto kids (skateboarders)
DGMS	dgms	Don't get me started.
DGOAI	dgoai	Don't go on about it.
DGOT	dgot	Don't go over there.
DGT	dgt	Don't go there.
DGTB	dgtb	Don't go there, boyfriend.
DGTG	dgtg	Don't go there, girlfriend.
DGTH	dgth	Don't go there, honey.
DGTWM	dgtwm	Don't go there with me.
DGYPIAB	dgypiab	Don't get your panties in a bunch.
DH	dh	dear/darling husband
DH	dh	dickhead
DHAC	dhac	don't have a clue
DHCP	dhcp	Dynamic Host Configuration Protocol
DHL	dhl	shipping company
DHLY	dhly	Does he like you?
DHS	dhs	Department of Health Services
DHS	dhs	Department of Homeland Security
DHU	dhu	dinosaur hugs (used to show support)
DHV	dhv	demonstration of higher value

UPPERCASE	LOWERCASE	MEANING
DHYB	dhyb	Don't hold your breath.
DIACF	diacf	die in a car fire
DIAF	diaf	die in a fire
DIAH	diah	die in a hole
DIAO	diao	cool, hip
DIB	dib	Dumb Israeli Bastard (ethnic slur/derogatory)
DIBS	dibs	a claim
DIC	dic	Do I care?
DICK	dick	penis
DIDDO	diddo	(same as "ditto")
DIEZ	diez	dies
DIFF	diff	difference
DIG	dig	enjoy, like
DIG	dig	understand
DIGG	digg	social bookmarking Web site
DIGITS	digits	telephone number
DIGS	digs	home, lodgings
DIH	dih	dick in hand
DIIK	diik	darned if I know
DIKHED	dikhed	dickhead
DIKU	diku	Do I know you?
DIKY	diky	Do I know you?
DIL	dil	daughter-in-law
DILF	dilf	dad I'd like to fuck
DILIGAF	diligaf	(same as "DILLIGAF")
DILLIC	dillic	Do I look like I care?/Does it look like I care?
DILLIFC	dillifc	Do I look like I fucking care?
DILLIGAD	dilligad	Do I look like I give a damn?
DILLIGAF	dilligaf	Do I look like I give a fuck?
DILLIGAS	dilligas	Do I look like I give a shit?
DIME	dime	$10 of a drug
DIME	dime	very attractive person
DIMER	dimer	(same as "10")
DIMM	dimm	dual in-line memory module
DIN	din	didn't
DIN DIN	din din	dinner
DIN'T	din't	didn't
DINERO	dinero	money
DING	ding	just hit new level in RPG
DINGBAT	dingbat	stupid person, idiot
DINK	dink	double income, no kids
DINKY	dinky	dual income, no kids yuppie
DINKY	dinky	tiny, small
DINT	dint	did not, didn't
DIP	dip	leave
DIPPED	dipped	fashionable
DIRL	dirl	die in real life
DIRT	dirt	gossip
DIRT	dirt	low-grade marijuana
DIS	dis	did I say
DIS	dis	this
DISO	diso	desperately in search of
DISS	diss	disrespect
DISSING	dissing	being disrespectful

UPPERCASE	LOWERCASE	MEANING
DISTRO	distro	distribution (software, music, etc.)
DIT	dit	details in thread
DITD	ditd	down in the dumps, sad
DITTO	ditto	the same, me too, I agree
DITYID	dityid	Did I tell you I'm distressed?
DITZY	ditzy	acting dumb and innocent
DIV	div	stupid person
DIVA	diva	talented, but arrogant, female performer
DIY	diy	Do it yourself.
D.DIZZY	dizzy	crazy, mad
DJ	dj	dinner jacket
DJ	dj	disc jockey
DJ	dj	Dow Jones
DJM	djm	Don't judge me.
DJU	dju	Did you?
DK	dk	don't know
DKDC	dkdc	don't know, don't care
DKE	dke	dike (homosexual slur/derogatory)
DKFS	dkfs	don't know for sure
DKIE	dkie	dookie (poop)
DKM	dkm	Don't kill me.
DKNY	dkny	Donna Karan New York
DKP	dkp	dragon kill points (MMORPG)
DKY	dky	Don't kid yourself.
DKY	dky	don't know yet
DL	dl	down low
DL	dl	download
DLAM	dlam	Don't laugh at me.
DLBBB	dlbbb	Don't let (the) bedbugs bite.
DLC	dlc	downloadable content
DLDO	dldo	dildo (sexual toy)
DLF	dlf	dropping like flies
DLL	dll	dynamic link library (computer file)
DLN	dln	Don't look now.
DLS	dls	dirty little secret
DLTBBB	dltbbb	Don't let the bedbugs bite.
DLTM	dltm	Don't lie to me.
DLV	dlv	demonstration of lower value
DM	dm	death match
DM	dm	direct message
DM	dm	do me
DM	dm	doesn't matter/don't matter
DM	dm	don't mind/do mind
DM	dm	*Dungeon Master* (online gaming)
DMA	dma	direct memory access
DMA$$	dma$$	dumass (idiot)
DMAF	dmaf	do me a favor
DMAF	dmaf	don't make a fuss
DMAL	dmal	drop me a line
DMAZZ	dmazz	dumass (idiot)
DMB	dmb	Dave Matthews Band
DMBA	dmba	dumbass (idiot)
DMBA$$	dmba$$	dumbass (idiot)
DMBASS	dmbass	dumbass (idiot)

UPPERCASE	LOWERCASE	MEANING
DMBAZZ	dmbazz	dumbass (idiot)
DMBFK	dmbfk	dumbfuck (idiot)
DMBSH@T	dmbsh@t	dumbshit (idiot)
DMBSHT	dmbsht	dumbshit (idiot)
DMC	dmc	deep, meaningful conversation
DMCA	dmca	Digital Millennium Copyright Act
DMG	dmg	damage
DMI	dmi	Don't mention it.
DMIID	dmiid	Don't mind if I do.
DMN	dmn	damn
DMNO	dmno	dude man no offense
DMSH@T	dmsh@t	dumshit (idiot)
DMSHT	dmsht	dumshit (idiot)
DMT	dmt	dimethyl tryptamine (drug)
DMTA	dmta	Dirty minds think alike.
DMU	dmu	don't mess up
DMV	dmv	Department of Motor Vehicles
DMW	dmw	dead man walking
DMWM	dmwm	don't mess with me
DMX	dmx	Dark Man X (rapper)
DMY	dmy	Don't mess yourself.
DMZ	dmz	demilitarized zone
DN	dn	doing nothing
DN	dn	don't know
DN	dn	down
DNA	dna	deoxyribonucleic acid
DNA	dna	did not attend
DNA	dna	does not apply
DNC	dnc	Democratic National Committee
DNC	dnc	does not compute (I do not understand)
DND	dnd	do not disturb
DNDC	dndc	don't know, don't care
DNDP	dndp	Do not double post.
DNF	dnf	did not finish
DNFTT	dnftt	Do not feed the troll.
DNIMB	dnimb	dancing naked in my bra
DNK	dnk	do not know
DNM	dnm	deep and meaningful
DNM	dnm	does not matter
DNO	dno	don't know
DNPMPL	dnpmpl	damn near pissed my pants laughing
DNR	dnr	dinner (SMS)
DNR	dnr	do not resuscitate
DNRTA	dnrta	did not read the article
DNRTFA	dnrtfa	did not read the fucking article
DNS	dns	did not start
DNS	dns	Domain Name Service
DNT	dnt	don't
DNW	dnw	do not want
DOA	doa	dead on arrival
DOA	doa	deteriorate on approach
DOAW	doaw	daughter of a whore
DOB	dob	date of birth
DOBE	dobe	idiot

UPPERCASE	LOWERCASE	MEANING
DOC	doc	doctor
DOC	doc	drug of choice
DOD	dod	day of defeat
DODGY	dodgy	of questionable legality, morality, integrity
DOE	doe	depends on experience
DOF	dof	depth of field
DOG	dog	telephone
DOG	dog	ugly person
DOG FOOD	dog food	heroin
DOGG	dogg	friend
DOH	doh	expression of frustration, realization
DOHC	dohc	dual overhead cam
DOI	doi	duh
DOIN	doin	doing
DOKE	doke	diet Coke
DOL	dol	dying of laughter
DOLF	dolf	a German, referring to Adolf Hitler (ethnic slur/derogatory)
DOLO	dolo	alone, solo
DOMO	domo	thank you (Japanese)
DON	don	denial of normal
DON	don	top man, Mafia boss
DONCHA	doncha	don't you
DONE	done	drunk, intoxicated
DONNO	donno	don't know
DONT	dont	don't
DONTCHA	dontcha	don't you
DOOD	dood	dude
DOODE	doode	(same as "dude")
DOODZ	doodz	dudes
DOOFUS	doofus	stupid person
DOOM	doom	classic fps
DOPE	dope	cool, awesome
DOPE	dope	heroin
DORB	dorb	adorable
DORK	dork	silly, socially inept person
DOS	dos	dad over shoulder
DOS	dos	denial of service (attack)
DOS	dos	Disk Operating System
DOSH	dosh	money
DOSHA	dosha	marijuana
DOSSER	dosser	lazy person
DOSSER	dosser	vagrant, tramp
DOT	dot	someone of South Asian descent (ethnic slur/derogatory)
DOT	dot	damage over time
DOTA	dota	*Defense of the Ancients* (game)
DOTC	dotc	dancing on the ceiling
DOUCHE	douche	idiot
DOUGH	dough	money, cash
DOUGIE	dougie	dance style
DOW	dow	*Dawn of War* (game)
DOW	dow	Dow Jones Industrial Average
DOWNER	downer	someone or something that brings the mood down

UPPERCASE	LOWERCASE	MEANING
DOWNS	downs	Down syndrome
DOYPOV	doypov	depends on your point of view
DP	dp	display picture
DPI	dpi	Don't push it.
DPI	dpi	dots per inch
DPMO	dpmo	Don't piss me off.
DPRSD	dprsd	depressed
DPS	dps	damage per second (MMORPG)
DPSHT	dpsht	dipshit (idiot)
DPYN	dpyn	Don't pick your nose.
DQ	dq	disqualified
DQMOT	dqmot	Don't quote me on this.
DQYDJ	dqydj	Don't quit your day job.
DR	dr	didn't read
DR	dr	double rainbow
DR00D	dr00d	druid
DRAG	drag	dressed as a woman
DRAG	drag	inhale smoke from cigarette or joint
DRAM	dram	dynamic random-access memory
DRC	drc	don't really care
DRINKY POO	drinky poo	alcoholic drink
DRIVE BY	drive by	recce, check out
DRM	drm	digital rights management
DRM	drm	dream
DRO	dro	hydroponically grown marijuana
DROOD	drood	druid
DROVE	drove	mad, angry
DRT	drt	dead right there
DS	ds	darling/dear son
DS	ds	double standard
D'S	d's	Dayton rims
DSD	dsd	do some damage
DSIDED	dsided	decided
DSL	dsl	digital subscriber line
DSLAM	dslam	Digital Subscriber Line Access Multiplexer
DSLR	dslr	digital single-lens reflex (camera)
DSS	dss	department of social services
DSU	dsu	don't screw up
DT	dt	double-team
DT	dt	downtown
DTA	dta	don't trust anyone
DTB	dtb	don't text back
DTC	dtc	down to cuddle
DTD	dtd	Document Type Definition
DTD	dtd	drunk till dawn
DTE	dte	down to earth
DTH	dth	down to hang
DTL	dtl	damn the luck
DTMS	dtms	Does that make sense?
DTP	dtp	disturbing the peace
DTR	dtr	define the relationship
DTRT	dtrt	do the right thing
DTS	dts	don't think so
DTS	dts	down the shore

UPPERCASE	LOWERCASE	MEANING
DTS	dts	down to snuggle
DTT	dtt	Don't touch that.
DTTD	dttd	Don't touch that dial.
DTTM	dttm	Don't talk to me.
DTTML	dttml	Don't talk to me, loser.
DTTPOU	dttpou	Don't tell the police on us.
DTTRIAA	dttriaa	Don't tell the RIAA.
DTYT	dtyt	Don't take your time.
DU JOUR	du jour	of the day (French)
DU2H	du2h	damn you to hell
DUB	dub	twenty (dollars, dollars of drugs, inch rims)
DUB DUB DUB	dub dub dub	www, World Wide Web
DUB SACK	dub sack	a $20 bag of marijuana
DUBS	dubs	twenty-inch wheels
DUCES	duces	good-bye
DUCWIC	ducwic	Do you see what I see?
DUCY	ducy	Do you see why?
DUDE	dude	a name for anyone (esp. surfers, skaters)
DUDETTE	dudette	female dude
DUECES	dueces	misspelling of deuces
DUGI	dugi	Do you get it?
DUGT	dugt	Did you get this/that/these/those/them?
DUH	duh	of course
DUI	dui	driving under the influence
DUK	duk	Did you know?
DULM	dulm	Do you like me? / Do you love me?
DUM	dum	Do you masturbate?
DUN	dun	don't
DUN	dun	son
DUNNA	dunna	don't know
DUNNO	dunno	don't know
DUNO	duno	don't know
DUNZO	dunzo	done, over, finished
DUPE	dupe	duplicate
DUR	dur	Do you remember?
DUR	dur	duh
DURS	durs	damn, you are sexy
DUS	dus	does
DUSS	duss	run away
DUST	dust	angel dust, PCP
DUSTY	dusty	ugly
DUTCH	dutch	joint
DUTCH	dutch	split the cost
DUTMA	dutma	don't you text me again
DUTTY	dutty	dirty
DV	dv	digital video
DV8	dv8	deviate
DVD	dvd	digital versatile disc
DVD+R	dvd+r	digital versatile disc recordable
DVD+RW	dvd+rw	digital versatile disk rewritable
DVDA	dvda	double vaginal, double anal
DVD-R	dvd-r	digital versatile disc recordable
DVD-RAM	dvd-ram	digital versatile disc random-access memory

UPPERCASE	LOWERCASE	MEANING
DVDRIP	dvdrip	video copied from a dvd
DVD-RW	dvd-rw	digital versatile disk rewritable
DVI	dvi	digital video interface
DVR	dvr	digital video recorder
DW	dw	darling/dear wife
DW	dw	Don't worry.
DWAG	dwag	misspelling of dawg
DWAI	dwai	Don't worry about it.
DWB	dwb	driving while black
DWBH	dwbh	Don't worry, be happy.
DWBI	dwbi	Don't worry 'bout it.
DWEEB	dweeb	dork, nerd
DWF	dwf	divorced white female
DWI	dwi	deal with it
DWIOYOT	dwioyot	deal with it on your own time
DWISNWID	dwisnwid	do what I say not what I do
DWL	dwl	dying with laughter
DWM	dwm	divorced white male
DWMT	dwmt	Don't waste my time.
DWN	dwn	down
DWO	dwo	Driving While Oriental (ethnic slur/derogatory)
DWP	dwp	drunk while posting
DWPKOTL	dwpkotl	deep wet passionate kiss on the lips
DWS	dws	driving while stupid
DWT	dwt	don't wanna talk
DWT	dwt	driving while texting
DWTS	dwts	*Dancing with the Stars* (TV Show)
DWU	dwu	Don't wait up.
DWWWI	dwwwi	surfing the World Wide Web while intoxicated
DWY	dwy	Don't wet yourself.
DX	dx	horror, disgust, sadness
DXC	dxc	deathcore (music style)
DXNRY	dxnry	dictionary
DY2H	dy2h	damn you to hell
DYA	dya	do you
DYAC	dyac	damn you autocorrect
DYCOTFC	dycotfc	do you cyber on the first chat
DYEC	dyec	don't you ever care
DYFH	dyfh	do your fucking homework
DYFI	dyfi	Did you find it?
DYFM	dyfm	dude, you fascinate me
DYGTP	dygtp	Did you get the picture?
DYH	dyh	do your homework
DYHWIH	dyhwih	Do you hear what I hear?
DYJ	dyj	do your job
DYJHIW	dyjhiw	Don't you just hate it when...
DYK	dyk	Did you know?
DYK	dyk	dyke (homosexual slur/derogatory)
DYKWIM	dykwim	Do you know what I mean?
DYLH	dylh	Do you love/like her?/Do you love/like him?
DYLM	dylm	Do you love/like me?
DYLOS	dylos	Do you like oral sex?
DYM	dym	Do you mean?
DYM	dym	Do you mind?

UPPERCASE	LOWERCASE	MEANING
DYNK	dynk	Do you not know?
DYNM	dynm	Do you know me?
DYNWUTB	dynwutb	Do you know what you are talking about?
DYOFDW	dyofdw	Do your own fucking dirty work.
DYOR	dyor	Do your own research.
DYT	dyt	Don't you think?
DYTH	dyth	Damn you to hell.
DYW2GWM	dyw2gwm	Do you want to go with me?
DYWTMUSW	dywtmusw	Do you want to meet up somewhere?
DZ	dz	drop zone
E	e	ecstasy
E!	e!	Entertainment (TV)
E&OE	e&oe	errors and omissions excluded
E.G.	e.g.	example
E_E	e_e	tired, exhausted
E>	e>	heartlike
E1	e1	everyone
E123	e123	easy as one, two, three
E2EG	e2eg	ear-to-ear grin
E4U2S	e4u2s	easy for you to say
EA	ea	Electronic Arts
EAD	ead	eat a dick
EAK	eak	eating at keyboard
EAPFS	eapfs	everything about Pittsburgh fucking sucks
EB	eb	eyeball
EBCAK	ebcak	error between chair and keyboard
EBITDA	ebitda	earnings before interest, taxes, depreciation, and amortization
EBKAC	ebkac	error between keyboard and chair
EBONY	ebony	dark skin tone
EBT	ebt	electronic benefits transfer
ECC	ecc	error correction code
ECF	ecf	error carried forward
ECG	ecg	electrocardiogram
ECO	eco	ecological/economical
ECT	ect	misspelling of "etc."
ECW	ecw	Extreme Championship Wrestling
ED	ed	erase display
E-DATING	e-dating	online dating
EDD	edd	estimated delivery date
EDDRESS	eddress	e-mail address
EDI	edi	electronic data interchange
EDJ	edj	energy drink junkie
EDM	edm	electronic dance music
EDUMACATION	edumacation	education
EEDYAT	eedyat	idiot
EEE	eee	expression of excitement
EEG	eeg	extremely evil grin
EEJIT	eejit	idiot
EEK	eek	expression of surprise, distress
EEPROM	eeprom	erasable eprom
EF	ef	fuck
EF4T	ef4t	effort
EFA	efa	edited for accuracy

UPPERCASE	LOWERCASE	MEANING
EFCT	efct	effect
EFFFL	efffl	extrafriendly friends for life
EFFIN	effin	fucking
EFFING	effing	fucking
EFG	efg	epic fail guy
EF·ING	ef·ing	fucking
EG	eg	evil grin
EG	eg	for example (*exempli gratia*)
EGL	egl	elegant gothic Lolita
EH	eh	What? Huh?
EHLP	ehlp	help
EI	ei	eat it
EIDE	eide	Enhanced Integrated Drive Electronics
EIL	eil	explode into laughter
EIP	eip	editing in progress
EL	el	Chicago's elevated rail system
EL!T	el!t	elite
ELBOW	elbow	a pound of marijuana
ELE	ele	everybody love everybody
ELEO	eleo	extremely low earth orbit
ELF	elf	every lady's fantasy
ELITE	elite	skillful, quality, professional
ELLO	ello	hello
ELNS	elns	*eller noe sånt* (or something like that – Norwegian)
ELO	elo	hello
ELOL	elol	evil laugh out loud
EM	em	e-mail
EM	em	them
EMA	ema	e-mail address
EMAW	emaw	every man a wildcat
EMCEE	emcee	MC, master of ceremonies
EMFBI	emfbi	Excuse me for butting in.
EMM	emm	e-mail me
EMO	emo	emotional
EMOTICON	emoticon	sequence of characters representing an emotion, e.g., :)
EMP	emp	Eat my pussy.
EMS	ems	emergency medical service
EMSG	emsg	e-mail message
ENAT	enat	every now and then
ENDZ	endz	area where you live
ENE	ene	Northerner
ENIT	enit	Isn't it?
ENNIT	ennit	expression of agreement
ENO	eno	awesome, cool
ENOF	enof	enough
ENT	ent	isn't
ENUF	enuf	enough
ENUFF	enuff	enough
EOB	eob	end of business
EOC	eoc	end of conversation
EOD	eod	end of day
EOD	eod	end of discussion
EOE	eoe	equal opportunity employer

UPPERCASE	LOWERCASE	MEANING
EOF	eof	end of file
EOG	eog	end of grade
E-OK	e-ok	electronically OK
EOL	eol	end of lecture/end of life
EOM	eom	end of message
EOR	eor	end of rant
EOS	eos	end of show
EOS	eos	end of story
EOT	eot	end of thread (i.e., end of discussion)
EOT	eot	end of transmission
EOTW	eotw	end of the world
EOTWAWKI	eotwawki	end of the world as we know it
EP	ep	extended play
EPA	epa	emergency parent alert
E-PEEN	e-peen	online ego
EPIC	epic	extremely awesome
EPIC FAIL	epic fail	total failure
EPIN	epin	epic win
EPROM	eprom	electronically programmable rom
EPS	eps	Encapsulated PostScript
EQ	eq	*EverQuest* (game)
EQ2	eq2	*EverQuest2* (game)
EQE	eqe	easy, quick, efficient
ER	er	emergency room
ER	er	indicating hesitation
ERB	erb	herb, marijuana
ERE	ere	here
ERK	erk	irk, annoy
ERM	erm	awkward conversation filler
ERP	erp	erotic role-play
ERRYTHIN	errythin	everything
ERS2	ers2	*eres tz*/are you (Spanish SMS)
ES	es	erase screen
ESA	esa	European Space Agency
ESAD	esad	eat shit and die
ESADYFA	esadyfa	eat shit and die, you fucking asshole
ESADYFFB	esadyffb	eat shit and die, you fat fucking bastard
ESB	esb	*Empire Strikes Back* (*Star Wars*)
ESBM	esbm	Everyone sucks but me.
ESC	esc	escape
ESD	esd	electrostatic discharge
ESE	ese	friend, homeboy (Hispanic)
ESH	esh	donkey (Armenian)
ESKI	eski	type of urban music
ESL	esl	eat shit, loser
ESL	esl	English as second language
ESMF	esmf	eat shit, motherfucker
ESP	esp	extrasensory perception
ESPN	espn	Entertainment and Sports Programming Network
ESRB	esrb	Entertainment Software Rating Board
EST	est	Eastern standard time
EST	est	established
ET	et	extraterrestrial
ETA	eta	edited to add

UPPERCASE	LOWERCASE	MEANING
ETA	eta	estimated time of arrival
ETC	etc	et cetera (and so on)
ETD	etd	estimated time of departure
ETF	etf	*Escape the Fate* (band)
ETID	etid	*Every Time I Die* (band)
ETLA	etla	extended three-letter acronym
ETMDA	etmda	explain it to my dumb ass
ETP	etp	eager to please
EU	eu	European Union
EUA	eua	end-user agreement
EUB	eub	extremely ugly boy
EUC	euc	excellent used condition
EUG	eug	extremely ugly girl
EULA	eula	end-user license agreement
EUP	eup	Enterprise Unified Process
EV	ev	expected value
EV1	ev1	everyone
EVA	eva	ever
EVAA	evaa	ever
EVAR	evar	ever
EVERCRACK	evercrack	*EverQuest* (game)
EVERY1	every1	everyone
EVL	evl	evil laugh
EVN	evn	even
EVO	evo	evolution
EVR	evr	ever
EVRY	evry	every
EVRY1	evry1	everyone
EVRYTIN	evrytin	everything
EVT	evt	*ei voi tietää* (Finnish for "How am I supposed to know?")
EVVK	evvk	couldn't care less (Finnish)
EW	ew	exclamation of disgust
EWBA	ewba	everything will be all right
EWE	ewe	Epilogue, what epilogue? (*Harry Potter*)
EWG	ewg	evil wicked grin (in fun, teasing)
EWI	ewi	e-mailing while intoxicated
EWW	eww	expression of disgust
EX	ex	example
EX	ex	former girlfriend, boyfriend, wife, husband etc.
EX-BF	ex-bf	ex-boyfriend
EXE	exe	Windows program file
EX-GF	ex-gf	ex-girlfriend
EXP	exp	experience
EXPO	expo	exposition, large-scale public exhibition
EXTRA	extra	over the top, excessive
EY	ey	hey
EYC	eyc	excitable, yet calm
EYEBALL	eyeball	look at
EYEZ	eyez	eyes
EYO	eyo	hey, yo(u)
EZ	ez	easy
EZI	ezi	easy

UPPERCASE	LOWERCASE	MEANING
EZPZ	ezpz	very easy
EZY	ezy	easy
F	f	female
F U	f u	fuck you
F#CKING	f#cking	fucking
F&E	f&e	forever and ever
F.M.L.	f.m.l.	fuck my life
F.U.	f.u.	fuck you
F/O	f/o	fuck off
F@	f@	fat
F@G	f@g	fag (homosexual slur/derogatory)
F@GGIT	f@ggit	faggit (homosexual slur/derogatory)
F@GGOT	f@ggot	faggot (homosexual slur/derogatory)
F@GGOTCK	f@ggotck	faggotcock (homosexual slur/derogatory)
F@GTARD	f@gtard	fagtard (homosexual idiot)
F'N	f'n	fucking
FOOK	f00k	fuck
F2F	f2f	face-to-face
F2P	f2p	files to peers
F2P	f2p	free to play
F2T	f2t	free to talk
F4C3	f4c3	face
F4EAA	f4eaa	friends forever and always
F4F	f4f	female for female
F4M	f4m	female for male
F5	f5	refresh
F8	f8	fate
F9	f9	fine
FAAK	faak	falling asleep at keyboard
FAB	fab	fabulous
FABU	fabu	fabulous
FACE PALM	face palm	slap forehead with the palm of your hand
FACKA$$	facka$$	fuckass (idiot)
FACKASS	fackass	fuckass (idiot)
FACKAZZ	fackazz	fuckass (idiot)
FADE	fade	haircut
FADE	fade	kill, disgrace
FADED	faded	high, stoned, drunk
FAE	fae	from
FAF	faf	funny as fuck
FAFWOA	fafwoa	for a friend without access (when about to ask a silly question)
FAG	fag	cigarette
FAGGIT	faggit	faggot
FAH	fah	fucking a hot
FAH	fah	funny as hell
FAI	fai	forget about it
FAIC	faic	for all I care
FAIL	fail	suck
FAM	fam	family
FAMALAM	famalam	family, close friend
FAMO	famo	friend, dude, family member etc.
FANKLE	fankle	area between foot and ankle

UPPERCASE	LOWERCASE	MEANING
FANNYING	fannying	wasting time, messing about
FANTABULOUS	fantabulous	fantastic and fabulous
FAO	fao	for attention of
FAP	fap	fucking a pissed
FAP	fap	masturbate
FAPPING	fapping	masturbating
FAQ	faq	Frequently Asked Questions
FA-Q	fa-q	fuck you
FAQL	faql	frequently asked questions list
FARG	farg	fuck
FASHIZZLE	fashizzle	for sure
FASHO	fasho	for sure
FAT32	fat32	32-bit file allocation table
FATA$$	fata$$	fatass (a fat person)
FATAZZ	fatazz	fatass (a fat person)
FAUX PAS	faux pas	social blunder (French for "false step")
FAV	fav	favorite
FAVE	fave	favorite
FAWK	fawk	fuck
FAWOMFT	fawomft	frequently argued waste of my fucking time
FAY	fay	fuck all, y'all
FB	fb	facebook
FB	fb	fuck, buddy
FBC	fbc	facebook chat
FBF	fbf	facebook friend
FBF	fbf	fat boy food (e.g., pizza, burgers, fries)
FBFR	fbfr	facebook friend
FBI	fbi	Federal Bureau of Investigation
FBI	fbi	female body inspector
FBI	fbi	fucking brilliant idea
FBIMCL	fbimcl	fall back in my chair laughing
FBK	fbk	facebook
FBM	fbm	fine by me
FBO	fbo	Facebook official
FBOW	fbow	for better or worse
FBTW	fbtw	fine, be that way
FBW	fbw	fly-by-wire
FC	fc	fingers crossed
FC	fc	fruit cake
FC	fc	full combo
FCBK	fcbk	Facebook
FCFS	fcfs	first come, first served
FC'INGO	fc'ingo	for crying out loud
FCK	fck	fuck
FCKD	fckd	fucked
FCKIN	fckin	fucking
FCKING	fcking	fucking
FCKM3HDBAYB	fckm3hdbayb	fuck me hard, baby
FCKU	fcku	fuck you
FCOL	fcol	for crying out loud
FCS	fcs	for Christ's sake
FCUK	fcuk	fuck
FDA	fda	Food and Drug Administration
FDDI	fddi	Fiber Distributed Data Interface

UPPERCASE	LOWERCASE	MEANING
FDR	fdr	Franklin Delano Roosevelt
FE	fe	fair enough
FE	fe	fatal error
FEAE	feae	for ever and ever
FEAT	feat	featuring
FECK	feck	fuck
FEDEX	fedex	Federal Express (shipping company)
FEDS	feds	FBI agents, police
FEDZ	fedz	police
FEE	fee	female
FEENING	feening	craving, wanting really badly
FEH	feh	expression of dismissal, disgust
FEITCTAJ	feitctaj	Fuck 'em if they can't take a joke.
FELLAS	fellas	close friends
FELLER	feller	fellow, man
FER	fer	for
FERR	ferr	for
FETCH	fetch	cool, trendy, awesome
FF	ff	*Final Fantasy* (game)
FF	ff	follow Friday (Twitter slang)
FF	ff	friendly fire
FF5	ff5	*Family Force 5* (band)
FFA	ffa	free for all
FFCL	ffcl	falling from chair laughing
FFR	ffr	*Flash Revolution* (game)
FFR	ffr	for future reference
FFS	ffs	for fuck's sake
FFS	ffs	for fucking sake
FFT	fft	food for thought
FFTL	fftl	*From First to Last* (band)
FFXI	ffxi	*Final Fantasy XI*
FG	fg	fag (homosexual slur/derogatory)
FG	fg	family guy
FG	fg	fat girl
FG	fg	fucking gay (homosexual slur/derogatory)
FGBG	fgbg	fagbag (homosexual slur/derogatory)
FGFKR	fgfkr	fagfucker (homosexual slur/derogatory)
FGI	fgi	fucking Google it
FGJ	fgj	for great justice
FGOVT	fgovt	fuck government
FGS	fgs	for god's sake
FGSSU	fgssu	For god's sake, shut up.
FGT	fgt	faggot
FHE	fhe	firsthand experience
FHM	fhm	*For Him Magazine*
FI	fi	forget it
FI	fi	fuck it
FI9	fi9	fine
FIBIJAR	fibijar	Fuck it, buddy, I'm just a reserve.
FIC	fic	fan fiction
FICCL	ficcl	Frankly, I couldn't care less.
FIF	fif	Fifth Amendment
FIF	fif	fuck, I'm fucking
FIFA	fifa	Fédération Internationale de Football Association

UPPERCASE	LOWERCASE	MEANING
FIFO	fifo	first in, first out
FIFY	fify	fixed it for you
FIGJAM	figjam	Fuck, I'm good, just ask me.
FIGMO	figmo	fuck it, got my orders
FIIC	fiic	fucked if I care
FIIK	fiik	fuck if I know
FIIOOH	fiiooh	Forget it, I'm out of here.
FIL	fil	father-in-law
FILO	filo	first in, last out
FIMH	fimh	forever in my heart
FIN	fin	finished
FINA	fina	about to do (something)
FINE	fine	fucked up, insecure, neurotic, emotional
F-ING	f-ing	fucking
FINK	fink	snitch, informer
FINNA	finna	going to
FIO	fio	figure it out
FiOS	fios	fiber optic service
FIRM	firm	gang of soccer hooligans
FIRM	firm	organized criminal gang
FIRME	firme	cool, good, nice
FISH	fish	first in still here
FIT	fit	good-looking, hot, sexy
FITB	fitb	fill in the blanks
FITE	fite	fight
FITTIN TO	fittin to	about to, getting ready to
FIV	fiv	five
FIVE O	five o	police
FIX	fix	a dose of drugs
FIXIN TO	fixin to	about to, getting ready to
FIZZLE	fizzle	fool
FJ	fj	foot job
FK	fk	fuck
FKA	fka	formerly known as
FKA$$	fka$$	fuckass (idiot)
FKASS	fkass	fuckass (idiot)
FKAZZ	fkazz	fuckass (idiot)
FKBAG	fkbag	fuckbag (idiot)
FKBOY	fkboy	fuckboy (idiot)
FKBRAIN	fkbrain	fuckbrain (idiot)
FKBUTT	fkbutt	fuckbutt (butt)
FKBUTTER	fkbutter	fuckbutter (sexual fluids)
FKED	fked	fucked (had intercourse)
FKER	fker	fucker
FKFACE	fkface	fuckface (idiot)
FKHEAD	fkhead	fuckhead (butt)
FKHOLE	fkhole	fuckhole (jerk)
FKIN	fkin	fucking
FKING	fking	fucking
FKN	fkn	fucking
FKNUT	fknut	fucknut (idiot)
FKNUTT	fknutt	fucknutt (idiot)
FKO	fko	fuckhole (jerk)
FKOFF	fkoff	fuckoff (go away)

UPPERCASE	LOWERCASE	MEANING
FKR	fkr	fucker (fornicator)
FKRSKR	fkrskr	fuckersucker (idiot)
FKS	fks	fucks (sexual act)
FKSTICK	fkstick	fuckstick (male genitalia)
FKTARD	fktard	fucktard (moron)
FKTART	fktart	fucktart (idiot)
FKU	fku	fuck you
FKUP	fkup	fuckup (idiot)
FKUU	fkuu	fuckbutt (butt)
FKWAD	fkwad	fuckwad (idiot)
FKWIT	fkwit	fuckwit (dummy)
FKWITT	fkwitt	fuckwitt (idiot)
FL	fl	fake laugh
FLA	fla	Florida
FLAFF	flaff	footloose and fancy-free
FLAG	flag	bandana
FLAGGED	flagged	banned
FLAKE	flake	unreliable person
FLAKE OUT	flake out	cancel at the last minute
FLAKY	flaky	unreliable
FLAME	flame	insult someone over the Internet
FLAMER	flamer	angry poster
FLAMES	flames	angry comments
FLEX	flex	show off
FLICKS	flicks	pictures
FLIR	flir	forward-looking infrared
FLK	flk	funny-looking kid
FLOABT	floabt	for lack of a better term
FLOG	flog	sell
FLOPS	flops	floating point operations per second
FLOSS	floss	show off
FLOSSING	flossing	showing off
FLOTUS	flotus	first lady of the United States
FLS	fls	flulike symptoms
FLTCH	fltch	feltch (sexual act)
FLUFF	fluff	humorous/romantic fan fiction
FLUID	fluid	fucking look it up, I did
FLY	fly	awesome, cool
FLY	fly	zipper
FLYFF	flyff	*Fly for Fun* (MMORPG)
FM	fm	frequency modulation (radio signal)
FM	fm	fuck me
FMA	fma	*Fullmetal Alchemist*
FMAH	fmah	fuck my asshole
FMAO	fmao	freezing my ass off
FMB	fmb	fuck me, bitch/baby
FMBB	fmbb	fuck me, baby
FMBO	fmbo	fuck my brains out
FMCG	fmcg	fast-moving consumer goods
FMDIDGAD	fmdidgad	Frankly, my dear, I don't give a damn.
FMFL	fmfl	fuck my fucking life
FMFLTH	fmflth	fuck my fucking life to hell
FMH	fmh	fuck me hard
FMHB	fmhb	fuck me hard, bitch

UPPERCASE	LOWERCASE	MEANING
FMI	fmi	for more information
FMIR	fmir	family member in room
FMITA	fmita	fuck me in the ass
FMJ	fmj	*Full Metal Jacket*
FML	fml	fuck my life
FMLA	fmla	family and medical leave of absence
FMLTWIA	fmltwia	fuck me like the whore I am
FMN	fmn	fuck me now
FMNB	fmnb	fuck me now, bitch
FMNKML	fmnkml	fuck me now, kiss me later
FMPH	fmph	fuck my pussy hard
FMQ	fmq	fuck me quick
FMR	fmr	fuck me running
FMTH	fmth	fuck me to hell
FMTKFYTFO	fmtkfytfo	for me to know, for you to find out
FMTYEWTK	fmtyewtk	far more than you ever wanted to know
FMUTA	fmuta	fuck me up the ass
FMUTP	fmutp	fuck me up the pussy
FMV	fmv	full-motion video
FN	fn	first name
FNA	fna	for necessary action
FNAR	fnar	for no apparent reason
FNB	fnb	football and beer
FNCI	fnci	fancy
FNE	fne	free and easy
FNG	fng	fucking new girl/guy
FNNY	fnny	funny
FNPR	fnpr	for no particular reason
FNX	fnx	thanks
FNY	fny	funny
FO	fo	fuck off
FO SHIZZLE	fo shizzle	for sure
FO SHO	fo sho	for sure
FO'	fo'	for
FO'SHIZZLE	fo'shizzle	for sure
FOA	foa	first of all
FOA	foa	fuck off, asshole
FOAD	foad	fuck off and die
FOAF	foaf	friend of a friend
FOAG	foag	fuck off and Google
FOAH	foah	fuck off, asshole
FOB	fob	a recent immigrant (ethnic slur/derogatory)
FOB	fob	fresh off the boat
FOBR	fobr	*Fall Out Boy Rock* (Web site)
FOC	foc	free of charge
FOCL	focl	falling off chair laughing
FOF	fof	full of fail
FOFL	fofl	fall on floor laughing
FOFO	fofo	.44 caliber gun
FOI	foi	freedom of information
FOIA	foia	Freedom of Information Act
FOL	fol	farting out loud
FOLDED	folded	drunk, wasted
FOLO	folo	follow

UPPERCASE	LOWERCASE	MEANING
FOMC	fomc	falling off my chair
FOMCL	fomcl	falling off my chair laughing
FOMO	fomo	fear of missing out
FOMOFO	fomofo	fuck off, motherfucker
FON	fon	freak of nature
FONE	fone	phone
FOO	foo	fool
FOOBAR	foobar	fucked up beyond all recognition
FOOCL	foocl	falls out of chair laughing
FOOD	food	marijuana
FOOK	fook	fuck
FOOPA	foopa	fat in belly area
FOPS	fops	fake cops (security guards, etc.)
FOR SHEEZE	for sheeze	for sure
FORTE	forte	area of expertise, strength
FOS	fos	full of shit
FOSHIZZLE	foshizzle	for sure
FOSHO	fosho	for sure
FOSS	foss	free, open-source software
FOTC	fotc	*Flight of the Concords*
FOTCL	fotcl	fell off the chair laughing
FOTM	fotm	flavor of the month
FOTR	fotr	*Fellowship of the Ring* (Tolkien)
FOUC	fouc	fuck off, you cunt
FOV	fov	field of view
FOX	fox	sexy, attractive woman
FOYB	foyb	fuck off, you bitch
FP	fp	first post
FPMITAP	fpmitap	federal pound-me-in-the-ass prison
FPOS	fpos	fucking piece of shit
FPS	fps	first-person shooter (video game term)
FPU	fpu	floating point unit
FR	fr	for real
FRAG	frag	kill
FRAGGED	fragged	killed
FRAK	frak	swear word from *Battlestar Galactica*
FRAP	frap	Frappuccino
FRAT	frat	fraternity
FRED	fred	fucking ridiculous electronic device
FREEBIE	freebie	item or service one gets for free
FREEBSD	freebsd	free Berkeley Software Distribution (UNIX like OS)
FREN	fren	friend
FRENS	frens	friends
FRESH	fresh	very good, cool
FRESHIE	freshie	immigrant
FRGT	frgt	forgot
FRIED	fried	high on drugs
FRIGGIN	friggin	freaking
FRILL	frill	for real
FRK	frk	freak
FRM	frm	from
FRND	frnd	friend
FRNDS	frnds	friends
FRO	fro	Afro hairstyle

UPPERCASE	LOWERCASE	MEANING
FROG	frog	offensive word for a French person
FRONT	front	pretend, falsely represent
FRONTING	fronting	misrepresenting oneself
FROOB	froob	free noob, nonpaying player
FRT	frt	fart
FRT	frt	for real though
FS	fs	for sure
FSAS	fsas	Famous Stars and Straps (clothing)
FSB	fsb	frontside bus
FSCK	fsck	file system (consistency) check
FSHO	fsho	for sure
FSM	fsm	female seeking male
FSM	fsm	flying spaghetti monster
FSOB	fsob	fucking son of a bitch
FSOD	fsod	front screen of death
FSOT	fsot	for sale or trade
FSR	fsr	for some reason
FST	fst	fast
FSU	fsu	friends stand united
FSU	fsu	fuck, shut up
FT	ft	fuck that
FT2T	ft2t	from time to time
FTA	fta	from the article
FTASB	ftasb	faster than a speeding bullet
FTB	ftb	fuck that bitch
FTBFS	ftbfs	failed to build from source
FTBOMH	ftbomh	from the bottom of my heart
FTD	ftd	fresh to death
FTF	ftf	face-to-face
FTF	ftf	first to find
FTF	ftf	fuck, that's funny
FTFA	ftfa	from the fucking article
FTFOI	ftfoi	for the fuck of it/for the fun of it
FTFW	ftfw	For the fucking win!
FTFY	ftfy	fixed that for you
FTIO	ftio	Fun time is over.
FTK	ftk	for the kids
FTK	ftk	for the kill
FTL	ftl	faster than light
FTL	ftl	for the loss
FTLOG	ftlog	for the love of God
FTLT	ftlt	for the last time
FTM	ftm	female to male
FTMFW	ftmfw	for the motherfucking win
FTMP	ftmp	for the most part
FTN	ftn	fuck that noise
FTP	ftp	File Transfer Protocol
FTR	ftr	for the record
FTRF	ftrf	fuck, that's really funny
FTS	fts	fuck that shit
FTSK	ftsk	*Forever the Sickest Kids* (band)
FTTB	fttb	for the time being
FTUW	ftuw	for the ultimate/über win
FTW	ftw	for the win

UPPERCASE	LOWERCASE	MEANING
FTW	ftw	fuck that whore/fuck the world
FU	fu	fuck you
FU2	fu2	fuck you too
FUA	fua	fuck you all
FUAH	fuah	fuck you, asshole
FUB	fub	fuck you, bitch
FUBAH	fubah	fucked up beyond all hope
FUBALM	fubalm	fucked up beyond all local maintenance
FUBAR	fubar	fouled up beyond all recognition
FUBB	fubb	fouled up beyond belief
FUBH	fubh	fucked up beyond hope
FUBOHIC	fubohic	fuck you bend over here it comes
FUBR	fubr	fucked up beyond recognition
FUBU	fubu	clothing brand
FUBU	fubu	fouled up beyond use
FUCKEN	fucken	fucking
FUCKTARD	fucktard	fucking retard
FUCLA	fucla	fuck UCLA
FUCTARD	fuctard	fucking retard (disability slur/derogatory)
FUD	fud	fear, uncertainty, and doubt
FUDH	fudh	fuck you, dickhead
FUDIE	fudie	fuck you and die
FUGLY	fugly	fucking ugly
FUHGET	fuhget	forget
FUH-Q	fuh-q	fuck you
FUJIMO	fujimo	Fuck you, jerk, I'm moving on.
FUK	fuk	fuck
FUKIN	fukin	fucking
FUKK	fukk	fuck
FUKKIN	fukkin	fucking
FUKN	fukn	fucking
FUKR	fukr	fucker
FUM	fum	fucked-up, messed up
FUMFER	fumfer	fuck you, motherfucker
FUNEE	funee	funny
FUNNER	funner	more fun
FUNY	funy	funny
FUQ	fuq	fuck you
FURTB	furtb	filled up and ready to burst
FUS	fus	fuck yourself
FUT	fut	fuck you too
FUTAB	futab	feet up, take a break
FUTCH	futch	femme + butch
FUU	fuu	fuck you up
FUX	fux	fuck
FUXING	fuxing	fucking
FUXOR	fuxor	fucker
FUXORED	fuxored	fucked
FUZZ	fuzz	police
FVCK	fvck	fuck
FW	fw	forward
FWB	fwb	friends with benefits
FWD	fwd	forward
FWIW	fwiw	for what it's worth

UPPERCASE	LOWERCASE	MEANING
FWM	fwm	fine with me
FWOB	fwob	friends with occasional benefits
FWOT	fwot	fucking waste of time
FWP	fwp	friend with privileges
FWTD	fwtd	fate worse than death
FX	fx	effects
FXE	fxe	foxy
FXP	fxp	file exchange protocol
FY	fy	fuck you
FYA	fya	for your amusement/for your attention
FYAD	fyad	fuck you and die
FYAH	fyah	fuck you, asshole
FYB	fyb	fuck you, bitch
FYC	fyc	fuck your couch
FYD	fyd	fuck your dad
FYE	fye	for your entertainment
FYEO	fyeo	for your eyes only
FYF	fyf	fuck your face
FYF	fyf	fuck your father
FYF411	fyf411	for your fucking information
FYFI	fyfi	for your fucking information
FYI	fyi	for your information
FYIFV	fyifv	fuck you, I'm fully vested
FYK	fyk	for your knowledge
FYL	fyl	for your love
FYM	fym	for your misinformation
FYM	fym	free your mind
FYM	fym	fuck your mom/mother
FYN	fyn	fine
FYP	fyp	fixed your post
FYR	fyr	for your records
FYR	fyr	for your review
FYRB	fyrb	fuck you right back
G	g	giggle
G	g	grin
G/F	g/f	girlfriend
G/G	g/g	got to go
G@@CH	g@@ch	gooch (female genitalia)
G@@K	g@@k	gook (Chinese person - ethnic slur/derogatory)
G@Y	g@y	gay
G'DAY	g'day	good day, hello
G'NITE	g'nite	good night
G0	g0	go
G00G13	g00g13	Google
G1	g1	good one
G2	g2	go to
G2/./	g2/./	go to hell
G2B	g2b	go to bed
G2BG	g2bg	got to be going
G2BL8	g2bl8	going to be late
G2CU	g2cu	glad to see you, good to see you
G2E	g2e	got to eat
G2F	g2f	got to fly
G2G	g2g	gotta go, got to go

UPPERCASE	LOWERCASE	MEANING
G2G2B	g2g2b	got to go to bed
G2G2TB	g2g2tb	got to go to the bathroom
G2G2W	g2g2w	got to go to work
G2G4AW	g2g4aw	got to go for a while
G2GB	g2gb	got to go, bye
G2GB2WN	g2gb2wn	got to go back to work now
G2GE	g2ge	got to go eat
G2GICYAL8ER	g2gicyal8er	Got to go, I'll see you later
G2GN	g2gn	got to go now
G2GP	g2gp	got to go pee
G2GPC	g2gpc	got to go, parents coming
G2GPP	g2gpp	got to go pee pee
G2GS	g2gs	got to go, sorry
G2H	g2h	go to hell
G2HB	g2hb	go to hell, bitch
G2K	g2k	good to know
G2P	g2p	got to pee
G2R	g2r	got to run
G2S	g2s	go to sleep
G2S	g2s	got to shit
G2T2S	g2t2s	got to talk to someone
G2TU	g2tu	got to tell you
G3Y	g3y	gay
G4B	g4b	going for breakfast
G4C	g4c	going for coffee
G4D	g4d	going for dinner
G4F	g4f	going for fuck
G4L	g4l	going for lunch
G4S	g4s	going for sex
G4U	g4u	good for you
G4Y	g4y	good for you
G8	g8	gate
G8	g8	great
G9	g9	genius
G9	g9	good night
GA	ga	go ahead
GAALMA	gaalma	Go away and leave me alone.
GAC	gac	get a clue
GAC	gac	guilty as charged
GAF	gaf	good as fuck
GAFC	gafc	get a fucking clue
GAFF	gaff	house
GAFI	gafi	get away from it
GAFIA	gafia	get away from it all
GAFJ	gafj	get a fucking job
GAFL	gafl	get a fucking life
GAFM	gafm	get away from me
GAG	gag	about to throw up
GAG	gag	joke
GAGA	gaga	crazy, infatuated
GAGF	gagf	go and get fucked
GAGFI	gagfi	gives a gay first impression
GAGP	gagp	go and get pissed
GAH	gah	expression of frustration

UPPERCASE	LOWERCASE	MEANING
GAH	gah	gay-ass homo
GAI	gai	gay
GAJ	gaj	get a job
GAL	gal	get a life
GAL	gal	girl
GAL PAL	gal pal	man who hangs around with girls
GALDEM	galdem	group of girls
GALFI	galfi	gives a lesbian first impression
GAMER	gamer	person who plays video games
GAMEZ	gamez	illegally obtained games
GAMMD	gammd	go ahead make my day
GANGSTA	gangsta	gangster
GANJA	ganja	marijuana, pot, cannabis, weed
GANK	gank	gang kill (MMORPG)
GANK	gank	kill
GANK	gank	steal
GAOEP	gaoep	generally accepted office etiquette principles
GAP	gap	gay-ass people
GAP	gap	Got a pic?
GARMS	garms	clothes
GAS	gas	flatulence
GAS	gas	Got a sec?
GAS	gas	greetings and salutations
GAS	gas	guitar acquisition syndrome
GASSED	gassed	have a high opinion of yourself
GASSING	gassing	talking
GAT	gat	gun
GAW	gaw	grandparents are watching
GAWD	gawd	god
GAWJUS	gawjus	gorgeous
GAWJUSS	gawjuss	gorgeous
GAYA$$	gaya$$	gayass (butt - homosexual slur/derogatory)
GAYAZZ	gayazz	gayass (butt - homosexual slur/derogatory)
GAYFK	gayfk	gayfuck (homosexual slur/derogatory)
GAYFKIST	gayfkist	gayfuckist (homosexual slur/derogatory)
GAYLRD	gaylrd	gaylord (homosexual slur/derogatory)
GAYTRD	gaytrd	gaytard (homosexual slur/derogatory)
GAYWD	gaywd	gaywad (homosexual slur/derogatory)
GB	gb	gigabyte
GB	gb	go back
GB	gb	good-bye
GB	gb	Great Britain
GB2	gb2	go back to
GBA	gba	game boy advance
GBFN	gbfn	good-bye for now
GBH	gbh	grievous bodily harm
GBIOUA	gbioua	go blow it out your ass
GBML	gbml	good-bye, my love
GBNF	gbnf	gone but not forgotten
GBP	gbp	Great Britain pounds (sterling)
Gbps	gbps	gigabits per second
GBTFS	gbtfs	go back to fucking school
GBTS	gbts	go back to school
GBTW	gbtw	get back to work

UPPERCASE	LOWERCASE	MEANING
GBU	gbu	God bless you
GBY	gby	God bless you
GBY	gby	good-bye
GC	gc	good condition
GCAD	gcad	get cancer and die
GCF	gcf	good clean fun
GCF	gcf	Google click fraud
GCSE	gcse	General Certificate of Secondary Education (UK)
GD	gd	gangsta disciple
GD	gd	good
GD&R	gd&r	grins, ducks, and runs
GD4U	gd4u	good for you
GDAY	gday	good day/hi
GDBY	gdby	good-bye
GDDM	gddm	goddamn
GDDMT	gddmt	goddamn it
GDED	gded	grounded
GDGD	gdgd	good, good
GDI	gdi	goddamn independent
GDI	gdi	goddamn it
GDIAF	gdiaf	go die in a fire
GDIH	gdih	go die in hell
GDILF	gdilf	granddad I'd like to fuck
GDMFPOS	gdmfpos	goddamn motherfucking piece of shit
GDO	gdo	guido (Italian - ethnic slur/derogatory)
GDR	gdr	grinning, ducking, running
GE	ge	good evening
GED	ged	general educational development
GEEZ	geez	Jesus
GEEZER	geezer	a guy, a bloke, a person
GEG	geg	interrupt a conversation
GEMO	gemo	gay emo
GEN	gen	information
GENIOUS	genious	misspelling of "genius"
GEOCACHE	geocache	scavenger hunt destination point
GET	get	git
GET DOWN	get down	party, dance
GETCHA	getcha	get you
GETO	geto	ghetto
GETTO	getto	ghetto
GEWD	gewd	good
GEY	gey	gay
GF	gf	girlfriend
GFA	gfa	grenade-free America
GFAD	gfad	go fuck a duck
GFADH	gfadh	go fuck a dead horse
GFAK	gfak	go fly a kite
GFAM	gfam	go fuck a monkey
GFAR2CU	gfar2cu	go find a rock to crawl under
GFAS	gfas	go fuck a sheep
GFC	gfc	global financial crisis
GFD	gfd	god-fucking-damn it
GFE	gfe	girlfriend experience
GFE2E	gfe2e	grinning from ear to ear

UPPERCASE	LOWERCASE	MEANING
GFF	gff	go fucking figure
GFF	gff	grenade-free foundation
GFG	gfg	good fucking game
GFGI	gfgi	go fucking Google it
GFI	gfi	go for it
GFI	gfi	good fucking idea
GFJ	gfj	good fucking job
GFL	gfl	get fucking lost
GFL	gfl	grounded for life
GFN	gfn	gone for now
GFO	gfo	go fuck off
GFTD	gftd	gone for the day
GFU	gfu	go fuck yourself
GFU	gfu	good for you
GFURS	gfurs	go fuck yourself
GFUS	gfus	go fuck yourself
GFX	gfx	graphics
GFY	gfy	go find yourself
GFY	gfy	go fuck yourself
GFY	gfy	good for you
GFYA	gfya	go find yourself, asshole
GFYA	gfya	go fuck yourself, asshole
GFYA	gfya	good for you, asshole
GFYD	gfyd	go fuck your dad
GFYF	gfyf	go fuck your father
GFYG	gfyg	go fuck your granny
GFYM	gfym	go fuck your mom
GFYM	gfym	go fuck your mother
GFYMF	gfymf	go fuck yourself, motherfucker
GFYS	gfys	go fuck yourself
GG	gg	brother (Mandarin Chinese text messages)
GG	gg	good game
GG	gg	gotta go
GGA	gga	good game, all
GGAL	ggal	go get a life
GGBB	ggbb	good game, bye-bye
GGE	gge	gotta go eat
GGE1	gge1	good game, everyone
GGF	ggf	go get fucked
GGG	ggg	Go, go, go!
GGG	ggg	good, giving, and game (in bed)
GGGG	gggg	god, god, god, god
GGL	ggl	giggle
GGMSOT	ggmsot	gotta get me some of that
GGN	ggn	gotta go now
GGNORE	ggnore	good game, no rematch
GGOH	ggoh	gotta get outta here
GGP	ggp	gotta go pee
GGPAW	ggpaw	gotta go, parents are watching
GGS	ggs	good games
GGS	ggs	gotta go shit
GGW	ggw	girls gone wild
GGY	ggy	go Google yourself
GGYA	ggya	go Google yourself, asshole

UPPERCASE	LOWERCASE	MEANING
GGYF	ggyf	go Google yourself, fucker
GH	gh	good half
GH	gh	guitar hero
GHB	ghb	gamma-hydroxybutyrate (drug)
GHD	ghd	good hair day
GHEI	ghei	gay
GHEY	ghey	gay
GHOST	ghost	leaving
GI	gi	American solider
GI	gi	good idea
GI	gi	government issue
GIA	gia	Google it, asshole
GIAR	giar	give it a rest
GIEF	gief	give
GIF	gif	Graphics Interchange Format
GIG	gig	gigabyte
GIG	gig	job
GIG	gig	live performance
GIGIG	gigig	get it, got it, good
GIGO	gigo	garbage in, garbage out
GILF	gilf	grandma I'd like to fuck
GIM	gim	Google instant messenger
GIMF	gimf	Google it, motherfucker
GIMME	gimme	give me
GIMP	gimp	uncool/stupid person
GIN	gin	gin (Aboriginal woman - ethnic slur/derogatory)
GINGER	ginger	person with red hair
GINGRICH	gingrich	hypocrite
GINNEL	ginnel	alley, passageway
GIR	gir	Google it, retard
GIRL	girl	guy in real life
GIS	gis	Geographic Information Systems
GIS	gis	Google image search
GIT	git	idiot
GITAR	gitar	guitar
GIV	giv	give
GIWIST	giwist	Gee, I wish I'd said that.
GIYF	giyf	Google is your friend
GJ	gj	good job/joke
GJA	gja	good job, asshole
GJIAL	gjial	go jump in a lake
GJMF	gjmf	good job, motherfucker
GJOAC	gjoac	go jump off a cliff
GJP	gjp	good job, partner
GJSU	gjsu	God, just shut up
GJT	gjt	good job, team
GJWHF	gjwhf	Girls just wanna have fun.
GJYI	gjyi	good job, you idiot
GK	gk	good kid
GK	gk	gook (Chinese - ethnic slur/derogatory)
GKY	gky	go kill yourself
GKYS	gkys	go kill yourselves
GL	gl	good luck
GL	gl	good-looking

UPPERCASE	LOWERCASE	MEANING
GL&HF	gl&hf	Good luck and have fun.
GL/HF	gl/hf	Good luck, have fun.
GL2U	gl2u	good luck to you
GLA	gla	Get lost, asshole.
GLA	gla	good luck, all
GLAG	glag	giggling like a girl
GLBT	glbt	gay, lesbian, bisexual, transgender
GLD	gld	good life decision
GLE1	gle1	good luck, everyone
GLEAK	gleak	spit
GLEEK	gleek	a fan of the TV show *Glee*
GLF	glf	group looking for
GLHF	glhf	good luck, have fun
GLI	gli	get lost, idiot
GLLN	glln	got laid last night
GLMF	glmf	get lost, motherfucker
GLNG	glng	good luck next game
GLNHF	glnhf	good luck and have fun
GLOCK	glock	semiautomatic pistol
GLOMP	glomp	hug very hard
GLOTR	glotr	good luck on the rebuild
GLTA	glta	good luck to all
GLTY	glty	good luck this year/good luck to you
GLU	glu	guys/girls like us
GLU2	glu2	good luck to you too
GLUCK	gluck	good luck
GLUX	glux	good luck
GLWS	glws	good luck with sale
GLWT	glwt	good luck with that
GLYASDI	glyasdi	God loves you and so do I.
GM	gm	General Motors
GM	gm	genetically modified
GM	gm	good morning
GM	gm	good move
GMA	gma	*Good Morning, America*
GMA	gma	grandma
GMAB	gmab	give me a break
GMABJ	gmabj	give me a blowjob
GMAFB	gmafb	give me a fucking break
GMAIL	gmail	Google Web e-mail service
GMAO	gmao	giggling my ass off
GMBH	gmbh	Gesellschaft mit beschränkter Haftung (LLC)
GMC	gmc	General Motors Corporation
GMFAB	gmfab	give me a fucking break
GMFAO	gmfao	giggling my fucking ass off
GMH	gmh	gives me hope
GMILF	gmilf	grandmother I'd like to fuck
GMO	gmo	genetically modified organism
GMOD	gmod	*Garry's Mod* (game)
GMOD	gmod	global moderator
GMT	gmt	Greenwich mean time
GMTA	gmta	great minds think alike
GMTYT	gmtyt	good morning to you too
GMV	gmv	got my vote

UPPERCASE	LOWERCASE	MEANING
GMY	gmy	good man yourself
GMYBS	gmybs	give me your best shot
GN	gn	good night
GN8	gn8	good night
GNA	gna	good night, asshole
GNAGFY	gnagfy	good night and go fuck yourself
GNARLY	gnarly	extreme
GND	gnd	girl next door
GNDN	gndn	goes nowhere, does nothing
GNE	gne	good night and everything
GNE1	gne1	good night, everyone
GNFB	gnfb	good night, Facebook
GNFPWLBN	gnfpwlbn	good news for people who love bad news
GNG	gng	going
GNGBNG	gngbng	gang bang
GNI	gni	good night, idiot
GNIGHT	gnight	good night
GNITE	gnite	good night
GNK	gnk	glitch no kill (gaming)
GNMF	gnmf	good night, motherfucker
GNN	gnn	get naked now
GNO	gno	girls/guys night out
GNO	gno	going to do
GNOC	gnoc	get naked on cam
GNOS	gnos	get naked on screen
GNR	gnr	*Guns N' Roses* (band)
GNRN	gnrn	get naked right now
GNSD	gnsd	good night, sweet dreams
GNST	gnst	goodnight, sleep tight
GNSTDLTBBB	gnstdltbbb	Good night, sleep tight; don't let the bed bugs bite.
GNU	gnu	GNU's not Unix, Linux OS
GOAT	goat	greatest of all time
GOB	gob	mouth
GOBLIN	goblin	gangster
GOC	goc	get on camera
GODSPEED	godspeed	good luck
GOG	gog	person from North Wales
GOI	goi	get over it
GOIA	goia	get over it, asshole
GOIN	goin	going
GOK	gok	God only knows
GOKID	gokid	got observers, keep it decent
GOKIL	gokil	crazy (Indonesian)
GOL	gol	giggle out loud
GOLD DIGGER	gold digger	person who loves someone just for their money
GOM	gom	idiot, fool
GOMB	gomb	get off my back
GOMD	gomd	guy/girl of my dreams
GOMEN	gomen	sorry
GOMER	gomer	get out of my emergency room, unwelcome patient
GOML	goml	get on my level
GOML	goml	get out of my life
GON	gon	go on
GONA	gona	gonna

UPPERCASE	LOWERCASE	MEANING
GONNA	gonna	going to
GOOD9	good9	good night
GOOG	goog	ecstasy pill
GOOH	gooh	get out of here
GOOMH	goomh	get out of my head
GOON	goon	stupid
GOON	goon	tough guy
GOONER	gooner	supporter of arsenal football club
GOP	gop	grand old party
GORG	gorg	gorgeous
GORK	gork	God only really knows.
GORM	gorm	germless person
GOS	gos	game of soldiers
GOS	gos	girlfriend over shoulder
GOS?	gos?	Gay or straight?
GOSAD	gosad	go suck a dick
GOSH	gosh	exclamation of surprise or shock
GOSU	gosu	skillful person (Korean)
GOTC	gotc	get on the computer
GOTCHA	gotcha	I got you, I understand
GOTTA	gotta	got to...
GOTTA	gotta	Have you got a...?
GOTY	goty	game of the year
GOU	gou	good on you
GOW	gow	*Gears of War* (game)
GOW	gow	*God of War* (game)
GOYA	goya	get off your ass
GOYHH	goyhh	get off your high horse
GP	gp	general principle
GP	gp	good point
GPA	gpa	grade point average
GPB	gpb	gotta pee bad
GPC	gpc	generic pack of cigarettes
GPC	gpc	get/post/cookie (Web pages)
GPL	gpl	general public license
GPOY	gpoy	gratuitous picture of yourself
GPOYW	gpoyw	gratuitous picture of yourself Wednesday
GPRS	gprs	general packet radio services
GPS	gps	Global Positioning System
GPU	gpu	graphics processing unit
GPWM	gpwm	good point well made
GQ	gq	*Gentlemen's Quarterly* (magazine)
GQ	gq	suave, well-dressed man
GR	gr	gotta run
GR&D	gr&d	grinning, running, and ducking
GR8	gr8	great
GRASS	grass	marijuana
GRATS	grats	congratulations
GRATZ	gratz	congratulations
GRE	gre	Graduate Record Examination
GREEN	green	environmentally beneficial
GREEN	green	inexperienced
GREEN	green	marijuana
GRENADE	grenade	ugly girl in a group

UPPERCASE	LOWERCASE	MEANING
GRFX	grfx	graphics
GRILL	grill	tooth jewelry
GRILLZ	grillz	metal teeth
GRL	grl	girl
GRMBL	grmbl	grumble
GRNGO	grngo	gringo (foreigner· ethnic slur/derogatory)
GRO	gro	guest relations officer
GRODY	grody	disgusting, nasty, gross
GROG	grog	beer
GRONK	gronk	idiot, fool
GROOL	grool	great and cool
GROOVY	groovy	cool, awesome
GROSS	gross	unpleasant, disgusting
GROUSE	grouse	great, amazing
GRR	grr	anger, frustration
GRRL	grrl	girl
GRTG	grtg	getting ready to go
GRUB	grub	food
GRULE	grule	hard work, nuisance
GRVY	grvy	groovy
GRWG	grwg	get right with god
GS	gs	good shot
GSAD	gsad	go suck a dick
GSAVE	gsave	global struggle against violent extremists
GSD	gsd	getting shit done
GSFG	gsfg	go search fucking Google
GSI	gsi	go suck it
GSM	gsm	global system for mobile communications
GSOH	gsoh	good sense of humor
GSP	gsp	get some pussy
GSR	gsr	gunshot residue
GSTA	gsta	gangster
GSTQ	gstq	God save the queen.
GT	gt	get
GT	gt	good try
GT	gt	*Gran Turismo* (game)
GT	gt	grand touring
GTA	gta	*Grand Theft Auto* (game)
GTAS	gtas	go take a shit
GTB	gtb	go to bed
GTBOSH	gtbosh	glad to be of some help
GTFA	gtfa	Go the fuck away.
GTFBTW	gtfbtw	Get the fuck back to work.
GTFH	gtfh	Go to fucking hell.
GTFO	gtfo	Get the fuck out.
GTFOI	gtfoi	Get the fuck over it.
GTFON	gtfon	Get the fuck out, noob.
GTFOOH	gtfooh	Get the fuck out of here.
GTFOOMF	gtfoomf	Get the fuck out of my face.
GTFU	gtfu	Grow the fuck up.
G,.GTG	gtg	got to go
GTGBB	gtgbb	got to go, bye-bye
GTGFN	gtgfn	got to go for now
GTGMMILOMS	gtgmmiloms	got to go, my mum is looking over my shoulder

UPPERCASE	LOWERCASE	MEANING
GTGN	gtgn	got to go now
GTGP	gtgp	got to go pee
GTGPP	gtgpp	got to go pee pee
GTGTB	gtgtb	got to go to bed
GTGTWN	gtgtwn	got to go to work now
GTH	gth	go to hell
GTHA	gtha	go the hell away
GTHB	gthb	go to hell, bitch
GTHBA	gthba	good times had by all
GTHMF	gthmf	go to hell, mothafucka
GTHO	gtho	get the hell out
GTHU	gthu	grow the heck up
GTHYFAH	gthyfah	go to hell, you fucking asshole
GTI	gti	high-performance hatchback (e.g., VW Golf)
GTK	gtk	good to know
GTL	gtl	gym, tan, laundry
GTLD	gtld	generic tld
GTM	gtm	giggling to myself
GTN	gtn	getting
GTO	gto	Gran Turismo Omologato
GTOG	gtog	got to go
GTP	gtp	got to pee
GTR	gtr	getting ready/got to run
GTRM	gtrm	going to read mail
GTS	gts	going to school
GTS	gts	good times
GTSY	gtsy	good to see you
GTTP	gttp	get to the point
GTTS	gtts	got the T-shirt
GTTY	gtty	good talking to you
GTW	gtw	got to work
GU	gu	grow up
GUAP	guap	money
GUCCI	gucci	good, awesome, high quality
GUD	gud	good
GUDD	gudd	good
GUFN	gufn	grounded until further notice
GUH	guh	annoyed, angry
GUI	gui	Graphical User Interface
GUID	guid	Globally Unique Identifier
GURL	gurl	girl
GURLZ	gurlz	girls
GURU	guru	expert
GUTI	guti	get used to it
GUUD	guud	good
GUV	guv	guvnor, boss
GV	gv	good vibes
GW	gw	good work
GWAAN	gwaan	go on
GWAP	gwap	money
GWARN	gwarn	go on
GWAS	gwas	game was a success
GWC	gwc	guy with camera
GWG	gwg	girl with glasses

UPPERCASE	LOWERCASE	MEANING
GWHTLC	gwhtlc	Glad we had this little chat.
GWI	gwi	get with it
GWIJD	gwijd	guess what I just did
GWM	gwm	gay white male
GWOP	gwop	money
GWORK	gwork	good work
GWP	gwp	gift with purchase
GWR	gwr	Guinness world records
GWRK	gwrk	good work
GWS	gws	get well soon
GWTF	gwtf	go with the flow
GWYTOSE	gwytose	Go waste your time on someone else.
GY	gy	gay
GYAL	gyal	girl
GYALDEM	gyaldem	group of girls
GYBOB	gybob	gaybob (homosexual slur/derogatory)
GYFS	gyfs	get your facts straight
GYHOOYA	gyhooya	get your head out of your ass
GYO	gyo	get your own
GYPO	gypo	get your penis out
GYST	gyst	get your shit together
GYT	gyt	get yourself tested
GZ	gz	congratulations
H	h	Harvard University
H	h	hug
H&K	h&k	hugs and kisses
H*R	h*r	*Homestar Runner* (game)
H/E	h/e	however
H/MO	h/mo	homo
H/O	h/o	hold on
H/T	h/t	hat tip
H/U	h/u	hold up
H/U	h/u	hook up, make out
H/W	h/w	homework
H@M@	h@m@	homo (homosexual - slur/derogatory)
H+K	h+k	hugs and kisses
H0	h0	ho (woman)
H1B	h1b	US employment visa
H1N1	h1n1	swine flu virus
H2	h2	*Halo 2* (game)
H2CUS	h2cus	hope to see you soon
H2G	h2g	had to go
H2G	h2g	honest to God
H2GTB	h2gtb	have to go to the bathroom
H2H	h2h	head to head
H2H	h2h	heart to heart
H2IK	h2ik	hell if I know
H2O	h2o	water
H2SYS	h2sys	hope to see you soon
H3	h3	*Halo 3* (game)
H3Y	h3y	hey
H4KZ0R5	h4kz0r5	hackers
H4X	h4x	hacks, cheats
H4X0R	h4x0r	hacker

UPPERCASE	LOWERCASE	MEANING
H4XR	h4xr	hacker
H4XRZ	h4xrz	hackers
H4XX0RZ	h4xx0rz	hacker
H4XXOR	h4xxor	hacker
H8	h8	hate
H80R	h80r	hater
H82SIT	h82sit	hate to say it
H83R	h83r	hater
H8ED	h8ed	hated
H8ER	h8er	hater
H8R	h8r	hater
H8RED	h8red	hatred
H8S	h8s	hates
H8T	h8t	hate
H8T0R	h8t0r	hater
H8T3R	h8t3r	hater
H8TE	h8te	hate
H8TR	h8tr	hater
H8TTU	h8ttu	hate to be you
H8U	h8u	I hate you
H9	h9	husband in room
H9	h9	really hate (h8+1)
HA	ha	sarcastic laugh
HABBO	habbo	online community/game
HABIBI	habibi	my darling (Arabic)
HABT	habt	How about this?
HACK	hack	break into computer systems or software
HAFL	hafl	heart attack from laughing
HAFTA	hafta	have to
HAG	hag	unattractive old woman
HAG1	hag1	have a good one
HAGD	hagd	have a good day
HAGE	hage	have a good evening
HAGL	hagl	have a good life
HAGN	hagn	have a good night
HAGO	hago	have a good one
HAGS	hags	have a great summer
HAGT	hagt	have a great time
HAI	hai	hello, hey, hi
HAI	hai	yes (Japanese)
HAISTK	haistk	How am I supposed to know?
HAIT	hait	hate
HAIZ	haiz	sigh
HAK	hak	here's a kiss
HAK	hak	hugs and kisses
HAKAS	hakas	have a kick-ass summer
HALP	halp	help
HAMMRD	hammrd	hammered
HAN	han	alone
HAN	han	how about now
HAND	hand	have a nice day
HANDLE	handle	half a gallon of liquor
HANDLE	handle	nickname, alias
HANG	hang	hang out, spend time with

UPPERCASE	LOWERCASE	MEANING
HANG UP	hang up	inhibition, emotional difficulty
HANL	hanl	have a nice life
HAPA	hapa	mixed race
HAR	har	sarcastic laugh
HARD LINES	hard lines	bad luck
HARF	harf	vomit, throw up
HASHTAG	hashtag	label on Twitter to aid searching
HASIAN	hasian	hot Asian
HATERZ	haterz	enemies
HAU	hau	How about you?
HAU	hau	How are you?
HAV	hav	have
HAVNT	havnt	haven't
HAWF	hawf	husband and wife forever
HAWK	hawk	knife
HAWT	hawt	having a wonderful time
HAWT	hawt	hot
HAWTIE	hawtie	hottie
HAWTSOME	hawtsome	hot and awesome
HAX	hax	hacking, hackers, hacks
HAX0R	hax0r	hacker
HAX0RED	hax0red	hacked
HAX0RZ	hax0rz	hackers
HAXER	haxer	hacker
HAXOR	haxor	hacker
HAXORING	haxoring	hacking
HAXORS	haxors	hackers
HAXORZ	haxorz	hackers
HAXX0R	haxx0r	hacker
HAXXOR	haxxor	hacker
HAXXZOR	haxxzor	hacker
HAXZ0R	haxz0r	hacker
HAXZOR	haxzor	hacker
HAY	hay	How are you?
HAYD	hayd	How are you doing?
HAYWIRE	haywire	crazy
HAZE	haze	type of marijuana
HB	hb	heeb (Jewish Person - ethnic slur/derogatory)
HB	hb	hug back
HB	hb	hurry back
HB4B	hb4b	hoes before bros
HBD	hbd	happy birthday
H-BDAY	h-bday	happy birthday
HBIB	hbib	hot but inappropriate boy
HBIC	hbic	head bitch in charge
HBII	hbii	How big is it?
HBN	hbn	How about now?
HBO	hbo	Home Box Office
HBP	hbp	*Half-Blood Prince* (*Harry Potter*)
HBT	hbt	How 'bout that?
HBTU	hbtu	happy birthday to you
HBTY	hbty	happy birthday to you
HBU	hbu	How about you?
HBY	hby	How about you?

UPPERCASE	LOWERCASE	MEANING
HC	hc	holy cow
HC	hc	How come?
HCBT1	hcbt1	He could be the one.
HCDAJFU	hcdajfu	He could do a job for us.
HCIB	hcib	How can it be?
HCIHY	hcihy	How can I help you?
HCIT	hcit	How cool is that?
HCO	hco	Hollister
HD	hd	high-definition
HDCP	hdcp	High-bandwidth Digital Content Protection
HDD	hdd	hard disk drive
HDF	hdf	*halt die fresse* ("shut up" in German)
HDJB	hdjb	handjob (sexual act)
HDL	hdl	*hab dich lieb* ("I love you" in German)
HDMI	hdmi	High-Definition Multimedia Interface
HDON	hdon	hard on (erection)
HDOP	hdop	help delete online predators
HDTV	hdtv	high definition televsion
HDU	hdu	How dare you?
HDV	hdv	high-definition video
HDY	hdy	How dare you?
HDYDI	hdydi	How do you do it?
HDYDT	hdydt	How did you do that?
HDYK	hdyk	How do/did you know?
HE	he	happy ending
HE	he	high explosives
HEA	hea	happily ever after
HEADS	heads	people
HEADS UP	heads up	advance notice
HEAT	heat	gun(s)
HEAVY	heavy	awesome, good
HEAVY	heavy	serious, intense
HECK	heck	mild expletive
HECTIC	hectic	cool, good
HEEB	heeb	a Jewish person (short for Hebrew - ethnic slur/derogatory)
HEH	heh	cynical laugh
HEH	heh	ha-ha
HELLA	hella	really, very
HENCH	hench	strong, muscular, well built
HERB	herb	stupid person
HESHE	heshe	person of unidentifiable gender
HEX	hex	curse
HEX	hex	hexadecimal (base 16)
HEY	hey	hello, hi
HEYA	heya	hey
HEYT	heyt	hate
HEYY	heyy	hey, you
HEYYA	heyya	hey, you
HF	hf	have fun
HFAC	hfac	holy flipping animal crackers
H-FDAY	h-fday	Happy Father's Day
HFD	hfd	Happy Father's Day
HFFA	hffa	hot from far away

UPPERCASE	LOWERCASE	MEANING
HFN	hfn	hell fucking no
HFS	hfs	hierarchical file system
HFS	hfs	Holy fucking shit!
HFSBM	hfsbm	Holy fucking shit, Batman.
HFWT	hfwt	have fun with that
HG	hg	hockey god
HG	hg	holy grail
HGB	hgb	*Hellogoodbye* (band)
HGH	hgh	haters gonna hate
HGHT	hght	height
HH	hh	ha-ha
HH	hh	holding hands
HHIAD	hhiad	holy hole in a doughnut
HHIADB	hhiadb	Holy hole in a donut, Batman.
HHIS	hhis	head hanging in shame
HHO1/2K	hho1/2k	ha-ha, only half kidding
HHOJ	hhoj	ha-ha, only joking
HHOK	hhok	ha-ha, only kidding
HHOS	hhos	ha-ha, only serious
HHVF	hhvf	ha-ha, very funny
HHWW	hhww	holding hands while walking
HHYB	hhyb	how have you been
HI	hi	hello
HI2U	hi2u	hello
HI2U2	hi2u2	hello to you too
HI5	hi5	social networking site
HICKEY	hickey	love bite
HIET	hiet	height
HIIK	hiik	hell if I know
HIJACK	hijack	start an off-topic discussion
HIMYM	himym	*How I Met Your Mother* (TV show)
HINKEY	hinkey	strange, unusual
HIP	hip	cool, stylish, contemporary
HIPSTER	hipster	person who is hip
HIT A LICK	hit a lick	get a lot of money very quickly
HIT ME UP	hit me up	call me later
HIT YOU UP	hit you up	call you later
HITH	hith	how in the hell
HIV	hiv	human immunodeficiency virus
HIW	hiw	husband is watching
HIWTH	hiwth	hate it when that happens
HIYA	hiya	hello
HIYBBPRQAG	hiybbprqag	copying somebody else's search results
HJ	hj	hand job
HK	hk	Hong Kong
HK	hk	hostile kids
HL	hl	*Half-Life* (game)
HL2	hl2	*Half-Life 2* (game)
HLA	hla	*hola*/hello (Spanish SMS)
HLA	hla	hot lesbian action
HLAS	hlas	hook, line, and sinker
HLB	hlb	horny little bastard
HLD	hld	hold
HLDN	hldn	hold on

UPPERCASE	LOWERCASE	MEANING
HLDON	hldon	hold on
HLL	hll	hell
HLM	hlm	he loves me
HLO	hlo	hello
HLP	hlp	help
HLY	hly	holy
HLYSHT	hlysht	holy shit
HM	hm	thinking
HMB	hmb	hit me back (reply)
HMB	hmb	hold me back
H-MDAY	h-mday	Happy Mother's Day
HMD	hmd	Happy Mother's Day
HMEWRK	hmewrk	homework
HMFIC	hmfic	head mother fucker in charge
HMIHY	hmihy	How may I help you?
HML	hml	hate my life
HMOJ	hmoj	holy mother of Jesus
HMP	hmp	help me, please
HMPF	hmpf	sound made when irritated
HMPH	hmph	expression of apathy or disagreement
HMPING	hmping	humping (sexual act)
HMS	hms	Her Majesty's ship (UK)
HMU	hmu	hit me up
HMUL	hmul	hit me up later
HMW	hmw	homework
HMWRK	hmwrk	homework
HNG	hng	horny net geek
HNGRY	hngry	hungry
HNIC	hnic	head nigger in charge
HNK	hnk	hugs and kisses
HNKY	hnky	honkey (white person - ethnic slur/derogatory)
HNOS	hnos	home network operating system
HNR	hnr	hit and run
HNY	hny	happy new year
HO	ho	head office
HO	ho	hold on
HOAS	hoas	hang on a second/hold on a second
HOAY	hoay	How old are you?
HOBO	hobo	itinerant worker
HOG	hog	Harley owner group
HOH	hoh	hard of hearing (disability slur/derogatory)
HOH	hoh	head of household
HOH	hoh	head over heels
HOHA	hoha	Hollywood hacker
HOLD	hold	borrow (money)
HOLD UP	hold up	wait a minute
HOLLA	holla	used by a man to express interest in a woman
HOLLA BACK	holla back	get back to me
HOLLAND	holland	hope our love lasts and never dies
HOLLER	holler	shout
HOLS	hols	holidays, vacation
HOM	hom	home
HOMEBOY	homeboy	closest friend
HOMEDOG	homedog	(same as "homeboy")

UPPERCASE	LOWERCASE	MEANING
HOMEGIRL	homegirl	closest female friend
HOMES	homes	homeboy
HOMESLICE	homeslice	homeboy
HOMEY	homey	homeboy/friend
HOMG	homg	(same as "OMG")
HOMIE	homie	good friend
HOMIE	homie	homeboy
HOMMIE	hommie	misspelling of "homie"
HOMO	homo	homosexual
HON	hon	honey
HONKIE	honkie	white person (ethnic slur/derogatory)
HONKY	honky	(same as "honkie")
HOOAH	hooah	(same as "hua")
HOOCHIE	hoochie	overly made-up woman with trashy dress sense
HOOD	hood	neighborhood, ghetto
HOODIE	hoodie	hooded sweatshirt
HOOK ME UP	hook me up	share with me
HOOKED	hooked	addicted
HOOPS	hoops	basketball
HOOPTY	hoopty	broke down automobile
HOOROO	hooroo	good-bye
HOP	hop	heroin
HOP OFF	hop off	leave me alone
HORNY	horny	turned on
HORSE	horse	heroin
HOS	hos	husband over shoulder
HOT	hot	healing over time
HOTT	hott	hot
HOTTIE	hottie	attractive person
HOVA	hova	Jehovah, God
HOWDEY	howdey	hello
HOWDY	howdy	How do you do?
HOWZ	howz	how's
HP	hp	*Harry Potter*
HP	hp	hit points
HPB	hpb	high ping bastard
HPOA	hpoa	hot piece of ass
HPPY	hppy	happy
HPY	hpy	happy
HPYBDY	hpybdy	happy birthday
HQ	hq	high quality
HQF	hqf	(same as "LOL")
HR	hr	hour
HR	hr	human resources
HRE	hre	here
HRH	hrh	His/Her Royal Highness
HRNY	hrny	horny
HRS	hrs	hours
HRU	hru	How are you?
HRUD	hrud	How are you doing?
HS	hs	headshot
HSATAABW	hsataabw	He's as thick as a bull's walt.
HSD	hsd	high school dropout
HSF	hsf	heat sink and fan

UPPERCASE	LOWERCASE	MEANING
HSIK	hsik	How should I know?
HSIT	hsit	How sad is that?
HSM	hsm	high school musical
HSP	hsp	highly sensitive person
HSPDA	hspda	High-Speed Packet Data Access
HSR	hsr	*Homestar Runner* (game)
HSS	hss	horseshit and splinters
HSWM	hswm	have sex with me
HT	ht	handheld transceiver
HT	ht	hat tip (thanks)
HT	ht	heard through
HT	ht	home time
HTB	htb	hang the bastards
HTC	htc	hit the cell
HTF	htf	how the fuck
HTFSIK	htfsik	How the fuck should I know?
HTFU	htfu	hurry the fuck up
HTH	hth	hope that/this helps
HTH	hth	how the hell
HTHFYS	hthfys	hope to hear from you soon
HTM	htm	hand to mouth
HTML	html	Hyper-Text Markup Language
HTR	htr	hater
HTSYS	htsys	hope to see you soon
HTTP	http	HyperText Transfer Protocol
HTTPS	https	HyperText Transport Protocol Secure
HTX	htx	Houston, Texas
HU	hu	hey, you
HU	hu	*Hollywood Undead* (band)
HUA	hua	Heard, understood, acknowledged
HUB	hub	head up butt
HUBBY	hubby	husband
HUCKLEBERRY	huckleberry	the man you're looking for
HUD	hud	heads-up display
HUFF	huff	low-grade weed
HUGGLE	huggle	hug and cuddle / hug and snuggle
HUGZ	hugz	hugs
HUH	huh	confused sound
HUN	hun	honey
HUNDO	hundo	hundred (dollars)
HUNGO	hungo	a Hungarian (ethnic slur/derogatory)
HUNNED	hunned	hundred (dollars)
HUR	hur	hair
HUR	hur	here
HURT	hurt	ugly, unattractive
HUSPAZ	huspaz	hurray (texting)
HUYA	huya	head up your ass
HUZZAH	huzzah	expression of triumph, joy
HV	hv	have
HVAC	hvac	heating, ventilating, air conditioning
HVE	hve	have
HVNT	hvnt	haven't
HW	hw	homework
HW/HW	hw/hw	help me with homework

UPPERCASE	LOWERCASE	MEANING
HWB	hwb	hottie with body
HWG	hwg	here we go
HWGA	hwga	here we go again
HWIK	hwik	How would I know?
HWK	hwk	homework
HWMBO	hwmbo	he who must be obeyed
HWMNBN	hwmnbn	he who must not be named
HWMS	hwms	hot, wild monkey sex
HWP	hwp	height-weight proportional
HWSNBN	hwsnbn	he who shall not be named
HWU	hwu	Hey, what's up?
HWYD	hwyd	How was your day?
HWZ	hwz	how is
HXC	hxc	*hardcore* (music)
HY	hy	hell yeah / hell yes
HY	hy	hi
HYB	hyb	How you been?
HYD	hyd	How you doing?
HYDRO	hydro	hydroponically grown marijuana
HYFB	hyfb	hope you feel better
HYG	hyg	here you go
HYH	hyh	have you heard
HYH	hyh	hold your horses
HYIP	hyip	high-yield investment program
HYK	hyk	how you know
HYNA	hyna	good-looking girl (Hispanic)
HYP	hyp	Harvard, Yale, Princeton
HYPER	hyper	overenergetic
HYPH	hyph	hyperactive, crazy
HYPO	hypo	hypodermic needle/syringe
HYS	hys	have your say
HYU	hyu	hit you up
HYUK	hyuk	lose, despite having a good lead
I <3 U	i <3 u	I love you.
I C	i c	I see.
I&I	i&i	intercourse and inebriation
I/O	i/o	Input/Output
I'MA	i'ma	I am going to
I<3 U	i<3 u	I love you.
I18N	i18n	internationalization
I8	i8	all right
I8U	i8u	I hate you.
IA	ia	I agree.
IA8	ia8	I already ate.
IAAA	iaaa	I am an accountant.
IAAD	iaad	I am a doctor.
IAAL	iaal	I am a lawyer.
IAB	iab	I am bored.
IABW	iabw	in a bad way
IAC	iac	in any case
IAE	iae	in any event
IAFH	iafh	I am fucking hot.
IAFI	iafi	I am from India.
IAG	iag	it's all good

UPPERCASE	LOWERCASE	MEANING
IAH	iah	I am horny.
IAI	iai	I am interested.
IAL	ial	I actually laughed.
IAL	ial	I ain't laughing.
IAMA	iama	I am mildly amused.
IANABS	ianabs	I am not a brain surgeon.
IANAC	ianac	I am not a crook.
IANACL	ianacl	I am not a copyright lawyer.
IANAD	ianad	I am not a doctor.
IANAL	ianal	I am not a lawyer. (this is an uninformed opinion)
IANALB	ianalb	I am not a lawyer, but...
IANARS	ianars	I am not a rocket scientist.
IANS	ians	I am not sure.
IANYL	ianyl	I am not your lawyer.
IAOOH	iaooh	I am out of here.
IAP	iap	I am pissed.
IAS	ias	in a second
IASB	iasb	I am so bored.
IASPFM	iaspfm	I am sorry; please forgive me.
IATB	iatb	I am the best.
IATEU	iateu	I hate you.
IAVB	iavb	I am very bored.
IAW	iaw	I agree with
IAW	iaw	in accordance with
IAW	iaw	in another window
IAWTC	iawtc	I agree with that/this comment.
IAWTCSM	iawtcsm	I agree with this comment so much.
IAWTP	iawtp	I agree with this post.
IAWY	iawy	I agree with you.
IB	ib	I'm back.
IB2D	ib2d	I beg to differ.
IB4TL	ib4tl	in before the lock
IBAN	iban	International Bank Account Number
IBB	ibb	I'll be back.
IBCD	ibcd	idiot between chair and desk
IBID	ibid	*ibidem* (in the same place)
IBK	ibk	idiot behind keyboard
IBM	ibm	International Business Machines
IBMTS	ibmts	I've been meaning to say
IBS	ibs	Internet bitch slap
IBS	ibs	irritable bowel syndrome
IBT	ibt	I'll be there.
IBTD	ibtd	I beg to differ.
IBTD	ibtd	in before the delete
IBTL	ibtl	in before the lock
IBW	ibw	I'll be waiting.
IBYP	ibyp	I beg your pardon.
IC	ic	I see.
ICAM	icam	I couldn't agree more.
ICANN	icann	Internet Corporation For Assigned Names and Numbers
ICAY	icay	I care about you.
ICB	icb	I can't believe...
ICBB	icbb	I can't be bothered.

UPPERCASE	LOWERCASE	MEANING
ICBI	icbi	I can't believe it.
ICBINB	icbinb	I can't believe it's not butter.
ICBIWOOP	icbiwoop	I chuckled, but it was out of pity.
ICBSST	icbsst	I can't believe she said that.
ICBT	icbt	I can't believe that.
ICBU	icbu	I can't believe you.
ICBW	icbw	it could be worse.
ICBYST	icbyst	I can't believe you said that.
ICCL	iccl	I could care less.
ICE	ice	crystal meth
ICE	ice	diamonds
ICE	ice	kill
ICEDI	icedi	I can't even discuss it.
ICF	icf	Internet Connection Firewall
ICFILWU	icfilwu	I could fall in love with you.
ICGUP	icgup	I can give you pleasure.
ICIC	icic	I see, I see.
ICK	ick	(same as "ugh")
ICMP	icmp	Internet Control Message Protocol
ICP	icp	*Insane Clown Posse* (band)
ICQ	icq	I seek you (instant messaging program)
ICR	icr	I can't remember.
ICS	ics	Internet Connection Sharing
ICSL	icsl	I couldn't/can't stop laughing
ICSRG	icsrg	I can still reach Google
ICT	ict	Information and Communication Technologies
ICTRN	ictrn	I can't talk right now.
ICTY	icty	I can't tell you.
ICU	icu	I see you.
ICU	icu	intensive care unit
ICUDK	icudk	in case you didn't know
ICUP	icup	I see you pee
ICW	icw	I care, why?
ICWUDT	icwudt	I see what you did there.
ICWUM	icwum	I see what you mean.
ICYDK	icydk	In case you didn't know.
ICYDN	icydn	In case you didn't know.
ICYMI	icymi	In case you missed it.
ID	id	identity
ID10T	id10t	idiot
IDBI	idbi	I don't believe it.
IDBTWDSAT	idbtwdsat	I don't believe they would do such a thing.
IDBY	idby	I don't believe you.
IDC	idc	I don't care.
IDD	idd	indeed
IDDI	iddi	I didn't do it.
IDDQD	iddqd	*Cheat Code for Doom* (game)
IDE	ide	Integrated Device Electronics or Integrated Development Environment
IDEC	idec	I don't even care.
IDEK	idek	I don't even know.
IDFBI	idfbi	I don't fucking believe it.
IDFC	idfc	I don't fucking care.
IDFK	idfk	I don't fucking know.

Internet and Computer Slang Dictionary

UPPERCASE	LOWERCASE	MEANING
IDFLI	idfli	I don't feel like it.
IDFM	idfm	it doesn't fucking matter.
IDFTS	idfts	I don't fucking think so.
IDGAC	idgac	I don't give a crap.
IDGAD	idgad	I don't give a damn.
IDGAF	idgaf	I don't give a fuck.
IDGAFF	idgaff	I don't give a flying fuck.
IDGAFS	idgafs	I don't give a fucking shit.
IDGARA	idgara	I don't give a rat's ass.
IDGAS	idgas	I don't give a shit.
IDGI	idgi	I don't get it.
IDHAC	idhac	I don't have a clue.
IDI	idi	I doubt it.
IDJIT	idjit	idiot
IDK	idk	I don't know.
IDKBIBT	idkbibt	I don't know but I've been told.
IDKE	idke	I don't know either.
IDKH	idkh	I don't know how.
IDKH2S	idkh2s	I don't know how to spell.
IDKT	idkt	I don't know that.
IDKW	idkw	I don't know why.
IDKWIWDWU	idkwiwdwu	I don't know what I would do without you.
IDKWTS	idkwts	I don't know what to say.
IDKWURTA	idkwurta	I don't know what you are talking about.
IDKWYM	idkwym	I don't know what you mean.
IDKY	idky	I don't know why/I don't know you
IDKYB	idkyb	I don't know why, but...
IDKYMB2	idkymb2	I didn't know your mom blogs too.
IDL	idl	I don't like...
IDLE	idle	inactive
IDLI	idli	I don't like it.
IDLT	idlt	I don't like that.
IDLU	idlu	I don't like you.
IDLY	idly	I don't love/like you.
IDLYITW	idlyitw	I don't like you in that way.
IDM	idm	I don't mind.
IDM	idm	intelligent dance music
IDM	idm	It doesn't matter.
IDN	idn	I don't know.
IDNK	idnk	I don't know.
IDNO	idno	I do not know.
IDONNO	idonno	I do not know.
IDOP	idop	it depends on price
IDOT	idot	idiot
IDR	idr	I don't remember.
IDRC	idrc	I don't really care.
IDRFK	idrfk	I don't really fucking know.
IDRGAF	idrgaf	I don't really give a fuck.
IDRK	idrk	I don't really know.
IDRTS	idrts	I don't really think so.
IDST	idst	if destroyed, still true
IDSW	idsw	I don't see why.
IDT	idt	I don't think.
IDTIS	idtis	I don't think I should.

UPPERCASE	LOWERCASE	MEANING
IDTKSO	idtkso	I don't think so.
IDTS	idts	I don't think so.
IDU	idu	I don't understand.
IDUNNO	idunno	I don't know.
IDUWYM	iduwym	I don't understand what you mean.
IDW	idw	I don't want...
IDW2	idw2	I don't want to.
IDW2N	idw2n	I don't want to know.
IDWK	idwk	I don't wanna know.
IDWT	idwt	I don't want to.
IDWTAI	idwtai	I don't wanna talk about it.
IDWTG	idwtg	I don't want to go.
IDYAT	idyat	idiot
IE	ie	*id est* (that is)
IE	ie	Internet Explorer
IEBKAC	iebkac	issue exists between keyboard and chair
IED	ied	improvised explosive device
IEEE	ieee	Institute of Electrical and Electronics Engineers
IEP	iep	Individualized Education Program
IETF	ietf	Internet Engineering Task Force
IFF	iff	identification: friend or foe
IFF	iff	if and only if
IFF	iff	Internet friends forever
IFFY	iffy	dodgy, unreliable
IFHU	ifhu	I fucking hate you.
IFHY	ifhy	I fucking hate you.
IFLU	iflu	I fucking love you.
IFTHTB	ifthtb	I find that hard to believe.
IFU	ifu	I fucked up.
IFWIS	ifwis	I forgot what I said.
IFYP	ifyp	I feel your pain.
IG	ig	I guess
IG	ig	ignorant
IG2G	ig2g	I got to go.
IG2R	ig2r	I got to run.
IG5OI	ig5oi	I got 5 on it.
IGAHP	igahp	I've got a huge penis.
IGALBOC	igalboc	I've got a lovely bunch of coconuts.
IGG	igg	I gotta go.
IGG	igg	ignore
IGGY	iggy	ignore you
IGHT	ight	all right
IGHT	ight	I got high tonight.
IGI	igi	I get it.
IGKYMFA	igkymfa	I'm gonna kick your motherfucking ass.
IGM	igm	I got mine.
IGMC	igmc	I'll get my coat.
IGN	ign	in game name
IGNB	ignb	I'm going now, bye.
IGNTS	ignts	I've got nothing to say.
IGP	igp	Integrated Graphics Processor
IGS	igs	I guess so.
IGTG	igtg	I got to go.
IGTGT	igtgt	I got to go tinkle.

UPPERCASE	LOWERCASE	MEANING
IGTKYA	igtkya	I'm going to kick your ass.
IGU	igu	I give up.
IGYB	igyb	I got your back.
IGYB	igyb	I've got your back.
IH2GP	ih2gp	I have to go pee.
IH2P	ih2p	I'll have to pass.
IH8	ih8	I hate.
IH8MB	ih8mb	I hate my brother.
IH8MF	ih8mf	I hate my father.
IH8MLB	ih8mlb	I hate my little brother.
IH8MLS	ih8mls	I hate my little sister.
IH8MM	ih8mm	I hate my mother.
IH8MP	ih8mp	I hate my parents.
IH8MS	ih8ms	I hate my sister.
IH8P	ih8p	I hate parents/people.
IH8U	ih8u	I hate you.
IH8USM	ih8usm	I hate you so much.
IH8Y	ih8y	I hate you.
IHAC	ihac	I have a customer.
IHAT3U	ihat3u	I hate you.
IHISTR	ihistr	I hope I spelled that right.
IHIWYDT	ihiwydt	I hate it when you do that.
IHM	ihm	I hate Mondays.
IHML	ihml	I hate my life.
IHMP	ihmp	I hate my parents.
IHNC	ihnc	I have no clue.
IHNFC	ihnfc	I have no fucking clue.
IHNFI	ihnfi	I have no fucking idea.
IHNI	ihni	I have no idea.
IHOP	ihop	International House of Pancakes
IHS	ihs	I hope so.
IHT	iht	I hate this.
IHT	iht	I heard that/this/them
IHTFP	ihtfp	I hate this fucking place.
IHTGTTBWIJD	ihtgttbwijd	I have to go to the bathroom; wait, I just did.
IHTP	ihtp	I have to poop.
IHTSM	ihtsm	I hate this so much.
IHTUTBR	ihtutbr	I have to use the bathroom.
IHU	ihu	I hate you.
IHURG	ihurg	I hate your guts.
IHUSB	ihusb	I hate you so bad.
IHUSFM	ihusfm	I hate you so fucking much.
IHUSM	ihusm	I hate you so much.
IHY	ihy	I hate you.
IHYA	ihya	I hate you all.
IHYSM	ihysm	I hate you so much.
IHYSMRN	ihysmrn	I hate you so much right now.
IIB	iib	Ignorance is bliss.
IIGH	iigh	all right
IIGHT	iight	all right, OK
IIH	iih	if I'm honest
IIIO	iiio	Intel Inside, Idiot Outside
IIL	iil	I'm in love.
IINM	iinm	if I'm not mistaken

UPPERCASE	LOWERCASE	MEANING
IIOK	iiok	Is it OK?
IIR	iir	idiot in room
IIRC	iirc	if I recall correctly
IIRC	iirc	if I remember correctly
IIS	iis	Internet Information Services
IISTGTBTIPI	iistgtbtipi	if it sounds too good to be true, it probably is
IITUWUTMAS	iituwutmas	If I tell you, will you tell me a secret?
IITYWIMIWHTKY	iitywimiwhtky	If I tell you what it means, I will have to kill you.
IITYWTMWYBMAD	iitywtmwybmad	If I tell you what this means, will you buy me a drink?
IITYWTMWYKM	iitywtmwykm	If I tell you what this means, will you kiss me?
IITYWYBMAD	litywybmad	If I tell you, will you buy me a drink?
IIUC	Iiuc	if I understand correctly
IIW2	iiw2	Is it Web 2.0?
IIWII	iiwii	It is what it is.
IJ	ij	I'm joking.
IJ	ij	inside joke
IJAF	ijaf	it's just a fact.
IJCOMK	ijcomk	I just came on my keyboard.
IJDK	ijdk	I just don't know.
IJDL	ijdl	I just died laughing.
IJEOMK	ijeomk	I just ejaculated on my keyboard.
IJF	ijf	I just farted.
IJGL	ijgl	I just got laid.
IJIT	ijit	idiot
IJP	ijp	Internet job posting
IJPMP	ijpmp	I just peed my pants.
IJPMP	ijpmp	I just pissed my pants.
IJPMS	ijpms	I just pissed myself.
IJR	ijr	I just remembered.
IJS	ijs	I'm just saying.
IJSABOMOMCIBSTG	ijsabomomcibstg	I just saved a bunch of money on my car insurance by switching to Geico.
IJWTK	ijwtk	I just want to know.
IK	ik	I know.
IKE	ike	(same as "dude")
IKE	ike	I know, eh.
IKEA	ikea	Swedish furniture store
IKHYF	ikhyf	I know how you feel.
IKI	iki	I know it.
IKLY	ikly	I kinda like you.
IKM	ikm	I know, man.
IKMTY	ikmty	I know more than you
IKR	ikr	I know really
IKR	ikr	I know, right?
IKT	ikt	I know that.
IKTR	iktr	I know that's right.
IKWUM	ikwum	I know what you mean/meant.
IKWYDLS	ikwydls	I know what you did last summer.
IKWYL	ikwyl	I know where you live.
IKWYM	ikwym	I know what you mean.
IKY	iky	I know you.

UPPERCASE	LOWERCASE	MEANING
IKYP	ikyp	I'll keep you posted.
IL	il	in love
ILBCNU	ilbcnu	I'll be seeing you.
ILBL8	ilbl8	I'll be late.
ILCUL8R	ilcul8r	I'll see you later.
ILD	ild	*ich liebe dich* (German for "I love you")
ILH	ilh	I love him/her.
ILHSM	ilhsm	I love him/her so much.
ILI	ili	I love it.
ILK2FKU	ilk2fku	I would like to fuck you.
ILL	ill	cool, tight, etc.
ILLEST	illest	best
ILLY	illy	fresh, cool
ILM	ilm	*i lige måde* (Danish for "the same to you")
ILM	ilm	Industrial Light and Magic
ILML	ilml	I love my life.
ILMO	ilmo	in loving memory of
ILMS	ilms	I love myself.
ILOTIBINLIRL	ilotibinlirl	I'm laughing on the Internet, but I'm not laughing in real life.
ILSHIPMP	ilshipmp	I laughed so hard, I peed my pants.
ILTF	iltf	I love to fuck.
ILU	ilu	I love you.
ILU2	ilu2	I love you too.
ILUAAF	iluaaf	I love you as a friend.
ILULAFKLC	ilulafklc	I love you like a fat kid loves cake.
ILUM	ilum	I love you, man.
ILUM	ilum	I love you more.
ILUSFM	ilusfm	I love you so fucking much.
ILUSM	ilusm	I love you so much.
ILUT	ilut	I love you too.
ILUVM	iluvm	I love you very much.
ILUVU	iluvu	I love you.
ILUVYA	iluvya	I love you.
ILUWAMH	iluwamh	I love you with all my heart.
ILVU	ilvu	I love you.
ILY	ily	I love you.
ILY2	ily2	I love you too.
ILY4E	ily4e	I love you forever.
ILY4EV	ily4ev	I love you forever.
ILYA	ilya	I love you all.
ILYAAF	ilyaaf	I love you as a friend.
ILYAAS	ilyaas	I love you as a sister.
ILYAL	ilyal	I like you a lot.
ILYAM	ilyam	I love you as a mate.
ILYB	ilyb	I love you, bitch.
ILYB	ilyb	I love you both.
ILYBBY	ilybby	I love you, baby.
ILYBTID	ilybtid	I love you, but then I don't.
ILYF	ilyf	I'll love you forever.
ILYG	ilyg	I love you guys/girls.
ILYGSM	ilygsm	I love you guys so much.
ILYK	ilyk	I'll let you know.
ILYKTHNXBAI	ilykthnxbai	I love you, 'k thanks, bye.

UPPERCASE	LOWERCASE	MEANING
ILYL	ilyl	I love you loads/I love you lots.
ILYLAB	ilylab	I love you like a brother.
ILYLABF	ilylabf	I love you like a best friend.
ILYLAFKLC	ilylafklc	I love you like a fat kid loves cake.
ILYLAS	ilylas	I love you like a sister.
ILYLC	ilylc	I love you like crazy.
ILYLT	ilylt	I'll love you long time.
ILYM	ilym	I love you more.
ILYMTYK	ilymtyk	I love you more than you know.
ILYMTYLM	ilymtylm	I love you more than you love me.
ILYSDM	ilysdm	I love you so damn much.
ILYSFM	ilysfm	I love you so fucking much.
ILYSFMB	ilysfmb	I love you so fucking much, baby.
ILYSM	ilysm	I love you so much.
ILYSMB	ilysmb	I love you so much, baby.
ILYSMIH	ilysmih	I love you so much, it hurts.
ILYSMM	ilysmm	I love you so much more.
ILYSMYDEK	ilysmydek	I love you so much, you don't even know.
ILYSVM	ilysvm	I love you so very much.
ILYT	ilyt	I love you too.
ILYVM	ilyvm	I love you very much.
ILYWAMH	ilywamh	I love you with all my heart.
IM	im	Instant Message
IM'D	im'd	instant messaged
IM26C4U	im26c4u	I am too sexy for you.
IMA	ima	I'm a
IMA	ima	I'm going to
IMAHO	imaho	in my absolutely honest opinion
IMAO	imao	in my arrogant opinion
IMAP	imap	Internet Message Access Protocol
IMB	imb	I'm back.
IMB	imb	I'm bored.
IMBA	imba	imbalanced
IMBO	imbo	in my biased opinion
IMCDO	imcdo	in my conceited dogmatic opinion
IMCO	imco	in my considered opinion
IMDB	imdb	Internet Movie Database
IME	ime	in my experience
IMED	imed	instant messaged
IMEO	imeo	in my educated opinion
IMF	imf	International Monetary Fund
IMFAO	imfao	in my fucking arrogant opinion
IMFO	imfo	in my fucking opinion
IMFS	imfs	I am fucking sorry
IMH	imh	I'm here
IMH	imh	in my head
IMHBCO	imhbco	in my humble but correct opinion
IMHE	imhe	in my humble experience
IMHO	imho	in my humble opinion
IMING	iming	instant messaging
IMK	imk	in my knowledge
IMM	imm	instant message me
IMMA	imma	I'm going to
IMMAO	immao	in my most arrogant opinion

UPPERCASE	LOWERCASE	MEANING
IMMD	immd	It made my day.
IMNERHO	imnerho	in my not even remotely humble opinion
IMNL	imnl	I'm not laughing.
IMNSHMFO	imnshmfo	in my not so humble motherfucking opinion
IMNSHO	imnsho	in my not so humble opinion
IMO	imo	in my opinion
IMOFO	imofo	in my own fucking opinion
IMOO	imoo	in my own opinion
IMPO	impo	in my personal opinion
IMPOV	impov	in my point of view
IMR	imr	I mean, really
IMS	ims	I'm sorry.
IMS	ims	irritable male syndrome
IMSB	imsb	I'm so bored.
IMSFB	imsfb	I'm so fucking bored.
IMSRY	imsry	I'm sorry.
IMTAW	imtaw	it may take awhile.
IMTM	imtm	I'm the man.
IMTS	imts	I meant to say
IMU	imu	I miss you.
IMUSM	imusm	I miss you so much.
IMUT	imut	I miss you terribly.
IMVHO	imvho	in my very humble opinion
IMVU	imvu	Instant Messaging Virtual Universe
IMWTK	imwtk	Inquiring minds want to know.
IMY	imy	I miss you.
IMY2	imy2	I miss you too.
IMYA	imya	I miss you already.
IMYSFM	imysfm	I miss you so fucking much.
IMYSM	imysm	I miss you so much.
IMYT	imyt	I miss you too.
IN THE BAG	in the bag	definite
IN2	in2	into
INAL	inal	I'm not a lawyer.
INB	inb	I'm not bothered.
INB4	inb4	in before (already mentioned)
INBD	inbd	it's no big deal.
INC	inc	incoming
INCRSE	incrse	increase
IND2P	ind2p	I need to pee
INDIE	indie	independent
INDY	indy	independent
INEF	inef	it's not even funny.
INET	inet	Internet
INFO	info	information
INH	inh	I need help.
INHO	inho	in my honest opinion
INHWH	inhwh	I need homework help.
INIT	init	initialization
INIT	init	isn't it
INK	ink	I never knew
INK	ink	tattoo
INKED	inked	tattooed
INMFP	inmfp	It's not my fucking problem.

UPPERCASE	LOWERCASE	MEANING
INMP	inmp	It's not my problem.
INNIT	innit	isn't it
INO	ino	I know.
INORITE	inorite	I know, right?
INPO	inpo	in no particular order
INRS	inrs	It's not rocket science.
INSIDER	insider	inside joke
INSTAGIB	instagib	instant kill
INSTAKILL	instakill	instant kill
INT	int	isn't it
INTARWEBS	intarwebs	Internet
INTEL	intel	intelligence
InterNIC	internic	Internet Network Information Center
INTERWEB	interweb	Internet
INTPFTPOTM	intpftpotm	I nominate this post for the post of the month.
INTTWMF	inttwmf	I am not typing this with my fingers.
INVU	invu	I envy you.
INWLY	inwly	I never wanna lose you.
INY	iny	I need you.
IOAB	ioab	I'm on a boat.
IOH	ioh	I'm out of here.
IOH	ioh	I'm outta here.
IOI	ioi	I'm over it.
IOI	ioi	indication of interest
IOIS	iois	indicators of interest
IOKIYA	iokiya	it's OK if you are
IOKIYAR	iokiyar	it's OK if you're a Republican
IOM	iom	Isle of Man
IOMH	iomh	in over my head
IOMW	iomw	I'm on my way.
ION	ion	in other news
IONNO	ionno	I don't know.
IONO	iono	I don't know.
IOTD	iotd	image of the day
IOU	iou	I owe you.
IOW	iow	in other words
IOYA	ioya	I'd own your ass.
IOYK	ioyk	if only you knew.
IP	ip	intellectual property
IP	ip	Internet Protocol
IPC	ipc	ignore post count
IPN	ipn	I'm posting naked.
IPO	ipo	initial public offering
IPOD	ipod	mp3 player from Apple
IPX	ipx	Internetwork Packet Exchange
IQ	iq	intelligence quotient
IR	ir	infrared
IR	ir	injured reserve
IR	ir	Internet Relay
IRA	ira	Irish Republican Army
IRAH	irah	insert relevant acronym here
IRC	irc	Internet Relay Chat
IRCOP	ircop	Internet Relay Chat operator
IRDC	irdc	I really don't care.

UPPERCASE	LOWERCASE	MEANING
IRDGAF	irdgaf	I really don't give a fuck.
IRDK	irdk	I really don't know.
IRGTGBTW	irgtgbtw	I've really got to get back to work.
IRHTGTTBR	irhtgttbr	I really have to go to the bathroom.
IRHY	irhy	I really hate you.
IRIE	irie	feeling good, all right
IRL	irl	in real life
IRLY	irly	I really like you.
IRLY	irly	I really love you.
IRMC	irmc	I rest my case.
IRQ	irq	Interrupt Request
IRS	irs	Internal Revenue Service
IRT	irt	in reply to
IRTF	irtf	I'll return the favor.
IS2G	is2g	I swear to God.
ISA	isa	Industry Standard Architecture
ISA	isa	*Insha'Allah* (Arabic for "Okay")
ISB	isb	I'm so bored.
ISBYA	isbya	I'm sorry, but you asked.
iSCSI	iscsi	Internet Small Computer Systems Interface
ISD	isd	Internet slang dictionary
ISDN	isdn	Integrated Services Digital Network
ISE	ise	internal server error
ISFLY	isfly	I so fucking love you.
ISG	isg	I speak geek.
ISH	ish	shit
ISH	ish	suffix indicating vagueness
ISHK	ishk	I should have known.
ISIANMTU	isianmtu	I swear I am not making this up.
ISJ	isj	inside joke
ISLY	isly	I still love you.
ISO	iso	in search of
ISO	iso	International Organization for Standardization
ISP	isp	Internet Service Provider
ISS	iss	I'm so sorry.
ISS	iss	International Space Station
ISTG	istg	I swear to god.
ISTM	istm	it seems to me
ISTR	istr	I seem to recall.
ISTR	istr	I seem to remember.
ISTWFN	istwfn	I stole this word from noslang.com.
ISWYDT	iswydt	I see what you did there.
ISWYM	iswym	I see what you mean.
IT	it	Information Technology
ITA	ita	I totally agree.
ITAI	itai	I'll think about it.
ITALY	italy	I trust and love you.
ITB	itb	in the butt
ITC	itc	in that case
ITC	itc	in this channel
ITD	itd	in the dark
ITE	ite	All right? (hello)
ITILU	itilu	I think I love you.
ITILY	itily	I think I love you.

UPPERCASE	LOWERCASE	MEANING
ITK	itk	in the know
ITMA	itma	It's that man again.
ITN	itn	I think not.
ITOY	itoy	I'm thinking of you.
ITP	itp	inside the perimeter
ITS	its	I think/thought so.
ITT	itt	in this thread
ITTET	ittet	in these tough economic times
ITV	itv	Independent TV (UK)
ITYF	ityf	I think you'll find
ITYK	ityk	I thought you knew.
ITYL	ityl	I'll tell you later.
ITYLTK	ityltk	I thought you'd like to know.
ITYRM	ityrm	I think you're mean.
ITYS	itys	I told you so.
ITZ	itz	in the zone
ITZ	itz	it's
ITZK	itzk	it's OK
IUCMD	iucmd	if you catch my drift
IUKWIM	iukwim	if you know what I mean
IUNNO	iunno	I don't know.
IUNO	iuno	I dunno.
IUSS	iuss	if you say so.
IVE	ive	I have
IVF	ivf	in vitro fertilization
IVR	ivr	Interactive Voice Response
IW2F	iw2f	I want to fuck.
IW2FU	iw2fu	I want to fuck you.
IW2MU	iw2mu	I want to meet you.
IWAA	iwaa	It was an accident.
IWALY	iwaly	I will always love you.
IWAWO	iwawo	I want a way out.
IWBRBL@R	iwbrbl@r	I will be right back later.
IWC	iwc	in which case
IWFU	iwfu	I wanna fuck you.
IWFUSB	iwfusb	I wanna fuck you so bad.
IWFY	iwfy	I want to fuck you.
IWFYBO	iwfybo	I will fuck your brains out.
IWG	iwg	It was good.
IWHI	iwhi	I would hit it.
IWHSWU	iwhswu	I want to have sex with you.
IWIAM	iwiam	idiot wrapped in a moron
IWIK	iwik	I wish I knew.
IWJK	iwjk	I was just kidding.
IWK	iwk	I wouldn't know.
IWLU4E	iwlu4e	I will love you forever.
IWM	iwm	it wasn't me.
IWMU	iwmu	I will miss you.
IWMY	iwmy	I will miss you.
IWS	iws	I want sex.
IWSN	iwsn	I want sex now.
IWSUL8R	iwsul8r	I will see you later.
IWTD	iwtd	I want to die.
IWTFU	iwtfu	I want to fuck you.

UPPERCASE	LOWERCASE	MEANING
IWTFY	iwtfy	I want to fuck you.
IWTHSWY	iwthswy	I want to have sex with you.
IWTLY	iwtly	I want to love you.
IWU	iwu	I want you.
IWUWH	iwuwh	I wish you were here.
IWY	iwy	I want you.
IWYB	iwyb	I want your body.
IWYN	iwyn	I want you now.
IWYTHMB	iwythmb	I want you to have my baby.
IYA	iya	hiya, hello
IYAM	iyam	if you ask me
IYBTYBA	iybtyba	If you believe that, you'll believe anything.
IYD	iyd	in your dreams
IYDK	iydk	if you didn't know
IYDM	iydm	if you don't mind
IYDMMA	iydmma	if you don't mind me asking
IYF	iyf	in your face
IYFD	iyfd	in your fucking dream
IYFLG	iyflg	if you're feeling less generous
IYFO	iyfo	in your fucking opinion
IYGM	iygm	if you get me
IYH	iyh	in your head
IYKWIM	iykwim	if you know what I mean
IYL	iyl	if you're lucky
IYL	iyl	It's your life.
IYM	iym	I am your man.
IYO	iyo	in your opinion
IYQ	iyq	I like you.
IYQVM	iyqvm	I like you very much.
IYSS	iyss	if you say so
IYSWIM	iyswim	if you see what I mean
IYT	iyt	all right
IYTE	iyte	all right
IYTT	iytt	if you think that
IYW	iyw	if you want/will
IYWT	iywt	if you want to
IZ	iz	is, it's
J	j	joking
J CAT	j cat	category j – mentally unstable person
J DUB	j dub	Jehovah's Witness
J/A	j/a	just asking
J/C	j/c	just curious
J/D	j/d	just discussing
J/F	j/f	just fucking
J/G	j/g	just getting
J/H	j/h	just hearing
J/J	j/j	just joking
J/K	j/k	just kidding
J/L	j/l	just listening
J/M	j/m	just making
J/M/S	j/m/s	just making sure
J/O	j/o	jack off
J/P	j/p	just playing
J/S	j/s	just saying

UPPERCASE	LOWERCASE	MEANING
J/T	j/t	just talking / just teasing / just thinking
J/W	j/w	just wondering / just watching
J@P	j@p	Jap (Japanese person - ethnic slur/derogatory)
J00	j00	you
J00R	j00r	your
J2BS	j2bs	just to be sure
J2C	j2c	just too cute
J2F	j2f	just too funny
J2LUK	j2luk	just to let you know
J2LYK	j2lyk	just to let you know
J4F	j4f	just for fun
J4G	j4g	just for grins
J4L	j4l	just for laughs
J4U	j4u	just for you
JA	ja	*yes* (German)
JAC	jac	just a second
JACK WAGON	jack wagon	loser
JACKA$$	jacka$$	jackass (idiot)
JACKASS	jackass	stupid person, idiot
JACKAZZ	jackazz	jackass (idiot)
JAFM	jafm	just a fucking minute
JAFO	jafo	just another fucking onlooker
JAFS	jafs	just a fucking salesman
JAFS	jafs	just a fucking second
JAILBREAK	jailbreak	crack an iPhone
JAJA	jaja	Spanish laugh
JALAUDLM	jalaudlm	just as long as you don't leave me
JAM	jam	just a minute
JAMBO	jambo	hello (Swahili)
JAND	jand	England (Nigerian)
JANK	jank	worthless, useless
JANOE	janoe	I know
JAP	jap	Jap (Japanese person - ethnic slur/derogatory)
JAP	jap	Jewish-American princess
JAPAN	japan	just always pray at night
JAPO	japo	Japo (Japanese person - ethnic slur/derogatory)
JARRIN	jarrin	annoying
JAS	jas	just a second
JAT	jat	just a thought
JATQ	jatq	Just answer the question.
JAVA	java	coffee
JAVA	java	programming language
JAWN	jawn	thing
JB	jb	jailbait
JB	jb	Jonas Brothers
JBH	jbh	just being honest
JBU	jbu	just between us
JBY	jby	Just be yourself.
JC	jc	Jesus Christ
JC	jc	junior college
JC	jc	just checking/curious
JC	jc	just chilling
J·C	j·c	just chilling
JCAM	jcam	just checking away message

UPPERCASE	LOWERCASE	MEANING
JCATH	jcath	just chilling at the house
JD	jd	Jack Daniel's
JDFI	jdfi	Just fucking do it.
JDI	jdi	Just do it.
JDM	jdm	Japanese domestic market
JEAL	jeal	jealous
JEBUS	jebus	Jesus
JEEZ	jeez	expression of annoyance
JEEZUS	jeezus	Jesus
JEJE	jeje	*LOL* in Spanish
JEJEMON	jejemon	people who type stupidly
JELLO	jello	jealous
JELLY	jelly	jealous
JEOMK	jeomk	just ejaculated on my keyboard
JERK	jerk	idiot
JERKA$$	jerka$$	jerkass (idiot)
JERKAZZ	jerkazz	jerkass (idiot)
JEST	jest	joke
JET	jet	leave quickly
JEWFRO	jewfro	curly Jewish hairstyle
JF	jf	just fooling
JFC	jfc	Jesus fucking Christ
JFDI	jfdi	Just fucking do it!
JFF	jff	just for fun
JFG	jfg	just for giggles
JFGI	jfgi	just fucking Google it
JFH	jfh	Just fuck her.
JFH	jfh	Just fuck him.
JFI	jfi	Just forget it.
JFJ	jfj	jump for joy
JFK	jfk	John Fitzgerald Kennedy
JFK	jfk	just for kicks
JFK	jfk	just fucking kidding
JFK	jfk	New York airport
JFL	jfl	just for laughs
JFLTS	jflts	just felt like typing something
JFN	jfn	just for now
JFO	jfo	Just fuck off.
JFR	jfr	just for reference
JFTR	jftr	just for the record
JFU	jfu	just for you
JFWY	jfwy	just fucking with you
JFY	jfy	just for you
JFYI	jfyi	just for your information
JG2H	jg2h	Just go to hell.
JGH	jgh	just got home
JGI	jgi	just Google it
JGIYN	jgiyn	Just Google it, you noob.
JGL	jgl	Just get lost.
JGOFF	jgoff	jagoff (idiot)
JGTFOOH	jgtfooh	Just get the fuck out of here.
JH	jh	just hanging
JHC	jhc	Jesus H Christ
JHEEZE	jheeze	(same as "OMG"), wow

UPPERCASE	LOWERCASE	MEANING
JHM	jhm	just hold me
JHO	jho	just hanging out
JIC	jic	just in case
JICYDK	jicydk	just in case you didn't know
JIFF	jiff	cocaine
JIFFY	jiffy	short period of time
JIG@BOO	jig@boo	jigaboo (African American · ethnic slur/derogatory)
JIT	jit	just in time
JIT	jit	young gangster
JJ	jj	just joking
JJ/K	jj/k	just joking
JJA	jja	just joking around
JJJ	jjj	Australian radio station
JK	jk	just kidding
JKA	jka	just kidding around
JKA$$	jka$$	jackass (idiot)
JKASS	jkass	jackass (idiot)
JKAZZ	jkazz	jackass (idiot)
JKING	jking	joking
JKL	jkl	just kidding, LOL/loser
JKLOL	jklol	just kidding, laughing out loud
JKN	jkn	joking
JKS	jks	jokes
JKZ	jkz	jokes
JLMA	jlma	just leave me alone
JLMK	jlmk	just let me know
JLS	jls	*Jack the Lad Swing* (band)
JLT	jlt	just like that
JLY	jly	Jesus loves you
JLYK	jlyk	just letting you know
JM	jm	just messing
JMA	jma	just messing around
JMHO	jmho	just my humble opinion
JML	jml	just my luck
JMO	jmo	just my opinion
JMS	jms	just making sure
JMT	jmt	just my thoughts
JN	jn	just now
JNGL BUNNY	jngl bunny	jungle bunny (African American · ethnic slur/derogatory)
JO	jo	yo
JOANING	joaning	putting someone down, making fun of
JOCKER	jocker	someone who copies another's style
JOHN DOE	john doe	general term for a man
JOINT	joint	rolled marijuana cigarette
JOM	jom	just one minute
JONES	jones	craving, desire
JONESING	jonesing	craving, wanting really badly
JOO	joo	you
JOOC	jooc	just out of curiosity
JOOCE	jooce	juice
JOOR	joor	your
JORTS	jorts	jean shorts
JP	jp	jackpot (online gaming, bingo games)

UPPERCASE	LOWERCASE	MEANING
JP	jp	just playin'
JPA	jpa	just playing around
JPEG	jpeg	Joint Photographic Experts Group (image file format)
JPG	jpg	Joint Photographic Experts Group (image file format)
JRE	jre	Java Runtime Environment
JRKA$$	jrka$$	jerkass (idiot)
JRKASS	jrkass	jerkass (idiot)
JRKAZZ	jrkazz	jerkass (idiot)
JRKOFF	jrkoff	jerk off (masturbate)
JROTC	jrotc	Junior Reserve Officers' Training Corps
JS	js	just saying
JSA	jsa	just stop already
JSING	jsing	just saying
JSON	json	JavaScript Object Notation
JSP	jsp	Java Server Page
JST	jst	just
JSTFU	jstfu	Just shut the fuck up.
JSU	jsu	Just shut up.
JSUK	jsuk	just so you know
JSUN	jsun	just so you know
JSUT	jsut	just
JSYK	jsyk	just so you know
JSYN	jsyn	just so you know
JT	jt	just teasing
JTAY	jtay	just thinking about you
JTB	jtb	just too bad
JTBS	jtbs	just to be sure
JTC	jtc	Join the club.
JTFO	jtfo	joke the fuck out
JTLUK	jtluk	just to let you know
JTLYK	jtlyk	just to let you know
JTM	jtm	*je t'aime* (I love you)
JTOI	jtoi	just thought of it
JTOL	jtol	just thinking out loud
JTTSIOWCTW	jttsiowctw	just testing to see if other Web sites copy this word
JTTY	jtty	just to tell you
JTUMLTK	jtumltk	just thought you might like to know
JTUSK	jtusk	just thought you should know
JTYLTK	jtyltk	just thought you'd like to know
JTYSK	jtysk	just thought you should know
JUAD	juad	jumping up and down
JUGGALO	juggalo	fan of ICP
JUICE	juice	respect, power
JUICED	juiced	happy, excited
JUNKIE	junkie	addict
JUS	jus	just
JUSS	juss	just
JUZ	juz	just
JUZT	juzt	just
JV	jv	joint venture
JV	jv	junior varsity, amateur
JW	jw	just wondering
JW2K	jw2k	just wanted to know
JWAS	jwas	just wait a second

UPPERCASE	LOWERCASE	MEANING
JWAS	jwas	just wait and see
JWD	jwd	job well done
JWG	jwg	just a wild guess
JWTK	jwtk	just wanted to know
JWTLYK	jwtlyk	just wanted to let you know
JWW	jww	just was wondering
JYEAH	jyeah	cool version of yeah
JYFIHP	jyfihp	jam your finger in her pussy
JZZ	jzz	jizz (semen)
K	k	OK
k/b	k/b	keyboard
K@@CH	k@@ch	kooch (female genitalia)
K@@TCH	k@@tch	kootch (female genitalia)
K1	k1	the best, awesome
K33L	k33l	Kill
K3U	k3u	I love you
K3WL	k3wl	cool
K8T	k8t	Katie
KA	ka	kick-ass
KAFM	kafm	keep away from me
KAFN	kafn	kill all fucking noobs
KAH	kah	kisses and hugs
KAM	kam	gorgeous, sexy
KAW	kaw	kick-ass work
KAWAII	kawaii	cute, pretty (Japanese)
KAY	kay	OK
KB	kb	keyboard
KB	kb	kick butt
KB	kb	kilobyte
KB	kb	kind bud
Kbps	kbps	Kilobits Per Second
KBPS	kbps	kilobytes per second
KD	kd	Kraft Dinner
KDE	kde	K Desktop Environment
KEED	keed	kid, joke
KEEL	keel	kill
KEK	kek	laughing out loud
KEK	kek	LOL in WOW
KEN	ken	know (Scottish)
KEW	kew	(same as "kewl")
KEWEL	kewel	cool
KEWL	kewl	cool
KEWT	kewt	cute
KEY	key	kilogram (of drugs)
KEYA	keya	I will key you later.
KEYGEN	keygen	software serial number generator
KEYME	keyme	Key me when you get in.
KF	kf	kinda funny
KFC	kfc	Kentucky Fried Chicken
KFY	kfy	kiss for you
KG	kg	kilogram
KGB	kgb	Russian secret police *(Komitet Gosudarstvennoy Bezopasnosti)*
KGO	kgo	OJ, go

UPPERCASE	LOWERCASE	MEANING
KH	Kh	Kingdom Hearts (RPG)
KHITBASH	khitbash	kick her in the box and shove her
KHUF	khuf	know how you feel
KHYF	khyf	know how you feel
KI	ki	kilogram (of cocaine/crack)
KIA	kia	killed in action
KIA	kia	know it all
KIAB	kiab	Karma is a bitch.
KIB	kib	OK, I'm back
KIBO	kibo	knowledge in, bullshit out
KIC	kic	keep it clean
KICKS	kicks	shoes, sneakers
KICKS	kicks	thrills
KIFF	kiff	cool
KIG	kig	keep it going
KIG	kig	keep it, gangsta
KIK	kik	a mistyped version of "LOL"
KILED	kiled	killed
KILLA	killa	good-quality weed
KIM	kim	keep it moving
KINDA	kinda	kind of
KINGS	kings	drinking game
KINO	kino	physical flirting, touching
KIO	kio	knock it off
KIP	kip	bed
KIP	kip	sleep
KIR	kir	keepin' it real
KIR	kir	kid in room
KIRF	kirf	keeping it real fake
KIS	kis	keep it simple
KISA	kisa	knight in shining armor
KISS	kiss	keep it simple, stupid
KIT	kit	keep in touch
KITE	kite	mail received in jail
KITFO	kitfo	Knock it the fuck off.
KITTEN	kitten	woman who dates older men
KIU	kiu	keep it up
KIV	kiv	keep in view
KIWF	kiwf	kill it with fire
KIWI	kiwi	a person from New Zealand
KIWI	kiwi	a small brown bird from New Zealand
KIWI	kiwi	kiwifruit
KJ	kj	killjoy
KK	kk	knock, knock
KK	kk	OK/OK, cool/OK, OK!
KKE	kke	kike (Jewish Person - ethnic slur/derogatory)
KKK	kkk	Ku Klux Klan
KKKK	kkkk	*LOL* in Korean
KKTHNXBYE	kkthnxbye	OK, thanks, bye
KKY	kky	kinky
KKZ	kkz	OK
KL	kl	cool
KLKL	klkl	cool, cool
KLUTZ	klutz	clumsy or stupid person

UPPERCASE	LOWERCASE	MEANING
KM	km	keep mum
KMA	kma	kiss my ass
KMAG	kmag	kiss my ass good-bye
KMAO	kmao	kick my ass off
KMB	kmb	kiss my butt
KMBA	kmba	kiss my black ass
KMFA	kmfa	kiss my fucking ass
KMFHA	kmfha	kiss my fat hairy ass
KMHBA	kmhba	kiss my hairy big ass
KMK	kmk	kiss my keister
KML	kml	killing myself laughing
KMN	kmn	kill me now
KMP	kmp	Keep me posted.
KMP	kmp	Kill me, please.
KMS	kms	kill myself
KMSL	kmsl	killing myself laughing
KMSLA	kmsla	kiss my shiny little ass
KMT	kmt	kiss my teeth
KMT	kmt	kiss my tushie
KMUF	kmuf	kiss me, you fool
KMWA	kmwa	kiss my white ass
KMYA	kmya	kiss my yellow ass
KNACKERED	knackered	drunk
KNEWB	knewb	new player
KNIM	knim	Know what I mean?
KNN	knn	fuck your mother
KNO	kno	know
KNOCK IT OFF	knock it off	stop it
KNOCKED	knocked	caught (selling drugs)
KNOCKED UP	knocked up	pregnant
KNOCKOUT	knockout	stunning person or thing
KNOT	knot	roll of paper money
KNP	knp	OK, no problem
KNT	knt	kunt (female genitalia)
KNW	knw	know
KO	ko	knockout
KO	ko	OK
KOC	koc	kiss on cheek
KOI	koi	*koibito* (Japanese for "lover")
KOKO	koko	most important thing
KOL	kol	*Kingdom of Loathing* (game)
KOL	kol	kiss on cheek
KOL	kol	kiss on lips
KOO	koo	cool
KOOL	kool	cool
KOOLIO	koolio	cool
KOOLS	kools	mentholated cigarettes
KOS	kos	kid over shoulder
KOS	kos	kill on sight
KOSHER	kosher	good, OK
KOTC	kotc	kiss on the cheek
KOTH	koth	*King of the Hill* (game)
KOTL	kotl	kiss on the lips

UPPERCASE	LOWERCASE	MEANING
KOTOR	kotor	*Knights of the Old Republic* (game)
KOTS	kots	keep on talking, shit
KOW	kow	knock on wood
KP	kp	Korean pride
KPC	kpc	keep parents clueless
KPC	kpc	keeping parents clueless
KR	kr	kind regards
KRAM	kram	smoke weed
KRO	kro	keep right on
KRT	krt	kraut (German - ethnic slur/derogatory)
KS	ks	kill steal
KSC	ksc	kind (of) sort (of) chuckle
KSS	kss	kiss
KSSD	kssd	kissed
KT	kt	Katie
KT	kt	kecp talking
KTB	ktb	OK, thanks, bye
KTBPA	ktbpa	(same as "KTBSPA")
KTBSPA	ktbspa	keep the Backstreet pride alive
KTC	ktc	kill the cat
KTF	ktf	keep the faith
KTFO	Ktfo	knocked the fuck out
KTHANXBI	kthanxbi	OK, thanks, bye
KTHNXBAI	kthnxbai	OK, thanks, bye
KTHNXBI	kthnxbi	OK, thanks, bye
KTHNXBYE	kthnxbye	OK, thanks, bye
KTHX	kthx	OK, thanks
KTHXBAI	kthxbai	OK, thanks, bye
KTHXBI	kthxbi	OK, thank you, good-bye
KTHXBI	kthxbi	OK, thanks, bye (usually used dismissively)
KTHXBYE	kthxbye	OK, thank you, good-bye
KTHXGB	kthxgb	OK, thanks, good-bye
KTHXMN	kthxmn	OK, thanks, man
KTHZ	kthz	OK, thanks
KTNX	ktnx	OK and thanks
KTY	kty	OK, thank you
KUDOS	kudos	respect and recognition
KUHL	kuhl	cool
KUL	kul	cool
KUSH	kush	high-grade marijuana
KUTE	kute	cute
KUTGW	kutgw	keep up the good work
KUWL	kuwl	cool
KVM	kvm	Keyboard, Video, and Mouse
KW	kw	kilowatt
KWAM	kwam	(same as "KWIM")
KWEL	kwel	cool
KWIK	kwik	quick
KWIM	kwim	Know what I mean?
KWIS	kwis	Know what I'm saying?
KWIT	kwit	quit
KWIZ	kwiz	quiz
KWL	kwl	cool
KWTSDS	kwtsds	Kiss where the sun don't shine.

UPPERCASE	LOWERCASE	MEANING
KYAG	kyag	Kiss your ass good-bye.
KYFAG	kyfag	Kss your fucking ass good-bye.
KYFC	kyfc	Keep your fingers crossed.
KYK	kyk	kyke (Jewish person - ethnic slur/derogatory)
KYKO	kyko	Keep your knickers on.
KYOOT	kyoot	cute
KYS	kys	kill yourself
KYSO	kyso	knock yourself out
L	l	laugh
L@U	l@u	laughing at you
LOLZ	lOlz	laugh out loud
L2	l2	learn to
L2G	l2g	like to go/love to go
L2K	l2k	like to come
L2M	l2m	listening to music
L2MS	l2ms	laughing to myself
L2P	l2p	learn to play
L2PK	l2pk	learn to player kill
L2R	l2r	learn to read
L337	l337	elite
L33T	l33t	elite
L4M3RZ	l4m3rz	lamers
L7	l7	square
L8	l8	late
L84SKOOL	l84skool	late for school
L8A	l8a	later
L8ER	l8er	later
L8ERS	l8ers	later
L8R	l8r	later
L8RG8R	l8rg8r	later, gator
L8RS	l8rs	later
L8RZ	l8rz	later
L8S	l8s	later
L8T	l8t	late
L8TA	l8ta	later
L8TER	l8ter	later
L8TR	l8tr	later
LA	la	Cantonese exclamation
LABTOP	labtop	laptop
LAD	lad	guy
LAFF	laff	laugh
LAFS	lafs	love at first sight
LAG	lag	slow response (computer, Internet)
LAGG	lagg	defeat
LAGNAF	lagnaf	Let's all get naked and fuck.
LAK	lak	love and kisses
LAL	lal	laughing a lot/little
LALB	lalb	laughing a little bit
LALOL	lalol	lots and lots of laughs
LAM	lam	leave a message
LAM	lam	run
LAMBO	lambo	Lamborghini
LAME	lame	stupid, unoriginal
LAMEA$$	lamea$$	lameass (loser)

UPPERCASE	LOWERCASE	MEANING
LAMEAZZ	lameazz	lameass (loser)
LAMEO	lameo	lame person
LAMER	lamer	annoying person
LAMF	lamf	like a motherfucker
LAMO	lamo	misspelling of "LMAO"
LAMP	lamp	hit
LAN	lan	Local Area Network
LAND MINE	land mine	ugly, skinny girl
LAPAD	lapad	lick a pussy and die
LAPPY	lappy	laptop computer
LAQ	laq	lame-ass quote
LARDA$$	larda$$	lardass (overweight individual)
LARDAZZ	lardazz	lardass (overweight individual)
LARP	larp	live action role-play
LART	lart	Luser Attitude Readjustment Tool
LASB	lasb	lame-ass stupid bitch
LASER	laser	light amplification by stimulated emission of radiation
LAT	lat	laugh at that
LAT	lat	living apart together
LATA	lata	later
LATE	late	dead
LATE	late	missed a period, possibly pregnant
LATERS	laters	see you later, good-bye
LATERZ	laterz	see you later, good-bye
LATES	lates	later
LATM	latm	laughing at the moment
LATN	latn	laugh at the newbies
LATR	latr	later
LATWTTB	latwttb	laughing all the way to the bank
LAU	lau	laughing at you
LAWD	lawd	lord
LAWL	lawl	(same as "LOL")
LAWL	lawl	laughing out loud with a Southern drawl
LAWL'D	lawl'd	laughed out loud
LAWLED	lawled	laughed out loud
LAWLS	lawls	(same as "LOL")
LAWLS	lawls	laughing out loud with a Southern drawl
LAWLZ	lawlz	(same as "LOL")
LAWLZ	lawlz	laughing out loud
LAWLZ	lawlz	laughing out loud with a Southern drawl
LAX	lax	lacrosse
LAZER	lazer	laser
LAZOR	lazor	laser
LBAY	lbay	laughing back at you
LBC	lbc	Long Beach, California
LBD	lbd	little black dress
LBDN	lbdn	look busy doing nothing
LBH	lbh	Let's be honest.
LBH	lbh	loser back home
LBM	lbm	little big man
LBNL	lbnl	last but not least
LBNR	lbnr	laughing but not really
LBO	lbo	laughing butt off
LBR	lbr	little boy's room

UPPERCASE	LOWERCASE	MEANING
LBR	lbr	loser beyond repair
LBRS	lbrs	*Lower Blackrock Spire* (WOW)
LBS	lbs	laughing but serious
LBS	lbs	pounds (weight)
LBVS	lbvs	laughing but very serious
LBW	lbw	leg before wicket (cricket)
LC	lc	lowercase
LCD	lcd	liquid crystal display
LCSNPC	lcsnpc	low-cost, small, notebook personal computer
LD	ld	later, dude
LD	ld	link dead (disconnection from Internet)
LD	ld	long distance
LDA	lda	long-distance affair
LDAP	ldap	Lightweight Directory Access Protocol
LDL	ldl	long-distance lover
LDN	ldn	London
LDO	ldo	like duh, obviously
LDR	ldr	long-distance relationship
LDS	lds	Latter-Day Saint
LE	le	law enforcement
LE	le	limited edition
LED	led	light-emitting diode
LEDGE	ledge	legend, legendary
LEE7	lee7	elite
LEES	lees	very attractive man/woman
LEET	leet	chat room language
LEET	leet	elite
LEGGO	leggo	let's go
LEGIT	legit	legitimate, real, legal
LEIK	leik	like
LEL	lel	LOL
LEME	leme	let me
LEMENO	lemeno	let me know
LEMME	lemme	let me
LEO	leo	law enforcement officer
LERK	lerk	leaving easy reach of keyboard
LESBO	lesbo	lesbian (homosexual slur/derogatory)
LESS THAN 3	less than 3	love
LESS THAN THREE	less than three	love
LEV	lev	low-emission vehicle
LEVA	leva	traitor
LEWL	lewl	LOL
LEZ	lez	lesbian
LEZBEAN	lezbean	lesbian
LEZBO	lezbo	lesbian (homosexual slur/derogatory)
LEZZIE	lezzie	lesbian (homosexual slur/derogatory)
LF	lf	let's fuck
LF	lf	looking for
LF1M	lf1m	looking for one more
LF2M	lf2m	looking for two more
LFD	lfd	left for day
LFG	lfg	looking for group
LFL	lfl	let's fuck later

UPPERCASE	LOWERCASE	MEANING
LFM	lfm	looking for mate
LFM	lfm	looking for more
LFMF	lfmf	learn from my fail
LFNAR	lfnar	laughing for no apparent reason
LFP	lfp	looking for party (in MMORPG)
LFP	lfp	looking for pussy
LFR	lfr	laughing for real
LFTSU	lftsu	look forward to seeing you
LFW	lfw	looking for work
LG	lg	little girl
LGB	lgb	lesbian/gay/bisexual
LGBNAF	lgbnaf	let's get butt naked and fuck
LGBTQ	lgbtq	lesbian, gay, bisexual, transgender, and queer
LGF	lgf	little green footballs
LGFB	lgfb	looks good from behind
LGH	lgh	Let's get high.
LGMH	lgmh	Love gives me hope
LGN	lgn	link goes nowhere
LGO	lgo	Life goes on.
LGOT	lgot	Let's go out tonight.
LGR	lgr	little girls room
LGS	lgs	Let's go shopping!
LGT	lgt	link goes to...
LGTM	lgtm	looks good to me
LH	lh	living hell
LH6	lh6	Let's have sex.
LHAO	lhao	laughing her ass off
LHH	lhh	laughing hella hard
LHM	lhm	Lord, have mercy/Lord, help me
LHO	lho	laughing head off
LHOS	lhos	Let's have online sex.
LHS	lhs	Let's have sex.
LHSRN	lhsrn	Let's have sex right now.
LHSX	lhsx	Let's have sex.
LHYW	lhyw	like hell you will
LI	li	laughing inside
LI	li	LinkedIn
LIB	lib	liberal
LIB	lib	lying in bed
LIC	lic	like I care
LICKED	licked	drunk or high
LIEC	liec	like I even care
LIEING	lieing	misspelling of "lying"
LIEK	liek	like
LIEKZ	liekz	likes
LIFO	lifo	last in first out
LIFO	lifo	last in, first out
LIFTED	lifted	high
LIG	lig	Let it go.
LIGAFF	ligaff	like I give a flying fuck
LIGAFS	ligafs	like I give a flying shit
LIGAS	ligas	like I give a shit
LIGIT	ligit	legitimate
LIH	lih	laugh in head

UPPERCASE	LOWERCASE	MEANING
LIHOP	lihop	let it happen on purpose
LIITA	liita	love is in the air
LIK	lik	like
LIK	lik	liquor
LIKE	like	(same as "um")
LIKE	like	introduction to a quote
LIKKLE	likkle	little
LIL	lil	little
LIM	lim	like it matters
LIMB	limb	laughing in my brain
LIME	lime	hang out, socialize
LIMH	limh	laughing in my head
LIMM	limm	laughing in my mind
LIMO	limo	limousine, luxury car
LIMT	limt	laughing in my tummy
LINE	line	a line of a powdered drug
LINGO	lingo	language
LIOL	liol	laughing insanely out loud
LIPSING	lipsing	kissing
LIQ	liq	liquor
LIRL	lirl	laughing in real life
LIS	lis	laughing in silence
LITE	lite	light
LIU	liu	look it up
LIV	liv	live
LIVE	live	exciting
LIYF	liyf	laughing in your face
LJ	lj	live journal
LK	lk	(same as "LOLK")
LK	lk	like
LKE	lke	like
LL	ll	laughing loudly, LOL
LLAB	llab	laughing like a bitch
LLAP	llap	live long and prosper
LLC	llc	laughing like crazy
LLC	llc	limited liability company
LLF	llf	laugh like fuck
LLGB	llgb	love, later, god bless
LLH	llh	laughing like hell
LLL	lll	loony liberal left
LLO	llo	misspelt "LOL"
LLOL	llol	literally "LOL"
LLOL	llol	literally laughing out loud
LLS	lls	laughing like *silly*
LLZ	llz	(same as "LOLz")
LM	lm	loudmouth
LM4A~##ZZZZ>	lm4a~##zzzz>	Let's meet for a joint.
LM4AQ	lm4aq	Let's meet for a quickie.
LMA	lma	Leave me alone.
LMAM	lmam	Leave me a message.
LMAMF	lmamf	Leave me alone, motherfucker.
LMAO	lmao	laughing my ass off
LMAOL	lmaol	laughing my ass out loud
LMAOMTOAOA	lmaomtoaoa	laugh my ass off many times over and over again

UPPERCASE	LOWERCASE	MEANING
LMAONADE	lmaonade	laughing my ass off
LMAOOL	lmaool	laughing my ass off out loud
LMAOOTF	lmaootf	laughing my ass off on the floor
LMAOROF	lmaorof	laughing my ass off rolling on the floor
LMAOROTF	lmaorotf	laughing my ass off rolling on the floor
LMAOWROTF	lmaowrotf	laughing my ass of while rolling on the floor
LMAOWTNTPM	lmaowtntpm	laughing my ass off whilst trying not to piss myself
LMAOXH	lmaoxh	laughing my ass off extremely hard
LMAP	lmap	Leave me alone, please.
LMB	lmb	lick my balls
LMBAO	lmbao	laughing my black ass off
LMBFWAO	lmbfwao	laughing my big fat white ass off
LMBO	lmbo	laughing my butt off
LMC	lmc	let me check
LMC	lmc	let me see
LMCAO	lmcao	laughing my crazy ass off
LMCLAO	lmclao	laughing my cute little ass off
LMD	lmd	lick my dick
LMFAO	lmfao	laughing my fucking ass off
LMFBO	lmfbo	laugh my fucking butt off
LMFFAO	lmffao	laughing my fucking fat ass off
LMFFO	lmffo	laughing my fucking face off
LMFHO	lmfho	laughing my fucking head off
LMFO	lmfo	laughing my face off
LMFPO	lmfpo	laughing my fucking pussy off
LMFR	lmfr	let's meet for real
LMFTO	lmfto	laughing my fucking tits off
LMG	lmg	Let me guess.
LMG	lmg	light machine gun
LMGDAO	lmgdao	laughing my goddamn ass off
LMGTFY	lmgtfy	Let me Google that for you.
LMHAO	lmhao	laughing my hairy ass off
LMHO	lmho	laughing my head off/laughing my heiny off
LMIP	lmip	Let's meet in person.
LMIRL	lmirl	Let's meet in real life.
LMK	lmk	Let me know.
LMKS	lmks	Let me know soon.
LMKWUT	lmkwut	Let me know what you think.
LML	lml	love my life
LMMFAO	lmmfao	laughing my motherfucking ass off
LMMFAOS	lmmfaos	laughing my motherfucking ass off silly
LMMFAS	lmmfas	laugh my motherfucking ass off
LMMFFAO	lmmffao	laughing my motherfucking fat ass off
LMNK	lmnk	Leave my name out.
LMO	lmo	leave me alone/leave me one
LMOA	lmoa	misspelling of "LMAO"
LMOAO	lmoao	laughing my other ass off
LMP	lmp	lick my pussy
LMPO	lmpo	laughing my panties off
LMS	lms	last man standing
LMS	lms	Leave me some.
LMS	lms	like my status
LMSAO	lmsao	laughing my sexy ass off
LMSO	lmso	laughing my socks off

UPPERCASE	LOWERCASE	MEANING
LMT	lmt	Let me think.
LMTAL	lmtal	Let me take a look.
LMTD	lmtd	limited
LMTFA	lmtfa	Leave me the fuck alone.
LMTO	lmto	laughing my tits off
LMTUS	lmtus	Let me tell you something.
LMTY	lmty	laughing more than you
LMVO	lmvo	laugh my vagina off
LMWAO	lmwao	laughing my white ass off
LN	ln	last name
LNIB	lnib	like new in box
LNK	lnk	link
LNT	lnt	lost in translation
LO	lo	hello
LO	lo	little one
LOA	loa	leave of absence
LOA	loa	list of acronyms
LOADED	loaded	drunk, intoxicated / rich, a lot of money
LOAF	loaf	head
LOB	lob	line of business
LOB	lob	throw
LOBFL	lobfl	laugh out bloody fucking loud
LOCAL	local	local public house, bar
LOF	lof	laughing on floor
LOFI	lofi	uncool
LOFL	lofl	laugh out fucking loud
LOFLMAO	loflmao	lying on floor laughing my ass off
LOI	loi	laughing on the inside
LOK	lok	LOL, OK
LOL	lol	laughing out loud
LOL	lol	lots of love
LOL@U	lol@u	laugh out loud at you
LOL'D	lol'd	laughed out loud
LOL2U	lol2u	laugh out loud to you
LOLAGE	lolage	the act of LOL
LOLAK	lolak	lots of love and kisses
LOLAROTF	lolarotf	laughing out loud and rolling on the floor
LOLAW	lolaw	laugh out loud at work
LOLCANO	lolcano	laugh out loud
LOLCAT	lolcat	cat picture with silly caption
LOLCITY	lolcity	the whole city laughs out loud
LOLD	lold	laughed out loud
LOLED	loled	past tense of LOL
LOLEES	lolees	laugh out loud
LOLERZ	lolerz	laugh out loud
LOLF	lolf	lots of love forever
LOLH	lolh	laughing out loud hysterically
LOLIN	lolin	laughing out loud
LOLING	loling	the act of laughing out loud
LOLIO	lolio	laugh out loud, I own
LOLK	lolk	LOL, OK
LOLL	loll	laugh out loud literally
LOLLAM	lollam	laughing out loud like a maniac
LOLLERCAUST	lollercaust	an extreme event of hilarity

UPPERCASE	LOWERCASE	MEANING
LOLLERCOASTER	lollercoaster	laugh out loud (a lot)
LOLLERSKATES	lollerskates	laughing out loud
LOLLY	lolly	money
LOLM	lolm	laugh out loud man
LOLN	loln	laughing out loud...not
LOLNGS	lolngs	laughing out loud never gonna stop
LOLO	lolo	crazy
LOLO	lolo	lots of love
LOLO	lolo	low rider
LOLOCOST	lolocost	laugh out loud
LOLOL	lolol	lots of laughing out loud
LOLOLZ	lololz	laughing out loud
LOLPIMP	lolpimp	laughing out loud peeing in my pants
LOLQ	lolq	laughing out loud quietly
LOLROF	lolrof	laughing out loud while rolling on the floor
LOLROTF	lolrotf	laughing out loud rolling on the floor
LOLS	lols	laughing out loud
LOLV	lolv	lots of love
LOLWTIME	lolwtime	laughing out loud with tears in my eyes
LOLWUT	lolwut	What?
LOLX	lolx	(same as "LOL")
LOLZ	lolz	laughing out loud (with sarcasm)
LOLZ	lolz	laughing out loud
LOLZA	lolza	(same as "LOL")
LOMG	lomg	like, "Oh my god"
LOML	loml	love of my life
LOMO	lomo	lights out, missionary only
LOMY	lomy	love of my life
LOO	loo	toilet
LOOL	lool	laughing outlandishly out loud
LOOMM	loomm	laughing out of my mind
LOONY	loony	crazy
LOOT	loot	money (often stolen)
LOP	lop	stupid person
LOPL	lopl	misspelling of "LOL"
LOQ	loq	laugh out quietly
LORL	lorl	laugh out really loud
LOS	los	line of site
LOTF	lotf	laughing on the floor
LOTI	loti	laughing on the inside
LOTR	lotr	*Lord of the Rings* (movie)
LOTTA	lotta	lot of
LOUD	loud	good-quality marijuana
LOV	lov	love
LOVL	lovl	laughing out very loud
LOVU	lovu	love you
LOW	low	unfair, immoral
LOW IT	low it	allow it, don't worry
LOW KEY	low key	don't tell anyone/quiet
LOWE	lowe	don't bother, forget it
LOWRIDER	lowrider	vehicle with modified suspension often hydraulically controlled
LOXEN	loxen	laughing out loud
LOXXEN	loxxen	laughing out loud

UPPERCASE	LOWERCASE	MEANING
LOZ	loz	*Legend of Zelda* (game)
LOZER	lozer	loser
LP	lp	long play (record)
LPB	lpb	low ping bastard
LPG	lpg	liquefied petroleum gas
LPI	lpi	lines per inch
LPIAW	lpiaw	large penis is always welcome
LPL	lpl	misspelling of "LOL"
LPMS	lpms	Life pretty much sucks.
LQ	lq	laughing quietly
LQ	lq	liquor
LQ	lq	lover's quarrel
LQ2M	lq2m	laughing quietly to myself
LQI	lqi	laughing quietly inside
LQTM	lqtm	laughing quietly to myself
LQTMS	lqtms	laughing quietly to myself
LQTS	lqts	laughing quietly to self
LQTY	lqty	laughing quietly to yourself
LRF	lrf	low-resolution fox, attractive at a distance
LRFL	lrfl	laughing really fucking loud
LRG	lrg	Lifted Research Group (clothing)
LRH	lrh	laughing really hard
LRL	lrl	laughing really loud
LRQTMS	lrqtms	laughing really quietly to myself
LS	ls	life story
LS	ls	lovesick
LSD	lsd	lysergic acid diethylamide
LSE	lse	London School of Economics
LSE	lse	low self-esteem
LSFW	lsfw	less safe for work
LSH	lsh	laughing so hard
LSHIC	lshic	laughing so hard, I'm crying
LSHID	lshid	laugh so hard, I die
LSHIPMP	lshipmp	laughing so hard, I piss my pants
LSHISMP	lshismp	laughed so hard, I shit my pants
LSHIWMS	lshiwms	laughing so hard, I wet myself
LSHMBH	lshmbh	laughing so hard, my belly hurts
LSHMSON	lshmson	laughing so hard, milk shot out nose
LSHRN	lshrn	laughing so hard right now
LSI	lsi	limited social interaction
LSMIH	lsmih	laughing so much it hurts
LSP	lsp	lovesick puppy
LSR	lsr	loser
LSS	lss	last-song syndrome
LSTM	lstm	laughing silently to myself
LSUDI	lsudi	Let's see you do it.
LSV	lsv	language, sex, violence
LT	lt	long time
LTB	ltb	looking to buy
LTD	ltd	live/living the dream
LTG	ltg	learn to Google
LTHTT	lthtt	laughing too hard to type
LTIC	ltic	laugh 'til I cry
LTIO	ltio	laughing 'til I orgasm

UPPERCASE	LOWERCASE	MEANING
LTIP	ltip	laughing until I puke
LTL	ltl	living the life
LTLWDLS	ltlwdls	let's twist like we did last summer
LTM	ltm	laughing to myself
LTM	ltm	listen to me
LTMQ	ltmq	laughing to myself quietly
LTMS	ltms	laughing to myself
LTNASL	ltnasl	long time no ASLize
LTNC	ltnc	long time no chat/long time no see
LTNS	ltns	long time no see
LTNSOH	ltnsoh	long time, no see or hear
LTNT	ltnt	long time no talk
LTNT	ltnt	long time no type
LTOD	ltod	laptop of death
LTP	ltp	lay the pipe
LTP	ltp	lost the plot
LTR	ltr	later
LTR	ltr	long-term relationship
LTS	lts	laugh to self
LTTPOT	lttpot	laughing to the point of tears
LTW	ltw	lead the way
LTY	lty	laugh to yourself
LTYWL	ltywl	love the way you lie
LU	lu	love you
LU2	lu2	love you too
LU2D	lu2d	love you to death
LU4L	lu4l	love you for life
LUA	lua	love you always
LUB	lub	laugh under breath
LUB	lub	love
LUBB	lubb	love
LUBE	lube	lubricant
LUF	luf	love
LUFF	luff	love
LUG	lug	lesbian until graduation (homosexual slur/derogatory)
LUH	luh	love
LUK	luk	look
LUKIN	lukin	looking
LUL	lul	lame uncomfortable laugh
LUL	lul	love you lots
LULAB	lulab	love you like a brother
LULAS	lulas	love you like a sister
LULS	luls	(same as "LOL")
LULZ	lulz	(same as "LOL")
LUMI	lumi	love you, mean it
LUMU	lumu	love you, miss you
LUN	lun	Logical Unit Number
LURK	lurk	read a forum but never post
LURKER	lurker	forum follower who never posts
LURV	lurv	love
LURVE	lurve	love
LUSER	luser	user who is a loser
LUSH	lush	drunk person
LUSH	lush	great, brilliant

UPPERCASE	LOWERCASE	MEANING
LUSM	lusm	love you so much
LUV	luv	love
LUVER	luver	lover
LUVUVM	luvuvm	love you very much
LUVV	luvv	love
LUVVIE	luvvie	stage actor
LUX	lux	luxury
LUZAR	luzar	loser
LV	lv	Las Vegas
LV	lv	level
LV	lv	Louis Vuitton
LV	lv	love
LVE	lve	love
LVL	lvl	level
LVM	lvm	left voice mail
LVN	lvn	loving
LVR	lvr	lover
LVYA	lvya	love you
LW	lw	lucky win
LWIH	lwih	look what I have
LWKM	lwkm	laugh wan kill me (LOL)
LWKMD	lwkmd	laugh wan kill me die (Same as LWKM, but on a funnier scale.)
LWM	lwm	laugh with me
LWN	lwn	last week's news
LWOS	lwos	laughing without smiling
LWP	lwp	laughing with passion
LXG	lxg	*League of Extraordinary Gentlemen*
LY	ly	love you
LY2	ly2	love you too
LYA	lya	love you always
LYAAB	lyaab	love you as a brother
LYAAF	lyaaf	love you always and forever
LYAAF	lyaaf	love you as a friend
LYAO	lyao	laugh your ass off
LYB	lyb	love you, bye
LYBO	lybo	laugh your butt off
LYF	lyf	life
LYF	lyf	love you forever
LYFE	lyfe	life
LYK	lyk	let you know
LYK	lyk	like
LYK3	lyk3	like
LYKE	lyke	like
LYL	lyl	love you lots
LYLAB	lylab	love you like a brother
LYLABA	lylaba	love you like a brother always
LYLAD	lylad	love you like a dad
LYLAF	lylaf	love you like a friend
LYLAFKLC	lylafklc	love you like a fat kid loves cake
LYLAM	lylam	love you like a mom
LYLAS	lylas	love you like a sister
LYLASA	lylasa	love you like a sister always
LYLC	lylc	love you like crazy

UPPERCASE	LOWERCASE	MEANING
LYLMB	lylmb	love you like my brother
LYLNO	lylno	love you like no other
LYLS	lyls	love you lots
LYLT	lylt	love you long time
LYM	lym	love you more
LYMI	lymi	love you, mean it
LYMYWY	lymywy	love you, miss you, want you
LYR	lyr	love you really
LYSFM	lysfm	love you so fucking much
LYSM	lysm	love you so much
LYT	lyt	love you too
LYVM	lyvm	love you very much
LZ	lz	landing zone
LZER	lzer	laser
LZR	lzr	loser
LZY	lzy	lazy
M	m	am
M$	m$	Microsoft
M$WXP	m$wxp	Microsoft Windows XP
M&D	m&d	mom and dad
M&M	m&m	small chocolate candy
M&S	m&s	Marks & Spencer
M.I.A	m.i.a	missing in action
M.O	m.o	make out
M/B	m/b	maybe
M/F	m/f	male/female
M/O	m/o	make out
m|n_	m|n_	fuck you (left hand)
M'KAY	m'kay	OK
M2	m2	me too
M2AF	m2af	message to all friends
M2D	m2d	make my day
M2FP	m2fp	my two (three, four, etc.) favorite people
M3	m3	BMW sports car
M3	m3	me
M33T	m33t	meet
M473S	m473s	friends
M473Z	m473z	friends
M4F	m4f	male for female
M4M	m4m	men for men, male for male
M4W	m4w	man looking for a woman
M4W	m4w	men for women
M8	m8	mate
M84L	m84l	mate for life
M8S	m8s	mates
M8T'S	m8t's	friends
M9	m9	mine
MA	ma	master of arts
MA	ma	mom alert
MABBY	mabby	maybe
MABE	mabe	maybe
MAC	mac	Macintosh
MAC	mac	Media Access Control
MAC Address	mac address	Media Access Control Address

UPPERCASE	LOWERCASE	MEANING
MACHING	maching	going at maximum speed (skiing or biking)
MACK	mack	flirt
MAD	mad	really, extremely
MADD	madd	Mothers against Drunk Driving
MAG	mag	magazine
MAGGOT	maggot	fan of the band Slipknot
MAH	mah	my
MAI	mai	my
MAL	mal	mean, bad, evil
MAMAW	mamaw	grandmother
MAMI	mami	sexy, baby
MAN U	man u	Manchester United Football Club
MANC	manc	person from Manchester
MANDEM	mandem	group of men, boys
MANET	manet	Mobile Ad Hoc Network
MANG	mang	man
MANKY	manky	nasty, dirty
MAO	mao	my ass off
MAP	map	man-alien-predator
MARK	mark	target, sucker
MARVY	marvy	marvelous
MARY JANE	mary jane	marijuana
MAS	mas	mildly amused smirk
MASC	masc	masculine
MASH UP	mash up	song made from bits of other songs
MASTERB8	masterb8	masturbate
MASTRB8	mastrb8	masturbate
MATE	mate	friend
MAUH	mauh	kiss
MAUI WOWIE	maui wowie	marijuana, weed from Hawaii
MAWOY	mawoy	may angels watch over you
MAWP	mawp	Murder All White People (ethnic slur/derogatory)
MAYB	mayb	maybe
MAYTE	mayte	mate
MB	mb	mamma's boy
MB	mb	megabyte
MBA	mba	married but available
MBA	mba	masters of business association
MBF	mbf	my best friend
MBFAM	mbfam	my brother from another mother
MBHSM	mbhsm	my boobs hurt so much
MBL8R	mbl8r	maybe later
MBN	mbn	must be nice
MBO	mbo	management buyout
MBO	mbo	must be off
Mbps	mbps	megabits per second
MBRFN	mbrfn	must be real fucking nice
MBS	mbs	mom behind shoulder
MC	mc	master of ceremonies
MC	mc	Merry Christmas
MCA	mca	Micro Channel Architecture
MCD	mcd	McDonald's
MCDS	mcds	McDonald's
MCK	mck	mick (Irish - ethnic slur/derogatory)

UPPERCASE	LOWERCASE	MEANING
MCL	mcl	much clown love
MCP	mcp	male chauvinist pig
MCR	mcr	*My Chemical Romance* (band)
MCS	mcs	my computer sucks
MCSE	mcse	Microsoft Certified Systems Engineer
MD	md	doctor of medicine
MD	md	managing director
MDIAC	mdiac	my dad is a cop
MDMA	mdma	ecstasy
MDR	mdr	*mort de rire* ("LOL" in French)
MDW	mdw	Memorial Day weekend
ME GUSTA	me gusta	*I like* (Spanish)
ME2	me2	me too
MEAN	mean	cool
MEATCURTAIN	meatcurtain	woman's private parts
MEATHEAD	meathead	muscular, but thick, person
MEATSPACE	meatspace	the real world
MEC	mec	dude
MED	med	medication
MEDS	meds	medications
MEEH	meeh	me
MEETER	meeter	person who likes to look at fat men
MEGO	mego	my eyes glaze over
MEGO	mego	my eyes glazed over
MEH	meh	indifference, equivalent to shoulder shrug
MEH	meh	whatever
MELT	melt	idiot
MEME	meme	an idea that spreads like a virus by word of mouth, e-mail, blogs, etc.
MENTHOL	menthol	mint-flavored cigarette
MEP	mep	member of the European Parliament
MERC	merc	injure or kill
MERC	merc	mercenary
MERK	merk	kill
MERT	mert	mate
MESOS	mesos	currency in the game *MapleStory*
MESSG	messg	message
METH	meth	methamphetamine (drug)
MEX	mex	low-grade marijuana from Mexico
MF	mf	motherfucker
MF2F4SX	mf2f4sx	meet face-to-face for sex
MFA	mfa	motherfucking asshole
MFAH	mfah	motherfucking asshole
MFAO	mfao	my fucking ass off
MFB	mfb	motherfucking bitch
MFC	mfc	Microsoft foundation classes
MFC	mfc	mildly fat chick
MFEO	mfeo	made for each other
MFF	mff	muff (female genitalia)
MFFDRVR	mffdrvr	muffdiver (homosexual slur/derogatory)
MFG	mfg	merge from current
MFG	mfg	*Mit Freundlichen Grüßen* (German for "with friendly greetings")
MFI	mfi	mad for it

UPPERCASE	LOWERCASE	MEANING
MFIC	mfic	motherfucker in charge
MFKR	mfkr	motherfucker
MFL	mfl	marked for later
MFLFS	mflfs	married female looking for sex
MFR	mfr	motherfucker
MFW	mfw	my face when...
MG	mg	machine gun
MG	mg	milligram
MGB	mgb	may God bless
MGBY	mgby	may God bless you
MGIWJSDCHMW	mgiwjsdchmw	my girlfriend is watching, Jeff, so don't call her my wife
MGMT	mgmt	management
MGS	mgs	*Metal Gear Solid* (game)
MH	mh	map hack
MHBFY	mhbfy	my heart bleeds for you
MHH	mhh	my head hurts
MHM	mhm	(same as "MHMM")
MHM	mhm	yes
MHMM	mhmm	yes, sure, OK
MHO	mho	my humble opinion
MHZ	mhz	megahertz
MI	mi	middle initial
MI	mi	myocardial infarction (heart attack)
MI6	mi6	military intelligence service 6
MIA	mia	missing in action
MIB	mib	*Men in Black* (movie)
MIB	mib	mint in box
MIC	mic	microphone
MID	mid	midgrade marijuana
MID	mid	mobile Internet device
MIDI	midi	Musical Instrument Digital Interface
MIFF	miff	annoy
MIH	mih	make it happen
MIHOP	mihop	made it happen on purpose
MIID	miid	my Internet is down
MIL	mil	mother-in-law
MILEAGE	mileage	value for money
MILF	milf	mom I'd like to fuck
MILL	mill	million (dollars)
MILTF	miltf	mom I'd like to fuck
MIMO	mimo	multiple input, multiple output
MIN	min	minute
MINES	mines	mine
MINGA	minga	minger, ugly person
MINGER	minger	ugly person
MINGING	minging	dirty, disgusting, ugly
MINS	mins	minutes
MINT	mint	nice, cool
MINTED	minted	rich, wealthy
MINX	minx	cheeky, mischievous girl
MIP	mip	minor in possession
MIPS	mips	million instructions per second
MIQ	miq	make it quick

UPPERCASE	LOWERCASE	MEANING
MIR	mir	mom in room
MIRIN	mirin	admiring
MIRL	mirl	meet in real life
MISB	misb	mint (condition) in sealed box
MISC.	misc.	miscellaneous
MISELF	miself	myself
MISH	mish	missionary position
MISO	miso	my Internet shut off
MISSION	mission	arduous or boring task
MIT	mit	Massachusetts Institute of Technology
MITE	mite	might
MIW	miw	mom is watching
MIWNLF	miwnlf	mom I would not like to fuck
MIXOLOGY	mixology	study of mixing drinks
MIZ	miz	miserable
MJ	mj	marijuana
MJ	mj	Michael Jackson/Michael Jordan
MK	mk	mm, OK
MK	mk	mmm...OK
MKAY	mkay	mmm, OK
MKAY	mkay	OK
ML	ml	much love
MLB	mlb	Major League Baseball
MLC	mlc	midlife crisis
MLE	mle	Emily
MLG	mlg	Major League Gaming
MLIA	mlia	My life is amazing/average.
MLIB	mlib	My life is bad.
MLIG	mlig	My life is great/good.
MLIM	mlim	My life is magic.
MLM	mlm	middle finger/fuck you
MLM	mlm	multilevel marketing
MLOD	mlod	mega laugh out loud of doom
MLP	mlp	my little pony
MLS	mls	My life sucks.
MLTR	mltr	multiple long-term relationships
MLYP	mlyp	much like your post
MM	mm	married man
MM	mm	sister (Mandarin Chinese text message)
MM2	mm2	Message Mode 2 (CS)
MMA	mma	meet me at...
MMAMP	mmamp	meet me at my place
MMAS	mmas	meet me after school
MMATC	mmatc	meet me around the corner
MMATP	mmatp	meet me at the park
MMBOCMB	mmbocmb	message me back or comment me back
MMC	mmc	multimedia card
MMD	mmd	make my day
MMI	mmi	me, myself, and I
MMIW	mmiw	my mom is watching
MMJ	mmj	medical marijuana
MMK	mmk	mm, OK/OK? (as a question)
MMK	mmk	OK? (as a question)
MML	mml	make me laugh

UPPERCASE	LOWERCASE	MEANING
MML8R	mml8r	meet me later
MMLFS	mmlfs	married man looking for sex
MMM	mmm	expression of pleasure or contentment
MMMKAY	mmmkay	OK
MMO	mmo	massive multiplayer online
MMO	mmo	short for MMORPG
MMORPG	mmorpg	massively multiplayer online role-playing game
MMS	mms	Multimedia Messaging Service
MMT	mmt	makes me think / meet me there
MMTYH	mmtyh	my mom thinks you're hot
MMV	mmv	mileage may vary
MMW	mmw	making me wet
MNC	mnc	mother nature calls
MNF	mnf	Monday Night Football
MNGE	mnge	minge (female genitalia)
MNGING	mnging	munging (sexual act)
MNGMT	mngmt	management
MNGR	mngr	manager
MNM	mnm	*Eminem* (rapper)
MNSG	mnsg	*mensaje* (Spanish for "message")
MNT	mnt	maybe next time/more next time
MO	mo	modus operandi (method of operation)
MO	mo	a Muslim · contraction of Mohammed (ethnic slur/derogatory)
MO PO	mo po	mounted police
MOAR	moar	more
MOBBING	mobbing	bullying
MOBO	mobo	motherboard
MOC	moc	marriage of convenience
MOC	moc	my own creation
MODEM	modem	modulator-demodulator
MOE	moe	a Muslim · contraction of Mohammed (ethnic slur/derogatory)
MOF	mof	matter of fact
MOFO	mofo	motherfucker
MOFO	mofo	my own fucking opinion
MOH	moh	Medal of Honor
MOH	moh	my other half
MOHAA	mohaa	Medal of Honor: Allied Assault
MOI	moi	me (French)
MOJO	mojo	charm, spell
MOL	mol	more or less
MOLL	moll	gangster's gf
MOMBOY	momboy	mamma's boy
MOMPL	mompl	moment, please
MON	mon	man
MONG	mong	complete idiot
MONROE	monroe	piercing between nose and upper lip
MOO	moo	matter of opinion/my own opinion
MOOBS	moobs	man boobs
MOOLAH	moolah	money
MOOS	moos	member of the opposite sex
MOP	mop	hair on head
MOQ	moq	minimum order quantity

UPPERCASE	LOWERCASE	MEANING
MOR	mor	more
MORF	morf	male or female
MORO	moro	tomorrow
MOS	mos	mom over shoulder
MOSH	mosh	push/shove at rock/punk concert
MOSS	moss	member of same sex
MOSS	moss	relax, chill
MOT	mot	Ministry of Transport test for car safety
MOTA	mota	marijuana, weed
MOTARDED	motarded	more retarded
MOTD	motd	match of the day
MOTD	motd	message of the day
MOTKU	motku	master of the known universe
MOTO	moto	master of the obvious
MOTOS	motos	member of the opposite sex
MOTWYW	motwyw	make of that what you will
MOU	mou	memorandum of understanding
MOXY	moxy	courage, confidence
MP	mp	*Mana Points* (online gaming)
MP	mp	member of parliament
MP	mp	military police
MP3	mp3	MPEG-1 Audio Layer-3 (music file)
MP4	mp4	MPEG layer 4 (music/video file)
MP5	mp5	Heckler and Koch submachine gun
MPA	mpa	Music Publishers Association
MPAA	mpaa	Motion Picture Association of America
MPAW	mpaw	my parents are watching
MPBIS	mpbis	most popular boy in school
MPD	mpd	multiple personality disorder
MPE	mpe	my point exactly
MPEG	mpeg	Moving Picture Experts Group (audio/visual file format)
MPG	mpg	miles per gallon
MPGIS	mpgis	most popular girl in school
MPH	mph	miles per hour
MPIH	mpih	my penis is hard
MPOS	mpos	multiple positions
MPTY	mpty	more power to you
MPUA	mpua	master pickup artist
MPV	mpv	multipurpose vehicle
MR	mr	mentally retarded
MRA	mra	man bra
MRAU	mrau	message received and understood
MRE	mre	meal, ready to eat
MRI	mri	Magnetic Resonance Imaging
MRP	mrp	manufacturer's recommended price
MRT	mrt	modified retweet (Twitter slang)
MS	ms	*MapleStory* (MMORPG)
MS	ms	Microsoft
MSDN	msdn	Microsoft Developer Network
MSDOS	msdos	Microsoft disk operating system
MSF	msf	male seeking female
MSFAM	msfam	my sister from another mister
MSFT	msft	Microsoft

UPPERCASE	LOWERCASE	MEANING
MSG	msg	message
MSG	msg	monosodium glutamate
MSGS	msgs	messages
MSH	msh	me so horny
MSI	msi	*Mindless Self Indulgence* (band)
MSIBO	msibo	my side is busting open
MSIE	msie	Microsoft's Internet Explorer
MSM	msm	mainstream media
MSMD	msmd	monkey see, monkey do
MSN	msn	Microsoft Network
MSNGR	msngr	messenger
MSR	msr	Mulder-Scully romance
MSRP	msrp	manufacturer's suggested retail price
MSSG	mssg	message
MSV	msv	Microsoft Vista
MT	mt	*Mistell* (game)
MTA	mta	more than anything
MTB	mtb	mountain bike
MTBF	mtbf	mean time between failures (reliability)
MTBMW	mtbmw	may the best man win
MTC	mtc	more to come
MTE	mte	my thoughts exactly
MTF	mtf	male to female
MTF	mtf	more to follow
MTFBWU	mtfbwu	May the force be with you.
MTFBWY	mtfbwy	May the force be with you.
MTG	mtg	*Magic: The Gathering* (game)
MTG	mtg	meeting
MTH	mth	month
MTHERFKER	mtherfker	motherfucker
MTHRFKR	mthrfkr	motherfucker
MTL	mtl	Montreal, Canada
MTL	mtl	more than likely
MTLBWY	mtlbwy	May the Lord be with you.
MTO	mto	Media TakeOut (gossip Web site)
MTR	mtr	matter
MTRFKR	mtrfkr	motherfucker
MTU	mtu	Maximum Transmission Unit
MTUK	mtuk	more than you know
MTV	mtv	Music Television
MTYK	mtyk	more than you know
MU	mu	miss you
MU	mu	multiuser
MUA	mua	Makeupalley (website)
MUAH	muah	multiple unsuccessful attempts (at/to) humor
MUAH	muah	the sound of giving a kiss
MUAHA	muaha	an evil laugh
MUAHZ	muahz	kisses
MUAK	muak	(same as "MUAH")
MUCHO	mucho	much, very
MUCK	muck	ugly
MUD	mud	*Multi-User Dungeon* (MMORPG)
MUD DUCK	mud duck	ugly woman
MUDDA	mudda	mother

UPPERCASE	LOWERCASE	MEANING
MUDKIP	mudkip	water *Pokémon*
MUDSHARK	mudshark	white woman dating black men
MUFC	mufc	Manchester United Football Club
MUG	mug	face
MUG	mug	idiot
MUG	mug	rob somebody
MUH	muh	me/my
MUL	mul	miss you lots
MULA	mula	money
MULLET	mullet	hairstyle
MULTI	multi	player with multiple online accounts
MULU	mulu	miss you, love you
MUM	mum	mom
MUNTED	munted	drunk, intoxicated
MURKED	murked	badly defeated, killed
MURSE	murse	male nurse
MUSH	mush	friend
MUSIQ	musiq	music
MUSM	musm	miss you so much
MUTHA	mutha	mother
MUTT	mutt	Mutt (a multiracial person - ethnic slur/derogatory)
MUVE	muve	multiuser virtual environment
MUVVA	muvva	mother
MUZIK	muzik	music
MVP	mvp	most valuable player
MW2	mw2	*Modern Warfare 2* (game)
MW3	mw3	*Modern Warfare 3* (game)
MWA	mwa	kiss
MWAH	mwah	kiss
MWC	mwc	married with children
MWF	mwf	married white female
MWHA	mwha	kiss
MWI	mwi	mad with it (drunk)
MWM	mwm	married white male
MWM	mwm	whatever (both hands)
MWSMIRL	mwsmirl	maybe we should meet in real life
MX	mx	motocross
MY	my	miss you
MY BAD	my bad	(flippant) apology
MY BOO	my boo	my boyfriend/girlfriend
MY FOOT	my foot	expression of disbelief
MY SIZE	my size	my type of girl
MYALY	myaly	miss you and love you
MYF	myf	miss your face
MYFB	myfb	mind your fucking business
MYGGWY	myggwy	May your god go with you.
MYKE	myke	man-dyke
MYL	myl	miss you loads
MYMP	mymp	make your mama proud
MYN	myn	mine
MYOB	myob	mind your own business
MYODB	myodb	mind your own damn business
MYOFB	myofb	mind your own fucking business
MYPL	mypl	my young Padawan learner

UPPERCASE	LOWERCASE	MEANING
MYSM	mysm	miss you so much
MYSPACE	myspace	a social networking site
MYSPCE	myspce	Myspace
N	n	and
N E	n e	any
N/A	n/a	not applicable
N/A/S/L	n/a/s/l	name, age, sex, location
N/C	n/c	no comment
N/C	n/c	not cool
N/M	n/m	never mind
N/N	n/n	nickname
N/O	n/o	no offense
N/T	n/t	no text (subject says it all)
N@GGER	n@gger	nigger (African American · ethnic slur/derogatory)
N@GGERS	n@ggers	niggers (African Americans · ethnic slur/derogatory)
N00B	n00b	newbie
N00BS	n00bs	newbies
N00DZ	n00dz	nudes
N00S	n00s	news
N1	n1	nice one
N199312	n199312	leet speak for "nigga/nigger" (African American · ethnic slur/derogatory)
N1994	n1994	leet speak for "nigga/nigger" (African American · ethnic slur/derogatory)
N2	n2	into
N2B	n2b	not too bad
N2BB	n2bb	nice to be back
N2BR	n2br	not to be rude
N2G	n2g	need to go
N2G	n2g	not too good
N2K	n2k	need to know
N2K	n2k	nice to know
N2M	n2m	not too much
N2MH	n2mh	not too much here
N2MHBU	n2mhbu	Not too much, how about you?
N2MHJC	n2mhjc	not too much here, just chilling
N2MU	n2mu	nice to meet you
N2MU	n2mu	Not too much, you?
N2N	n2n	need to know
N2P	n2p	need to pee
N3	n3	no-name noob
N4P	n4p	noob
N64	n64	Nintendo 64
N8	n8	night
N8V	n8v	native
NA	na	not announced
NA	na	not applicable/not available
NA4W	na4w	not appropriate for work
NAA	naa	not at all
NAB	nab	noob
NABD	nabd	not a big deal
NAC	nac	not a chain (letter)
NAC	nac	not a chance
NACKER	nacker	Irish gypsy, traveler

UPPERCASE	LOWERCASE	MEANING
NACKERED	nackered	tired, worn out
NADA	nada	nothing
NADDA	nadda	nothing
NADE	nade	grenade
NADT	nadt	not a darn thing
NAE	nae	no
NAFC	nafc	not appropriate for children
NAFKAM	nafkam	not away from keyboard anymore
NAFT	naft	not a fucking thing
NAFTA	nafta	North American Free-Trade Agreement
NAGA	naga	North American Ground Ape (a black person - ethnic slur/derogatory)
NAGL	nagl	not a good look
NAH	nah	no
NAHMEAN	nahmean	you know what I mean
NAIJA	naija	Nigerian
NAIL IT	nail it	complete, get right
NAK	nak	nursing at keyboard
NALGO	nalgo	not a lot going on
NALOPKT	nalopkt	Not a lot of people know that.
NAMASTE	namaste	Sanskrit greeting
NAMEAN	namean	Do you know what I mean?
NAMH	namh	not at my house
NANA	nana	grandmother
NANA	nana	not now, no need
NANG	nang	cool, wicked, good
NAO	nao	not as often
NAO	nao	now
NAP	nap	not a problem
NAPSTER	napster	file-sharing site
NARF	narf	random interjection
NARK	nark	informer
NARP	narp	nonathletic regular person
NARU	naru	not a registered user
NAS	nas	network-attached storage
NASA	nasa	National Aeronautics and Space Administration
NASCAR	nascar	National Association for Stock Car Auto Racing
NASDAQ	nasdaq	National Association of Securities Dealers Automated Quotation
NASL	nasl	name, age, sex, location
NAT	nat	Network Address Translation
NATCH	natch	naturally
NATI	nati	Cincinnati
NATM	natm	not at the moment
NATO	nato	no action, talk only
NATO	nato	North Atlantic Treaty Organization
NATTY	natty	natural light beer
NATTY	natty	smart, good, cool
NATTY LIGHT	natty light	natural light beer
NAW	naw	no
NAWIDT	nawidt	Never again will I do that.
NAWT	nawt	not
NAWW	naww	no
NAY	nay	no

UPPERCASE	LOWERCASE	MEANING
NAYL	nayl	in a while
NB	nb	not bad
NB	nb	*nota bene* (Latin for "please note")
NB,P	nb,p	nothing bad, parents
NBA	nba	National Basketball Association
NBC	nbc	National Broadcasting Company
NBD	nbd	no big deal
NBDY	nbdy	nobody
NBF	nbf	new best friend
NBFD	nbfd	no big fucking deal
NBM	nbm	nil by mouth
NBM	nbm	not before midnight
NBS	nbs	no bullshit
NBSB	nbsb	no boyfriend since birth
NBT	nbt	nothing but trouble
NBTD	nbtd	nothing better to do
NC	nc	no choice
NC	nc	no comment
NC	nc	not cool
NC-17	nc-17	no children under seventeen (movie rating)
NCAA	ncaa	National Collegiate Athletic Association
NCIS	ncis	*Naval Criminal Investigative Service* (TV show)
NCO	nco	noncommissioned officer
NCS	ncs	no-crap Sherlock
ND	nd	and
NDA	nda	nondisclosure agreement
NDI	ndi	neither do I
NDIT	ndit	no details in thread
NDN	ndn	Indian
NDP	ndp	new Democratic Party
NDR	ndr	nondelivery report/receipt
NDS	nds	Nintendo DS
NE	ne	any
NE1	ne1	anyone
NEA	nea	National Education Association
NEAT-O	neat-o	cool
NED	ned	noneducated delinquent
NEDAY	neday	any day
NEDM	nedm	*Not Even Doom Music* (game)
NEDN	nedn	any day now
NEE	nee	maiden name indicator
NEEK	neek	a cross between a nerd and a geek
NEET	neet	not in education, employment, or training
NEFIN	nefin	anything
NEFING	nefing	anything
NEG	neg	negative
NEGL	negl	not even gonna lie
NEI	nei	not enough information
NEIDA	neida	any idea
NEKKID	nekkid	naked
NEL	nel	no (Spanish)
NEMORE	nemore	anymore
NERD	nerd	intelligent but socially inept person
NERF	nerf	weaken

UPPERCASE	LOWERCASE	MEANING
NES	nes	Nintendo Entertainment System
NET	net	Internet
NetBIOS	netbios	Network Basic Input/Output System
NETHIN	nethin	anything
NETHING	nething	anything
NETWORK	network	two or more connected computers
NEVA	neva	never
NEVAH	nevah	never
NEVAR	nevar	never
NEVARZ	nevarz	never
NEVM	nevm	never mind
NEVR	nevr	never
NEW	new	clueless
NEWAIS	newais	anyways
NEWAY	neway	anyway
NEWAYS	neways	anyways
NEWAYZ	newayz	anyways
NEWB	newb	newbie, someone who is new
NEWBIE	newbie	new person/player
NEWEZ	newez	anyways
NEWFAG	newfag	newcomer
NEWPORT	newport	cigarette brand
NEY	ney	no
NF	nf	not funny
NFA	nfa	no further action
NFBSK	nfbsk	not for British schoolkids
NFC	nfc	no fucking chance
NFC	nfc	no fucking clue
NFD	nfd	no fucking deal
NFE	nfe	no fucking excuses
NFF	nff	not fucking fair
NFG	nfg	not fucking good
NFI	nfi	no fucking idea
NFL	nfl	National Football League
NFM	nfm	no further message
NFM	nfm	not for me
NFN	nfn	normal for Norfolk
NFR	nfr	not for real
NFS	nfs	need for sex
NFS	nfs	not for sale
NFT	nft	no further text
NFW	nfw	no fucking way
NFZ	nfz	no-fly zone
NG	ng	nice game
NG	ng	no good
NGAF	ngaf	nobody gives a fuck
NGGA	ngga	nigga (African American - ethnic slur/derogatory)
NGGR	nggr	nigger (African American - ethnic slur/derogatory)
NGGRS	nggrs	niggers (African Americans - ethnic slur/derogatory)
NGH	ngh	not gonna happen
NGL	ngl	not gonna lie
NGLT	nglt	niglet (African American child - ethnic slur/derogatory)
NGO	ngo	nongovernmental organization

UPPERCASE	LOWERCASE	MEANING
NGRO	ngro	negro - African american
NGU	ngu	never give up
NH	nh	nice hand (poker slang)
NHATM	nhatm	not here at the moment
NHF	nhf	no hard feelings
NHN	nhn	not here now
NHOI	nhoi	never heard of it
NHS	nhs	National Health Service
NI	ni	no idea
NI994	ni994	nigga (African American - ethnic slur/derogatory)
NIAMY	niamy	never in a million years
NIB	nib	new inbox
NIC	nic	Network Interface Card
NICE	nice	National Institute of Clinical Excellence
NICE	nice	nonsense in crappy existence
NICKED	nicked	arrested/stolen
NICKER	nicker	pound, quid (British currency)
NIFOC	nifoc	naked in front of computer
NIFOK	nifok	naked in front of keyboard
NIFOM	nifom	naked in front of monitor
NIGAB@@	nigab@@	nigaboo (African American - ethnic slur/derogatory)
NIGI	nigi	now I get it
NIGYSOB	nigysob	now I've got you, son of a bitch
NIGYYSOB	nigyysob	now I've got you, you son of a bitch
NIHAO	nihao	hello (Chinese)
NIK	nik	now I know
NIKE	nike	American sportswear company
NIMBY	nimby	not in my backyard
NIMROD	nimrod	stupid person, idiot
NIN	nin	Nine Inch Nails
NIN	nin	no, it's not
NINJA	ninja	Japanese warrior
NIP	nip	a Japanese person (ethnic slur/derogatory)
NIP	nip	nothing in particular
NIPS	nips	nipples
NIR	nir	noob in room
NIT	nit	idiot, nitwit
NIT	nit	new in town
NITE	nite	night/good night
NITM	nitm	not in the mood
NIYWFD	niywfd	not in your wildest fucking dreams
NIZZ	nizz	no
NIZZLE	nizzle	nigger
NJ	nj	nice job
NJ	nj	not joking
NJOY	njoy	enjoy
NJP	njp	nice job, partner
NK	nk	no kidding
NK	nk	not known
NKOTB	nkotb	new kid on the block
NKT	nkt	expression of annoyance
NKT	nkt	never knew that
NL	nl	Netherlands
NL	nl	no limit

UPPERCASE	LOWERCASE	MEANING
NLA	nla	no longer available
NLD	nld	nice lay down
NLI	nli	not logged in
NLM	nlm	no laughing matter
NLT	nlt	no later than...
NLYG	nlyg	never let you go
NM	nm	never mind
NM	nm	no message
NM	nm	not much/nothing much
NM U	nm u	Not much, you?
NMBR	nmbr	number
NME	nme	enemy
NME	nme	*New Musical Express* (magazine)
NMF	nmf	not my fault
NMFP	nmfp	not my fucking problem
NMG	nmg	*no mamcs guey* (OMG)
NMH	nmh	nodding my head
NMH	nmh	Not much here.
NMHAU	nmhau	Nothing much, how about you?
NMHM	nmhm	Nothing much here, man.
NMHU	nmhu	Nothing much here, you?
NMHWBY	nmhwby	Nothing much here, what about you?
NMI	nmi	need more info
NMJ	nmj	not my job
NMJB	nmjb	nothing much, just bored
NMJC	nmjc	not much, just chat
NMJC	nmjc	not much, just chilling
NMJCH	nmjch	nothing much, just chilling
NMJCU	nmjcu	Not much, just chilling, you?
NMJCU	nmjcu	Nothing much, just chilling, you?
NMJDHW	nmjdhw	nothing much, just doing homework
NMJFA	nmjfa	nothing much, just fucking around
NMN	nmn	no middle name
NMNHNLM	nmnhnlm	no money, no honey, nobody loves me
NMO	nmo	not my opinion
NMP	nmp	not my problem
NMR	nmr	not my responsibility
NMS	nms	not my style
NMT	nmt	not my type
NMU	nmu	Not much, you?
NMU	nmu	Nothing much, you?
NMW	nmw	no matter what
NMWH	nmwh	no matter what happens
NMY	nmy	nice meeting you
NN	nn	good night/night, night
NN	nn	no need
NN	nn	not nice
NN2R	nn2r	no need to respond
NNAA	nnaa	no, not at all
NNFAA	nnfaa	no need for an apology
NNITO	nnito	not necessarily in that order
NNR	nnr	no not really
NNTP	nntp	Network News Transfer Protocol
NNTR	nntr	no need to reply

UPPERCASE	LOWERCASE	MEANING
NO	no	know
NO	no	no offense
NO BIGGIE	no biggie	no big deal
NO PRO	no pro	no problem
NO WORRIES	no worries	OK, no problem
NO1	no1	no one
NO1CURR	no1curr	no one cares
NOAA	noaa	National Oceanic and Atmospheric Administration
NO-BRAINER	no-brainer	something that requires no thought before deciding
NOC	noc	naked on camera
NOC	noc	Network Operations Center
NOC	noc	no one cares
NOCAL	nocal	Northern California
NOD	nod	doze off
NOE	noe	know
NOES	noes	no
NOFI	nofi	no flame intended
NOH	noh	new overhauled
NOH8	noh8	no hate
NOK	nok	no one knows
NOK	nok	not OK
NOLM	nolm	no one loves me
NOM	nom	no offense meant
NOMB	nomb	none of my business
NOMMY	nommy	good, delicious
NOMNOM	nomnom	sound of eating
NOMS	noms	food
NOMW	nomw	not on my watch
NON	non	now or never
NONG	nong	idiot, twit
NONYA	nonya	none of your (business)
NOOB	noob	new, inexperienced person
NOOB	noob	someone who is new
NOOB TUBE	noob tube	grenade launcher attachment in CoD 4
NOOBIE	noobie	new person
NOOBLET	nooblet	new player
NOOBZ0R	noobz0r	newbie
NOODZ	noodz	nude pictures
NOOKIE	nookie	sex
NOP	nop	no problem
NOP	nop	normal operating procedure
NOPE	nope	no
NORCAL	norcal	Northern California
NORLY	norly	No, really?
NORM	norm	normal
NORWICH	norwich	knickers off, ready when I come home
NOS	nos	new old stock
NOSA	nosa	no, sir, just kidding
NOTA	nota	none of the above
NOTIN	notin	nothing
NOTTIE	nottie	unattractive person, not a hottie
NOTY	noty	no, thank you
NOUB	noub	none of your business
NOUT	nout	nothing (northern UK)

UPPERCASE	LOWERCASE	MEANING
NOV	nov	novice
NOWAI	nowai	no way
NOWIN	nowin	knowing
NOWL	nowl	knowledge
NOWT	nowt	nothing
NOYB	noyb	none of your business
NOYDB	noydb	none of your damn business
NOYFB	noyfb	none of your fucking business
NOYGDB	noygdb	none of your goddamn business
NP	np	no problem
NP4NP	np4np	naked pic for naked pic
NPA	npa	not paying attention
NPAA	npaa	no problem at all
NPBF	npbf	no problem, boyfriend
NPC	npc	nonplayable character
NPC	npc	nonplayer character
NPE	npe	nope
NPGF	npgf	no problem, girlfriend
NPH	nph	no problem here
NPI	npi	no pun intended
NPNT	npnt	no picture, no talk
NPO	npo	never pull out
NPR	npr	National Public Radio
NPR	npr	no purchase required
NPS	nps	no problems
NPZ	npz	no problems
NQ	nq	thank you
NQR	nqr	not quite right
NQT	nqt	newly qualified teacher
NR	nr	nice roll
NR	nr	no reply
NR	nr	no reserve
NR4U	nr4u	not right for you
NRA	nra	National Rifle Association
NRFB	nrfb	never removed from box
NRG	nrg	energy
NRI	nri	nonrepairable item
NRI	nri	nonresident Indian
NRL	nrl	National Rugby League
NRN	nrn	no reply necessary
NRN	nrn	no response necessary
NS	ns	nice
NS	ns	nice score
NS	ns	nice split
NSA	nsa	no strings attached
NSAS	nsas	no-strings-attached sex
NSF	nsf	not so fast
NSF	nsf	not sufficient funds
NSFA	nsfa	not safe for anyone
NSFL	nsfl	not safe for life
NSFMF	nsfmf	not so fast, my friend
NSFU	nsfu	no sex for you
NSFV	nsfv	not safe for viewing/vegetarians/vegans
NSFW	nsfw	not safe for work

UPPERCASE	LOWERCASE	MEANING
NSISR	nsisr	not sure if spelled right
NSM	nsm	not so much
NSN	nsn	not so nice
NSS	nss	no-shit Sherlock
NST	nst	no school today
NSTAAFL	nstaafl	no such thing as a free lunch
NSW	nsw	New South Wales
NT	nt	nice try
NT	nt	no, thanks
NTB	ntb	not that bothered
NTB	ntb	not too bad
NTBCW	ntbcw	not to be confused with
NTBN	ntbn	no text-back needed
NTD	ntd	nothing to do
NTFS	ntfs	New Technology File System
NTH	nth	nothing
NTHG	nthg	nothing
NTHIN	nthin	nothing
NTHN	nthn	nothing
NTIGAF	ntigaf	not that I give a fuck
NTIM	ntim	not that it matters
NTK	ntk	need to know
NTKB	ntkb	need-to-know basis
NTL	ntl	nevertheless
NTM	ntm	not too much
NTM	ntm	nothing much
NTMK	ntmk	not to my knowledge
NTMU	ntmu	nice to meet you
NTMY	ntmy	nice to meet you
NTN	ntn	no thanks needed
NTN	ntn	nothing
NTRLY	ntrly	not really
NTS	nts	note to self
NTS	nts	nothing to say
NTSTT	ntstt	not safe to talk
NTT	ntt	name that tune
NTT	ntt	need to talk
NTT	ntt	not touching that
NTTA	ntta	nothing to talk about
NTTAWWT	nttawwt	not that there's anything wrong with that
NTTIAWWT	nttiawwt	not that there is anything wrong with that
NTTU	nttu	not talking to you
NTTY	ntty	nice talking to you
NTW	ntw	not to worry
NTWF	ntwf	Neopian Times Writers Forum
NTXT	ntxt	no text
NTY	nty	no, thank you
NU	nu	new
NU	nu	no
NUB	nub	newcomer, rookie, amateur
NUB	nub	someone who should know better
NUF	nuf	enough
NUF	nuf	nothing
NUFF	nuff	enough

UPPERCASE	LOWERCASE	MEANING
NUFFIN	nuffin	nothing
NUFIN	nufin	nothing
NUH	nuh	no
NUKE	nuke	to attack with a nuclear weapon
NUM	num	tasty
NUMPTY	numpty	idiot
NUNYA	nunya	none of your (business)
NUT SCK	nut sck	nut sack (male genitalia)
NUTCASE	nutcase	crazy person
NUTIN	nutin	nothing
NUTSCK	nutsck	nutsack (male genitalia)
NUTTIN	nuttin	nothing
NUTZ	nutz	nuts, crazy, insane
NV	nv	envy
NV	nv	never
NVM	nvm	never mind
NVMD	nvmd	never mind
NVMDT	nvmdt	never mind then
NVMT	nvmt	never mind that
NVR	nvr	never
NVRAM	nvram	Non-Volatile Random Access Memory
NVRM	nvrm	never mind
NVRMND	nvrmnd	never mind
NW	nw	no way
NWB	nwb	a new person
NWIH	nwih	no way in hell
NWIM	nwim	not what I mean
NWLY	nwly	never wanna lose you
NWO	nwo	New World Order
NWO	nwo	no way out
NWOT	nwot	new without tags (eBay)
NWRUS	nwrus	no way are your serious
NWS	nws	not work-safe (for messages/sites containing adult content)
NWT	nwt	new with tags
NWTF	nwtf	now what the fuck
NWY	nwy	no way
NXT	nxt	next
NY	ny	New York
NY1	ny1	anyone
NYC	nyc	New York City
NYE	nye	New Year's Eve
NYERK	nyerk	replacement swearword
NYF	nyf	not your fault
NYK	nyk	not yet known
NYK	nyk	now you know
NYOB	nyob	not your own business
NYP	nyp	not your problem
NYPD	nypd	New York Police Department
NYSE	nyse	New York Stock Exchange
NYT	nyt	*New York Times*
NYT	nyt	not your type
NYWY	nywy	anyway
O	o	hugs

UPPERCASE	LOWERCASE	MEANING
O	o	oh
O	o	opponent
O	o	ounce (of drugs)
O	o	over
O GAWD	o gawd	oh, God
O RLY	o rly	Oh, really?
O&O	o&o	over and out
O.o	O.o	confused
O.O	O.O	wide-eyed
O.P.	o.p.	original poster
O/	o/	high five
O/\O	o/\o	high five
O/Y	o/y	oh, yeah
O:)	o:)	innocent, angelic
O:-)	o:-)	innocent, angelic
O[-<]:	O[-<]:	skateboarder
O_O	o_o	confused
O4U	o4u	only for you
O7	o7	salute
OA	oa	online auctions
OA	oa	overacting
OAN	oan	on another note
OAO	oao	over and out
OAOA	oaoa	over and over again
OAP	oap	old-age pensioner
OAR	oar	on a roll
OASIS	oasis	Organization for the Advancement of Structured Information Standards
OATUS	oatus	on a totally unrelated subject
OAUS	oaus	on an unrelated subject
OAW	oaw	on a Web site
OB	ob	oh, brother
OBBY	obby	oh, baby
OBE	obe	order of the British empire
OBE	obe	out-of-body experience/overcome by events
OBGJFIOYO	obgjfioyo	old but good job finding it on your own
OBGYN	obgyn	gynecologist (obstetrics and gynecology)
OBHWF	obhwf	one big happy Weasley family
OBL	obl	Osama bin Laden
OBO	obo	or best offer
OBS	obs	obviously
OBTW	obtw	oh, by the way
OBV	obv	obviously
OBVI	obvi	obviously
OBVS	obvs	obviously
OBX	obx	Outer Banks, North Carolina
OC	oc	of course
OC	oc	Orange County
OC	oc	original character
OCC	occ	occupation
OCD	ocd	obsessive compulsive disorder
OCGG	ocgg	oh, crap, gotta go
OCO	oco	oh, come on
OCR	ocr	Optical Character Recognition

UPPERCASE	LOWERCASE	MEANING
OCT	oct	on company time
OD	od	overdoing it
OD	od	overdose
ODAY	oday	software illegally obtained before it was released
ODBC	odbc	Open Database Connectivity
ODEE	odee	(same as "od")
ODG	odg	oh, dear God
ODL	odl	oh, dear Lord
ODST	odst	*Orbital Drop Shock Trooper* (game)
ODT	odt	on dis ting
ODTAA	odtaa	one damn thing after another
OE	oe	operator error
OE	oe	or else
OE	oe	Outlook Express
OED	oed	Oxford English Dictionary
OEM	oem	original equipment manufacturer
OF10	of10	often
OFC	ofc	of course
OFCOL	ofcol	oh, for crying out loud
OFH	ofh	old folks' home
OFN	ofn	old fucking news
OFOC	ofoc	overwhelming feelings of concern
OFTC	oftc	out for the count
OFTN	oftn	often
OFTPC	oftpc	off topic
OFWGKTA	ofwgkta	*Odd Future Wolf Gang Kill Them All* (rapper)
OG	og	old git
OG	og	original gangster
OGIM	ogim	oh God, it's Monday
OGW	ogw	oh, guess what
OH	oh	other half
OH	oh	overheard
OH NOES	oh noes	Oh shit!
OH NOEZ	oh noez	Oh no!
OHAC	ohac	own house and car
OHAI	ohai	oh, hi
OHIC	ohic	oh, I see
OHIM	ohim	oh hell, it's Monday
OHK	ohk	oh OK
OHKO	ohko	one-hit knockout
OHN	ohn	Oh hell, no!
OHNOEZ	ohnoez	oh no
OHS	ohs	operator headspace
OHT	oht	one-handed typing
OHY	ohy	oh, hell yeah
OI	oi	hey
OI	oi	operator indisposed
OIB	oib	oh, I'm back
OIBMPC	oibmpc	Oops, I broke my computer.
OIC	oic	oh, I see
OICIC	oicic	oh, I see, I see
OICU	oicu	oh, I see you
OICWYDT	oicwydt	Oh, I see what you did there.
OIDIA	oidia	Oops, I did it again.

UPPERCASE	LOWERCASE	MEANING
OIK	oik	unpleasant, unpopular person
OIY	oiy	hey
OIYD	oiyd	only in your dreams
OJ	oj	only joking
OJ	oj	orange juice
OJD	ojd	Obsessive Jonas (Brothers) Disorder
OJSU	ojsu	oh, just shut up!
OJT	ojt	on-job training
OK	ok	OK
OK	ok	only kidding
OKI	oki	okeydoke
OKIES	okies	OK
OKW/E	okw/e	OK, whatever
OL	ol	office lady
OL	ol	old lady
OL	ol	online
OLAP	olap	Online Analytical Processing
OLD BAG	old bag	grumpy old woman
OLDFAG	oldfag	long-established member of an online community
OLE	ole	Object Linking and Embedding
OLED	oled	organic light-emitting diode
OLL	oll	online love
OLLG	ollg	one less lonely girl
OLPC	olpc	one laptop per child
OM	om	oh man/oh my
OM	om	old man
OM NOM	om nom	sound of eating
OMA	oma	oh, my Allah
OMAA	omaa	oh, my aching *a* (butt)
OMB	omb	on my break
OMD	omd	oh, my days
OMDB	omdb	over my dead body
OMDG	omdg	oh, my dear God
OMDZ	omdz	oh, my days
OMFG	omfg	oh, my fucking god
OMFGN	omfgn	oh, my fucking god noob
OMFGSH	omfgsh	oh, my fucking gosh
OMFJ	omfj	oh, my fucking Jesus
OMFL	omfl	oh, my fucking Internet connection is slow
OMFSM	omfsm	oh, my flying spaghetti monster
OMFWTG	omfwtg	Oh, my fuck what the god?
OMG	omg	oh, my god
OMG'S	omg's	oh, my gods
OMGA	omga	oh, my giddy aunt
OMGD	omgd	oh, my god, dude/oh, my gosh, dude
OMGF	omgf	Oh, my god...Fuck!
OMGG	omgg	oh, my gosh, girl
OMGICFBI	omgicfbi	oh, my god, I can't fucking believe it
OMGIH	omgih	oh, my god in heaven
OMGIHV2P	omgihv2p	oh, my god, I have to pee
OMGINBD	omginbd	oh, my god, it's no big deal
OMGN	omgn	oh, my goodness
OMGNA	omgna	oh, my gosh, not again
OMGNY	omgny	oh, my god, no way

UPPERCASE	LOWERCASE	MEANING
OMGOSH	omgosh	oh, my gosh
OMGROFLMAO	omgroflmao	oh, my god, roll on the floor laughing my ass off
OMGSH	omgsh	oh, my gosh
OMGTY	omgty	oh, my god, thank you
OMGUKK	omgukk	Oh, my god, you killed Kenny.
OMGWTF	omgwtf	Oh, my god, what the fuck?
OMGWTFBBQ	omgwtfbbq	Oh, my god, what the fuck?
OMGWTFHAX	omgwtfhax	Oh, my god, what the fuck, hacks!
OMGWTFIT	omgwtfit	Oh, my god, what the fuck is that?
OMGWTFNIPPLES	omgwtfnipples	Oh, my god, what the fuck?
OMGYG2BK	omgyg2bk	Oh, my god, you got to be kidding.
O.OMGYKKYB	omgykkyb	Oh, my god, you killed Kenny, you bastards.
OMGZ	omgz	(same as "OMG")
OMGZ	omgz	oh, my god
OMGZORS	omgzors	oh, my god
OMHG	omhg	oh, my hell god
OMJ	omj	oh, my Jesus
OMJC	omjc	oh, my Jesus Christ
OML	oml	oh, my lord
OMMFG	ommfg	oh, my motherfucking god
OMS	oms	oh, my science
OMSJ	omsj	Oh, my sweet Jesus!
OMT	omt	one more thing/one more time
OMW	omw	on my way
OMWH	omwh	on my way home
OMWN	omwn	on my way now
OMY	omy	Oh, my!
OMZ	omz	oh, my Zeus
ON	on	drunk, high
ON ONE	on one	under the influence of drugs
ON9	on9	online
ON9	on9	stupid (Chinese)
ONCO	onco	or nearest cash offer
ONE	one	one love, good-bye
ONG	ong	misspelling of "OMG"
ONL	onl	online
ONNA	onna	oh no, not again
ONNTA	onnta	oh no, not this again
ONO	ono	or nearest offer
ONOEZ	onoez	oh no
ONOZ	onoz	oh no
ONS	ons	one-night stand
ONTD	ontd	oh no, they didn't
ONUD	onud	oh no, you didn't
ONYD	onyd	oh no, you didn't
OO	oo	object orientated
OO	oo	over and out
OO	oo	surprised
O-O	o-o	shock
OOAK	ooak	one of a kind
OOB	oob	out of business
OOBL	oobl	out of breath, laughing

Internet and Computer Slang Dictionary

UPPERCASE	LOWERCASE	MEANING
OOC	ooc	out of character
OOC	ooc	out of control/character/context
OOF	oof	out of office
OOFT	ooft	sound made when impressed by something
OOH	ooh	out of here
OOHM	oohm	out of his/her mind
OOI	ooi	out of interest
OOMF	oomf	one of my friends/followers
OOML	ooml	out of my league
OOMM	oomm	out of my mind
OOO	ooo	out of office/ out of the office
OOP	oop	Object-Oriented Programming
OOP	oop	out of place
OOPS	oops	word said after doing something wrong
OOS	oos	out of style
OOSOOM	oosoom	out of sight, out of mind
OOT	oot	out of town
OOTB	ootb	out of the blue
OOTB	ootb	out of the box
OOTC	ootc	obligatory on-topic comment
OOTD	ootd	one of these days
OOTD	ootd	outfit of the day
OOTO	ooto	out of the office
OOW	oow	on our way
OP	op	on phone
OP	op	operator
OP	op	original poster
OPA	opa	Greek exclamation
OPB	opb	other people's business
OPK	opk	other people's kids
OPM	opm	other people's money
OPPS	opps	misspelling of "oops"
OPS	ops	oops
OREO	oreo	a black person (ethnic slur/derogatory)
ORG	org	online reality games
ORG	org	organization
ORGY	orgy	orgasm
ORITE	orite	all right, hello
ORKUT	orkut	Google's social network
ORLSX	orlsx	oral sex
ORLY	orly	oh, really
ORN	orn	oh, really now
ORPG	orpg	online role-playing game
ORZ	orz	frustration, despair
OS	os	operating system
OSBUTCTT	osbutctt	Only sad bastards use this crappy text talk.
OSD	osd	on screen display
OSIF	osif	Oh shit, I forgot.
OSIFGT	osifgt	Oh shit, I forgot.
OSINTOT	osintot	Oh shit, I never thought of that.
OSLT	oslt	or something like that
OSM	osm	awesome
OSPF	ospf	open shortest path first
OSSIM	ossim	awesome

155

UPPERCASE	LOWERCASE	MEANING
OST	ost	original sound track
OSY	osy	oh, screw you
OT	ot	off topic
OTA	ota	over the air
OTAY	otay	OK
OTB	otb	off the boat
OTB	otb	off to bed
OTC	otc	off the chain
OTC	otc	over-the-counter
OTD	otd	on the dot
OTD	otd	out the door
OTE	ote	over the edge
OTF	otf	off-topic forum
OTFCU	otfcu	on the floor cracking up
OTFL	otfl	on the floor laughing
OTFLMAO	otflmao	on the floor laughing my ass off
OTFLMFAO	otflmfao	on the floor laughing my fucking ass off
OTFLOL	otflol	on the floor laughing out loud
OTFP	otfp	on the fucking phone
OTFT	otft	over the fucking top
OTI	oti	on the Internet
OTK	otk	over the knee
OTL	otl	like orz stick figure on hands and knees
OTL	otl	out to lunch
OTLTA	otlta	one thing led to another
OTM	otm	of the moment
OTM	otm	one-track mind
OTOH	otoh	on the other hand
OTOOH	otooh	on the other hand
OTP	otp	on the phone
OTP	otp	one true pairing
OTR	otr	on the run
OTS	ots	on the side
OTS	ots	over the shoulder
OTT	ott	over the top
OTTH	otth	on the third hand
OTTOMH	ottomh	off the top of my head
OTW	otw	off to work
OTW	otw	on the way
OTW	otw	on the whole
OTY	oty	over to you
OTZ	otz	frustration, despair
OU	ou	open university
OUCH	ouch	interjection said when experiencing pain
OUGHTA	oughta	ought to
OUNCE	ounce	28 grams of drugs (usually marijuana)
OUTTA	outta	out of
OVA	ova	original video animation
OVA	ova	over
OVNO	ovno	or very near offer
OVO	ovo	obviously
OW	ow	oh, well
OW	ow	other woman
OW	ow	ouch

UPPERCASE	LOWERCASE	MEANING
OWAYS	oways	Oh wow, are you serious?
OWLING	owling	crouching and staring like an owl
OWN	own	beat, dominate (gaming)
OWNED	owned	dominated
OWNED	owned	made to look bad
OWNM	ownm	oh well, never mind
OWNT	ownt	made to look bad
OWNZ	ownz	owns
OWNZER	ownzer	one who makes others look bad
OWNZORZ	ownzorz	owned
OWT	owt	anything
OWT	owt	out
OWTTE	owtte	or words to that effect
OWW	oww	oops, wrong window
OX	ox	sharp blade
OXY	oxy	OxyContin (or oxycodone), painkiller
OY	oy	oh yeah
OYE	oye	listen up
OYFE	oyfe	open your fucking eyes
OYG	oyg	oh, your god
OYID	oyid	oh yes, I did
OYO	oyo	on your own
OYR	oyr	oh yeah, right
OZ	oz	Australia
OZ	oz	ounce
P	p	partner
P	p	penny, pence
P!ATD	p!atd	*Panic! at the Disco* (band)
P&C	p&c	point and click
P&L	p&l	peace and love
P&L	p&l	profit and loss
P&P	p&p	party and play
P&P	p&p	postage and packaging
P)	p)	pirate
P.O.B.	p.o.b.	parent over back
P.O.S	p.o.s	parent over shoulder
P/OED	p/oed	pissed off
P/U	p/u	pick up
P/W	p/w	password
P/X	p/x	part exchange
P@@N	p@@n	poon (female genitals)
P@@NANI	p@@nani	poonani (female genitalia)
P@@NANY	p@@nany	poonany (vagina)
P@@NTANG	p@@ntang	poontang (female genitalia)
P@W	p@w	parents are watching
P^S	p^s	parent over shoulder
P00P	p00p	poop
P0WN	p0wn	make to look bad
P2C2E	p2c2e	process too complicated to explain
P2P	p2p	parent to parent
P2P	p2p	pay to play
P2P	p2p	peer to peer
P33N	p33n	penis
P3N0R	p3n0r	penis

UPPERCASE	LOWERCASE	MEANING
P3N15	p3n15	penis
P3N1S	p3n1s	penis
P4P	p4p	pic for pic
P4P	p4p	pound for pound
P90X	p90x	type of workout schedule
P911	p911	parent alert/parent near
PA	pa	personal assistant
PAC	pac	gangsta rapper Tupac Shakur
PACH	pach	parents are coming home
PACHS	pachs	parents are coming home soon
PAD	pad	house, room
PAE	pae	pimping ain't easy
PAF	paf	phone a friend
PAG	pag	parents are gone
PAH	pah	parents at home
PAKI	paki	Paki (Pakistani person – ethnic slur/derogatory)
PAN	pan	personal area network
PAN@@CH	pan@@ch	panooch (femail genitalia)
PANSY	pansy	sissy, unmanly person
PANTS	pants	rubbish
PANTS	pants	trousers
PANTS	pants	underpants
PAPARAZZI	paparazzi	photojournalists
PAPER	paper	money
PAR	par	disrespect
PARA	para	paralytic, very drunk
PARNTS	parnts	parents
PARTY POOPER	party pooper	a person who ruins the mood with his/her attitude
PAS	pas	parent at side
PASII	pasii	put a sock in it
PAT	pat	patrol
PATCH	patch	correction applied to a computer program
PATD	patd	*Panic! at the Disco* (band)
PATT	patt	party all the time
PAW	paw	parents are watching
PAX	pax	peace
PAYCE	payce	peace
PAYE	paye	pay as you earn
PAYG	payg	pay as you go
PB	pb	peanut butter
PB	pb	personal best
PB&J	pb&j	peanut butter and jelly
PBB	pbb	parent behind back
PBCAKB	pbcakb	problem between chair and keyboard
PBIAB	pbiab	payback is a bitch
PBJ	pbj	peanut butter and jelly
PBKC	pbkc	problem between keyboard and chair
PBLY	pbly	probably
PBM	pbm	parent behind me
PBOOK	pbook	phonebook
PBP	pbp	please be patient
PBQ	pbq	please be quiet
PBR	pbr	Pabst Blue Ribbon (beer)

UPPERCASE	LOWERCASE	MEANING
PBS	pbs	Public Broadcasting Service
PBUH	pbuh	peace be upon him
PBWU	pbwu	peace be with you
PBWY	pbwy	peace be with you
PC	pc	Personal Computer
PC	pc	politically correct
PC 4 PC	pc 4 pc	picture comment for picture comment
PC4PC	pc4pc	picture comment for picture comment
PCB	pcb	please come back
PCB	pcb	printed circuit board
PCBD	pcbd	page cannot be displayed
PCD	pcd	Pussycat Dolls
PCE	pce	good-bye
PCE	pce	peace
PCENT	pcent	percent
PCI	pci	Peripheral Component Interconnect
PCI-X	pci-x	Peripheral Component Interconnect Extended
PCKR	pckr	pecker (penis)
PCKRHEAD	pckrhead	peckerhead (idiot)
PCM	pcm	please call me
PCO	pco	please come over
PCP	pcp	phencyclidine, angel dust
PCRS	pcrs	parents can read slang
PD	pd	public domain
PDA	pda	Personal Digital Assistant
PDA	pda	public display of affection
PDBAZ	pdbaz	please don't be a zombie
PDF	pdf	Portable Document Format
PDFS	pdfs	please don't fucking shout
PDG	pdg	pretty damn good
PDH	pdh	pretty darn happy
PDOA	pdoa	public display of affection
PDP	pdp	pretty darn precious
PDQ	pdq	pretty damn quick
PDS	pds	please don't shoot
PDS	pds	please don't stalk
PE	pe	physical education
PEACE	peace	good-bye
PEACE OUT	peace out	good-bye
PEAK	peak	humiliating
PEANUS	peanus	penis
PEAR	pear	pear shaped, wrong
PEAROAST	pearoast	repost
PEBCAC	pebcac	problem exists between chair and computer
PEBCAK	pebcak	problem exists between chair and keyboard
PEBKAC	pebkac	problem exists between keyboard and chair
PEBMAC	pebmac	problem exist between monitor and chair
PEEP DIS	peep dis	check out what I'm telling you
PEEPS	peeps	people
PEEPZ	peepz	people
PEER TO PEER	peer to peer	computer network without a central server
PEERS	peers	people in the same group, equals in age, background, etc.

UPPERCASE	LOWERCASE	MEANING
PEN	pen	penitentiary, jail, prison
PEN0R	pen0r	penis
PEN15	pen15	penis
PENDEJO	pendejo	idiot, fool
PENG	peng	good-looking person
PENG A LENG	peng a leng	really sexy, very fit
PENISFCKR	penisfckr	penisfucker (homosexual slur/derogatory)
PENISPFFR	penispffr	penispuffer (homosexual slur/derogatory)
PENOR	penor	penis
PEON	peon	low-ranking person
PEOPLES	peoples	people
PEPS	peps	people
PERF	perf	perfect
PERO	pero	but
PERV	perv	pervert
PERVING	perving	flirting in a creepy way
PERVY	pervy	perverted, creepy
PEWP	pewp	poop
PEWPEW	pewpew	laser sound
PEX	pex	Please explain?
PEZZAS	pezzas	parents
PF	pf	profile
PFA	pfa	please find attached
PFB	pfb	please find below
PFC	pfc	pretty fucking cold
PFC	pfc	private first class
PFF	pff	expression of disagreement
PFFT	pfft	expression of dismissal
PFH	pfh	pretty fucking hot
PFM	pfm	please forgive me
PFM	pfm	pretty fucking mad
PFO	pfo	please fuck off
PFOS	pfos	parental figure over shoulder
PFT	pft	an exclamation of disbelief
PFT	pft	pretty fucking tight
PFY	pfy	pimply faced youth
PG	pg	page
PG	pg	parental guidance
PG-13	pg-13	parental guidance if under 13 (movie rating)
PGDA	pgda	pretty goddamn awesome
PGP	pgp	pretty good privacy (encryption)
PH	ph	pantyhose
PH	ph	pussyhead
PH#	ph#	phone number
PH33R	ph33r	fear
PH34R	ph34r	fear
PHAG	phag	fag (homosexual - slur/derogatory)
PHAIL	phail	fail
PHAT	phat	pretty hot and tasty/pretty hot and tempting
PHAYL	phayl	fail
PHB	phb	pointy-haired boss (from *Dilbert*)
PHD	phd	doctor of philosophy
PHEAR	phear	fear
PHEW	phew	expression of relief

UPPERCASE	LOWERCASE	MEANING
PHISHING	phishing	scamming method used to get personal information
PHLR	phlr	peace, hugs, love, respect
PHM	phm	please help me
PHOAR	phoar	expression of lust, physical attraction
PHONY	phony	fake object or person
PHP	php	Hypertext Preprocessor
PHP	php	personal home page
PHQ	phq	fuck you
PHR33	phr33	free
PHREAK	phreak	freak
PHREAKER	phreaker	phone hacker
PHUCK	phuck	fuck
PHUCKER	phucker	fucker
PHUK	phuk	fuck
PHUN	phun	fun
PHUX	phux	fuck
PHUXOR	phuxor	fuck
PHWOAR	phwoar	acknowledgment that a person is fit, sexy, hot
PI	pi	ratio of circle's diameter to its circumference
PIC	pic	partner in crime
PIC	pic	picture
PICCIES	piccies	pictures
PICNIC	picnic	problem in chair, not in computer
PICS	pics	pictures
PIECE	piece	gun, weapon
PIECE	piece	pipe for smoking drugs
PIECE	piece	work of graffiti (masterpiece)
PIF	pif	marijuana
PIFF	piff	purple weed
PIG	pig	police officer
PIGS	pigs	the police
PIHB	pihb	pee in his/her butt
PIIHB	piihb	put it in her butt
PIITB	piitb	put it in the butt
PIM	pim	personal information manager
PIMA	pima	pain in my ass
PIMFA	pimfa	pain in my fucking ass
PIMHA	pimha	pain in my hairy ass
PIMP	pimp	peeing in my pants
PIMPL	pimpl	pissing in my pants laughing
PIN	pin	personal identification number
PINCHED	pinched	caught, arrested
PING	ping	send a packet to a computer and wait for its return (packet Internet groper)
PINK TOE	pink toe	white girl
PINO	pino	Filipino
PIP	pip	peeing in pants (laughing hard)
PIPS	pips	easy, not difficult
PIR	pir	parent in room
PIR	pir	parents in room
PIRLOS	pirlos	parent in room looking over shoulder
PISS	piss	put in some sugar
PISSED	pissed	angry
PISSED	pissed	drunk

UPPERCASE	LOWERCASE	MEANING
PISSED OFF	pissed off	mad, angry
PITA	pita	pain in the ass
PITCH	pitch	contribute money
PITFA	pitfa	pain in the fucking ass
PITME	pitme	peace in the Middle East
PITR	pitr	parent in the room
PITRTUL	pitrtul	parents in the room, text you later
PIW	piw	parent is watching
PIX	pix	pictures
PJ	pj	cheap alcoholic beverage
PJ	pj	poor/personal joke
PJ'S	pj's	pajamas, night wear
PK	pk	player kill (MMORPG)
PKB	pkb	pot, kettle, black
PKEMON	pkemon	Pokémon
PKER	pker	player killer
PKI	pki	public key infrastructure
PKING	pking	player killing
PKIT	pkit	please keep in touch
PKMN	pkmn	Pokémon
PKS	pks	painkillers
PL	pl	OK (typo)
PL	pl	parent looking
PL0X	pl0x	please
PL8	pl8	plate
PLA	pla	People's Liberation Army
PLAC	plac	parent looking at computer
PLAMS	plams	parents looking at my screen
PLANK	plank	idiot, stupid person
PLANKING	planking	lying facedown in an unusual place
PLARS	plars	party like a rock star
PLASTIC	plastic	credit card
PLATCS	platcs	parent looking at the computer screen
PLC	plc	public limited company
PLD	pld	played
PLE'S	ple's	please
PLEAZ	pleaz	please
PLEB	pleb	commoner, inferior person
PLEEZ	pleez	please
PLEEZE	pleeze	please
PLEZE	pleze	please
PLH	plh	peace, love, and happiness
PLI	pli	potential love interest
PLIES	plies	American rapper
PLIZ	pliz	please
PLL	pll	pretty little liar
PLLCK	pllck	pollock (Polish person - ethnic slur/derogatory)
PLMA	plma	please leave me alone
PLMK	plmk	please let me know
PLOCKS	plocks	please
PLOM	plom	parents looking over me
PLOMB	plomb	parents looking over my back
PLOMS	ploms	parent looking over my shoulder
PLONKER	plonker	idiot

UPPERCASE	LOWERCASE	MEANING
PLOS	plos	parents looking over shoulder
PLOX	plox	please
PLOXXORZ	ploxxorz	please
PLS	pls	please
PLSE	plse	please
PLU	plu	people like us
PLUMBUM	plumbum	plumber's crack
PLUR	plur	peace, love, unity, and respect
PLX	plx	please
PLYWM	plywm	play with me
PLZ	plz	please
PLZKTHX	plzkthx	Please? OK, thank you
PLZTHX	plzthx	Please? Thanks
PLZTLME	plztlme	please tell me
PM	pm	post meridiem (afternoon)
PM	pm	private message
PMA	pma	positive mental attitude
PMB	pmb	private message box
PMD	pmd	put me down
PMF	pmf	pardon my French
PMFI	pmfi	pardon me for interrupting
PMFJI	pmfji	pardon me for jumping in
PMFSL	pmfsl	piss my fucking self, laughing
PMG	pmg	oh my god
PMIGBOM	pmigbom	put mind in gear, before opening mouth!
PMITA	pmita	pound me in the ass
PMITAP	pmitap	pound me in the ass prison
PMJI	pmji	pardon for my jumping in
PMJI	pmji	pardon my jumping in
PML	pml	pissing myself laughing
PMO	pmo	pissing me off
PMP	pmp	peeing/pissing my pants
PMPL	pmpl	piss my pants laughing
PMSFL	pmsfl	pissed myself fucking laughing
PMSL	pmsl	pee/piss myself laughing
PMSL	pmsl	pissed myself laughing
PMT	pmt	premenstrual tension
PMU	pmu	power management unit
PNBF	pnbf	potential new boyfriend
PNG	png	Portable Network Graphic (image file format)
PNHLGD	pnhlgd	parents not home, let's get dirty
P-NIS	p-nis	penis
PNISBNGR	pnisbngr	penisbanger (homosexual - slur/derogatory)
PNL	pnl	peace and love
PNP	pnp	party and play
PNR	pnr	passenger name record
PNS	pns	penis
PNTA	pnta	punta (female dog)
PNUS	pnus	penis
PNW	pnw	Pacific Northwest
PO	po	piss off
PO PO	po po	police
PO'D	po'd	pissed off
POA	poa	plan of action

UPPERCASE	LOWERCASE	MEANING
POAHF	poahf	put on a happy face
POB	pob	parent over back
POC	poc	piece of crap
POCKET DIAL	pocket dial	accidentally make a call with the phone in your pocket
POCKO	pocko	pocket
POD	pod	passed out drunk
POED	poed	pissed off
POETS	poets	piss off early, tomorrow's Saturday
POF	pof	plenty of fish (dating site)
POI	poi	point(s) of interest
POIDH	poidh	pics or it didn't happen
POKER FACE	poker face	expressionless face
POKEY	pokey	prison
POL	pol	parent overlooking
POLE	pole	A Polish person (ethnic slur/derogatory)
POLY	poly	polyamory, loving more than one person at a time
POMG	pomg	oh my god (variation)
POMS	poms	parent over my shoulder
PON	pon	(same as "PWN")
PONED	poned	powerfully owned, dominated
PONR	ponr	point of no return
POO	poo	poop
POOL SHARK	pool shark	good pool player
POONTANG	poontang	female genitalia
POOTER	pooter	computer
POP	pop	popular (music)
POP A SQUAT	pop a squat	sit down
POP3	pop3	Post Office Protocol v3 (for e-mail)
POPO	popo	police officer(s)
POPPER	popper	amyl nitrate
POPPERS	poppers	amyl nitrate (recreational drug)
POPPIN	poppin	going on, happening
POPPING	popping	dance style
POPS	pops	father
POQ	poq	piss off quick
PORCH MONKEY	porch monkey	person who sits on their porch, lazy person
POS	pos	parent over shoulder
POSC	posc	piece-of-shit computer
POSCS	poscs	parents over shoulder, change subject
POSE	pose	suppose
POSMBRI	posmbri	parent over shoulder, might be reading it
POSS	poss	possibly
POST	post	hang out
POT	pot	marijuana
POT HEAD	pot head	person who smokes weed
POTC	potc	*Pirates of the Caribbean*
POTO	poto	*Phantom of the Opera*
POTS	pots	parents over the shoulder (parents watching, I can't really talk)
POTS	pots	plain old telephone service
POTUS	potus	president of the United States
POTW	potw	patient of the week (*House*)
POV	pov	point of view

UPPERCASE	LOWERCASE	MEANING
POV	pov	privately owned vehicle
POW	pow	prisoner of war
POWN	pown	(same as "PWN")
POZ	poz	HIV positive
PP	pp	pee pee
PPB	ppb	parts per billion
PPC	ppc	Pay Per Click
PPGA	ppga	Plastic Pin Grid Array
PPI	ppi	Pixels Per Inch
PPL	ppl	pay per lead
PPL	ppl	people
PPLE	pple	people
PPLS	ppls	people
PPLZ	pplz	people
PPM	ppm	Pages Per Minute
PPOR	ppor	post proof or recant
PPP	ppp	Point to Point Protocol
PPPoE	pppoe	Point-to-Point Protocol over Ethernet
PPPPPPP	ppppppp	prior proper planning prevents piss-poor performance
PPPW	pppw	per person, per week
PPS	pps	post-postscript
PPT	ppt	Microsoft Powerpoint
PPTP	pptp	Point-to-Point Tunneling Protocol
PPU	ppu	pending pick-up
PPU	ppu	please pick up
PPV	ppv	pay-per-view
PR	pr	public relations
PR0	pr0	professional
PR0N	pr0n	porn
PR0NZ	pr0nz	porn
PRAM	pram	Parameter Random Access Memory
PRANG	prang	scared
PRATT	pratt	stupid person
PRAWN	prawn	girl who is good-looking except for her face
PRBLM	prblm	problem
PRCK	prck	prick (penis)
PRD	prd	period
PREE	pree	watch, stare at
PREGGERS	preggers	pregnant
PREGGO	preggo	pregnant
PREGO	prego	pregnant
PREP	prep	prepare
PRESH	presh	awesome, cool
PRESH	presh	precious
PRFCT	prfct	perfect
PRI	pri	pretty
PRIT	prit	ugly
PRN	prn	porn
PRNCPL	prncpl	principal
PRNCSS	prncss	princess
PRNOSCRN	prnoscrn	porn on screen
PRO	pro	professional
PRO BONO	pro bono	for (public) good (Latin)
PROB	prob	probably

UPPERCASE	LOWERCASE	MEANING
PROB	prob	problem
PROBLY	probly	probably
PROBS	probs	probably
PROBZ	probz	probably
PROC	proc	Programmed Random Occurrence
PROD	prod	product
PROD	prod	protestant
PROG	prog	program
PROG	prog	progressive rock music
PROGGY	proggy	computer program
PROJECT	project	same as hood
PROLLY	prolly	probably
PROLLZ	prollz	probably
PROM	prom	Programmable Read-Only Memory
PRON	pron	porn
PROPS	props	Proper Respect and Acknowledgment
PROPS	props	respect, recognition
PROXIE	proxie	proxy
PROXY	proxy	agent, middleman
PRP	prp	please reply
PRSN	prsn	person
PRT	prt	party
PRT	prt	please retweet (Twitter slang)
PRTY	prty	party
PRV	prv	private
PRVRT	prvrt	pervert
PRW	prw	parents are watching
PRY	pry	probably
PS	ps	Photoshop
PS	ps	PlayStation
PS	ps	postscript
PS & QS	ps & qs	pints and quarts
PS & QS	ps & qs	please and thank you
PS/2	ps/2	computer port for keyboard or mouse
PS/2	ps/2	Personal System/2
PS1	ps1	PlayStation 1
PS2	ps2	PlayStation 2
PS3	ps3	PlayStation 3
PSA	psa	public service announcement
PSBMS	psbms	parent standing by my side
PSD	psd	Photoshop data file
PSH	psh	dismissive expression
PSHAW	pshaw	expression of disbelief, skepticism
PSI	psi	pounds per square inch (pressure)
PSM	psm	personal short message
PSN	psn	PlayStation network
PSOS	psos	parent standing over shoulder
PSP	psp	PlayStation portable
PSSY	pssy	pussy
PST	pst	Pacific Standard Time
PST	pst	please send tell
PSTN	pstn	public switched telephone network
PSU	psu	power supply unit
PSYCHED	psyched	excited, pumped up

UPPERCASE	LOWERCASE	MEANING
PT	pt	phantasy tour
PT	pt	physical training
PT33N	pt33n	preteen
PTB	ptb	pass the buck
PTB	ptb	please text back
PTB	ptb	powers that be
PTBB	ptbb	pass the barf bag
PTDR	ptdr	*pete de rire* (French for "LOL")
PTFO	ptfo	passed the fuck out
PTHC	pthc	preteen hardcore
PTI	pti	Pardon the interruption.
PTIYPASI	ptiypasi	put that in your pipe and smoke it
PTL	ptl	praise the Lord
PTMM	ptmm	Please tell me more.
PTO	pto	paid/personal time off
PTP	ptp	pay to play
PTP	ptp	peer to peer
PTSD	ptsd	posttraumatic stress disorder
PTW	ptw	play to win
PTW	ptw	professional time waster
PU	pu	That stinks!
PUA	pua	pickup artist
PUFF	puff	marijuana
PUG	pug	pickup group
PUH-LEAZE	puh-leaze	please
PUKKA	pukka	genuine, top quality
PUKS	puks	pick up kids
PULL	pull	make out with
PUM	pum	Potentially Unwanted Modification
PUMA	puma	woman who dates younger men
PUMPED	pumped	exhilarated, fired up
PUNK	punk	music genre
PUP	pup	Potentially Unwanted Program
PURDY	purdy	pretty
PURPLE	purple	strong marijuana
PURTY	purty	pretty
PUSH	push	sell (drugs)
PUTER	puter	computer
PV	pv	promotional video
PVE	pve	player versus environment (MMORPG)
PVM	pvm	player versus monster
PVP	pvp	player versus player
PVSP	pvsp	player versus player
PVT	pvt	pervert
PVT	pvt	private
PW	pw	parent watching
PWB	pwb	pussy-whipped bitch
PWCB	pwcb	parents watching close by
PWD	pwd	password
PWEASE	pwease	babyish form of please
PWN	pwn	made to look bad
PWN	pwn	own, dominate
PWN3D	pwn3d	owned
PWN3R	pwn3r	owner

UPPERCASE	LOWERCASE	MEANING
PWNAGE	pwnage	own age
PWND	pwnd	owned
PWNED	pwned	made to look bad
PWNED	pwned	owned, dominated
PWNED	pwned	perfectly owned
PWNER	pwner	owner
PWNT	pwnt	owned
PWNZ	pwnz	owns
PWNZOR	pwnzor	owner
PWOB	pwob	parent watching over back
PWOMS	pwoms	parent watching over my shoulder
PWOR	pwor	power
PWOR	pwor	proceeding with orders received
PWOS	pwos	parent was over shoulder
PWP	pwp	Plot? What plot?
PWT	pwt	poor white trash
PWW	pww	parents were watching
PXR	pxr	punk rocker
PXT	pxt	please explain that
PYDIM	pydim	put your dick in me
PYFCO	pyfco	put your freaking clothes on
PYP	pyp	play your position
PYT	pyt	pretty young thing
PZ	pz	peace
PZA	pza	pizza
PZLED	pzled	puzzled
Q	q	queue
Q	q	thank you
Q&A	q&a	question and answer
Q1	q1	first quarter
Q1	q1	*Quake 1* (game)
Q33R	q33r	queer (homosexual - slur/derogatory)
Q4U	q4u	question for you
Q8	q8	Kuwait
QA	qa	quality assurance
QA	qa	question and answer
QANTAS	qantas	Queensland and Northern Territory Aerial Service
QBE	qbe	Query By Example
QC	qc	quality control
QED	qed	I've made my point
QED	qed	*quod erat demonstrandum* (it has been proven)
QFE	qfe	question for everyone
QFE	qfe	quoted for emphasis
QFI	qfi	quoted for idiocy
QFI	qfi	quoted for irony
QFL	qfl	quit fucking laughing
QFMFT	qfmft	quoted for motherfucking truth
QFP	qfp	quoted for posterity
QFT	qft	quit fucking talking
QFT	qft	quoted for truth
QFT&GJ	qft&gj	quoted for truth and great justice
QIK	qik	quick
QK	qk	ninja
QL	ql	cool

UPPERCASE	LOWERCASE	MEANING
QL	ql	quit laughing
QLD	qld	Queensland
QLTM	qltm	quietly laughing to myself
QNA	qna	question and answer
QOOL	qool	cool
QOS	qos	*Quantum of Solace*
QOTD	qotd	quote of the day
QOTSA	qotsa	*Queens of the Stone Age* (band)
QOTY	qoty	quote of the year
QP	qp	quarter pound (of weed)
QPR	qpr	quite pathetic really
QPWD	qpwd	quit posting while drunk
QQ	qq	crying
QQ	qq	quick question
QQ	qq	quit
QQ	qq	tits
QQ (qq)	qq (qq)	crying eyes
QQ4U	qq4u	quick question for you
QR	qr	queer (homosexual · slur/derogatory)
QSL	qsl	confirmed
QSL	qsl	reply
QSO	qso	conversation
QT	qt	cutie
QT3.14	qt3.14	cutie pie
QTE	qte	cutie
QTPI	qtpi	cutie pie
QTY	qty	quantity
QUACK	quack	doctor
QUE	que	What?
QWERTYUIOP	qwertyuiop	bored
R	r	are
R&B	r&b	rhythm and blues
R&D	r&d	replicate and duplicate
R&D	r&d	research and development
R&R	r&r	rest and relaxation
R0X0RZ	r0x0rz	rocks
R5	r5	region 5 (DVD region)
R8	r8	rate
R8P	r8p	rape
R8PIST	r8pist	rapist
R8T	r8t	rate
RA	ra	resident advisor
RA2	ra2	*Red Alert 2* (game)
RA3	ra3	*Red Alert 3* (game)
RAC	rac	Rock Against Communism
RACHET	rachet	crazy, nasty
RAD	rad	radical, cool
RADAR	radar	radio detection and ranging
RAFL	rafl	(same as "ROFL")
RAGE	rage	party very hard, get wasted
RAGO	rago	whatever, OK
RAH	rah	pompous or superior person
RAID	raid	Redundant Array of Independent Disks
RAILS	rails	lines of cocaine

UPPERCASE	LOWERCASE	MEANING
RAK	rak	random act of kindness
RAM	ram	random-access memory
RANDOM	random	unexpected, unpredictable
RANGA	ranga	redhead (derogatory)
RANK	rank	disgusting, gross
RAOFLMAO	raoflmao	rolling around on floor laughing my ass off
RAP	rap	music genre
RAPID	rapid	cool, excellent
RAPPER	rapper	urban poet
RAR	rar	file compression type
RAS	ras	remote access server
RAT	rat	snitch, tattletale
RATM	ratm	*Rage Against the Machine* (band)
RAWK	rawk	rock
RAWKS	rawks	rocks
RAWR	rawr	right answer, wrong reason
RAWR	rawr	roar
RAZZ	razz	get drunk
RAZZ	razz	make fun of
RB@U	rb@u	right back at you
RBAU	rbau	right back at you
RBAY	rbay	right back at you
RBG	rbg	revolutionary but gangsta
RBM	rbm	right behind me
RC	rc	radio controlled
RC	rc	random chat
RCH	rch	a very small unit of measurement
RCI	rci	rectal-cranial inversion
RCKS	rcks	rocks
RCON	rcon	remote console
RCSA	rcsa	right click, save as
RCT	rct	roller-coaster tycoon
RCVD	rcvd	received
RD	rd	real deal
RDF	rdf	Resource Description Framework
RDJ	rdj	Robert Downey Jr.
RDM	rdm	random death match
RDR	rdr	*Red Dead Redemption* (game)
RDRAM	rdram	rambus dynamic random- access memory
RDRR	rdrr	har-de-har-har
RDY	rdy	ready
RE	re	regarding
RE	re	reply
RE/REHI	re/rehi	hello again
REDBONE	redbone	light-skinned colored person (ethnic slur/derogatory)
REDNECK	redneck	unsophisticated rural person from southeast USA
REEFA	reefa	(same as "reefer")
REEFER	reefer	marijuana
REF	ref	refugee
REFL	refl	rolling on the floor laughing
RE-GIFT	re-gift	pass an unwanted gift on to someone else
REGS	regs	low-quality marijuana
REGS	regs	regular
REHI	rehi	hello again

UPPERCASE	LOWERCASE	MEANING
REL	rel	relative
RELE	rele	really
RELLIES	rellies	relatives
REM	rem	rapid eye movement
REM	rem	rock band
RENTS	rents	parents
RENTZ	rentz	parents
REP	rep	repetition
REP	rep	represent
REP	rep	reputation
REP	rep	to represent
REPPIN	reppin	representing
RESH	resh	depressing
RESTECPA	restecpa	respect (Ali G)
RETRO	retro	old-fashioned style
REV	rev	make an engine go faster
REV	rev	reverend
REZ	rez	Indian reservation
RFA	rfa	real fucking asshole
RFC	rfc	request for comment
RFF	rff	really fucking funny
RFI	rfi	request for information
RFID	rfid	Radio-Frequency Identification
RFLMAO	rflmao	rolling on the floor laughing my ass off
RFN	rfn	right fucking now
RFP	rfp	request for proposal
RFR	rfr	real fucking rich
RFS	rfs	real fucking soon
RFT	rft	right first time
RFYL	rfyl	run for your life
RGB	rgb	red green blue
RGDS	rgds	regards
RGR	rgr	roger
RH	rh	road head
RHCP	rhcp	*Red Hot Chili Peppers* (band)
RHGIR	rhgir	really hot guy in room
RHINO	rhino	older man looking for a younger woman
RHIP	rhip	rank has its privileges
RHS	rhs	right-hand side
RIB	rib	make fun of
RICE	rice	race-inspired cosmetic enhancements
RICE	rice	an Asian person (ethnic slur/derogatory)
RICK ROLL	rick roll	trick someone with a link to Rick Astley video
RICL	ricl	rolling in chair laughing
RIF	rif	reduction in force
RIFK	rifk	rolling on the floor laughing
RIFRAF	rifraf	common people, trailer trash
RIHAD	rihad	rot in hell and die
RINGTONE	ringtone	sound a cell phone makes when receiving a call
RINO	rino	Republican in name only
RIP	rip	convert music on CD to MP3s
RIP	rip	rest in peace
RIPPED	ripped	stoned
RIPPED	ripped	well-defined muscles

171

UPPERCASE	LOWERCASE	MEANING
RISC	risc	Reduced Instruction Set Computing
RITE	rite	right
RITE	rite	write
RITJIVE	ritjive	nonvirgin
RJCT	rjct	reject
RKBA	rkba	right to keep and bear arms
RL	rl	real life
RLBF	rlbf	real-life boyfriend
RLF	rlf	real-life friend
RLG	rlg	really loud giggle
RLGF	rlgf	real-life girlfriend
RLLY	rlly	really
RLN	rln	real-life name
RLY	rly	really
RLZ	rlz	rules
RLZE	rlze	realize
RM	rm	room
RMA	rma	return merchandise authorization
RME	rme	rolling my eyes
RMJB	rmjb	rimjob (dirty sexual act)
RMLB	rmlb	read my lips, baby
RMMM	rmmm	read my mail, man
RMR	rmr	remember
RMSO	rmso	rock my socks off
RMT	rmt	real-money trading
RMV	rmv	results may vary
RN	rn	registered nurse
RN	rn	right now
RNA	rna	ribonucleic acid
RNB	rnb	renob (erection)
RNB	rnb	rhythm and blues
RNG	rng	random number generator
RNR	rnr	rock and roll
RNT	rnt	aren't
RO	ro	*Ragnarok Online* (MMORPG)
RO	ro	rock out
ROACH	roach	the end of a joint
ROAR	roar	right of admission reserved
ROCKBAND	rockband	music video game
ROCKIN	rockin	awesome
ROCKR	rockr	rocker
ROCKS	rocks	crack cocaine
RODGER	rodger	affirmative
ROE	roe	rules of engagement
ROF	rof	rate of fire
ROFALOL	rofalol	roll on the floor and laugh out loud
ROFC	rofc	rolling on floor crying
ROFFLE	roffle	rolling on the floor laughing
ROFFLE OUT LOUD	roffle out loud	rolling on the floor laughing out loud
ROFFLECAKE	rofflecake	rolling on the floor laughing
ROFFLECOPTERS	rofflecopters	rolling on the floor with laughter
ROFFLEOL	roffleol	rolling on the floor laughing out loud
ROFFLES	roffles	rolling on floor laughing

UPPERCASE	LOWERCASE	MEANING
ROFFLMFAO	rofflmfao	rolling on the floor laughing my fucking ass off
ROFL	rofl	rolling on floor laughing
ROFL&PMP	rofl&pmp	rolling on floor laughing and peeing my pants
ROFLAO	roflao	rolling on the floor laughing my ass off
ROFLASTC	roflastc	rolling on floor laughing and scaring the cat
ROFLCOPTER	roflcopter	rolling on floor laughing and spinning around
ROFLKMD	roflkmd	rolling on the floor laughing kicking my dog
ROFLLH	rofllh	rolling on the floor laughing like hell
ROFLMAO	roflmao	rolling on the floor laughing my ass off
ROFLMAOAPIMP	roflmaoapimp	rolling on the floor laughing my ass off and peeing in my pants
ROFLMAOOL	roflmaool	rolling on the floor laughing my ass off out loud
ROFLMAOPMP	roflmaopmp	rolling on the floor, laughing my ass off, pissing my pants
ROFLMAOUTS	roflmaouts	rolling on floor laughing my fucking ass off, unable to speak
ROFLMAOWPIMP	roflmaowpimp	rolling on floor laughing my ass off while peeing in my pants
ROFLMBFAO	roflmbfao	rolling on the floor laughing my big fat ass off
ROFLMBO	roflmbo	rolling on floor laughing my butt off
ROFLMFAO	roflmfao	rolling on the floor laughing my fucking ass off
ROFLMFAOPIMP	roflmfaopimp	rolling on the floor laughing my fucking ass off, pissing in my pants
ROFLMFAOPMP	roflmfaopmp	rolling on the floor laughing my fucking ass off, peeing my pants
ROFLMGAO	roflmgao	rolling on the floor laughing my gay ass off
ROFLMGDAO	roflmgdao	rolling on the floor laughing my goddamn ass off
ROFLMGDMFAO	roflmgdmfao	rolling on floor laughing my goddamn motherfucking ass off
ROFLMGO	roflmgo	rolling on floor laughing my guts out
ROFLMHO	roflmho	rolling on the floor laughing my head off
ROFLMIAHA	roflmiaha	rolling on the floor laughing myself into a heart attack
ROFLMMFAO	roflmmfao	rolling on the floor laughing my motherfucking ass off
ROFLOL	roflol	rolling on floor, laughing out loud
ROFLOLBAG	roflolbag	rolling on the floor laughing out loud, busting a gut
ROFLPIMP	roflpimp	rolling on the floor laughing, pissing in my pants
ROFLPMP	roflpmp	rolling on the floor laughing, peeing my pants
ROFLWTIME	roflwtime	rolling on the floor laughing with tears in my eyes
ROFPML	rofpml	rolling on the floor pissing myself laughing
ROFTL	roftl	misspelling of "ROTFL"
ROFWL	rofwl	rolling on the floor while laughing
ROG	rog	really old git
ROGER	roger	affirmative
ROGER THAT	roger that	I understand, OK
ROGL	rogl	rolling on ground laughing
ROGLMFAO	roglmfao	rolling on ground laughing my fucking ass off
ROH	roh	Ring of Honor (wrestling)
ROI	roi	return on investment
ROIDS	roids	steroids
ROJ	roj	affirmative
ROL	rol	rolling over laughing
ROLF	rolf	rolling on laughing floor
ROLL	roll	experience the effects of ecstasy
ROLLED	rolled	robbed, beaten

UPPERCASE	LOWERCASE	MEANING
ROLLIN	rollin	high on drugs
ROLMAO	rolmao	rolling over laughing my ass off
ROLMFAO	rolmfao	rolling over laughing my fucking ass off
ROM	rom	read-only memory
ROM COM	rom com	romantic comedy
ROMBL	rombl	rolled off my bed laughing
RONG	rong	wrong
ROOFLES	roofles	rolling on the floor laughing
ROOTS	roots	type of reggae music
ROR	ror	raughing out roud
ROSES	roses	money
ROTC	rotc	Reserve Officers' Training Corps
ROTF	rotf	rolling on the floor (laughing is implied)
ROTFALOL	rotfalol	roll on the floor and laugh out loud
ROTFFL	rotffl	roll on the fucking floor laughing
ROTFFLMAO	rotfflmao	rolling on the fucking floor laughing my ass off
ROTFFLMFAO	rotfflmfao	rolling on the fucking floor laughing my fucking ass off
ROTFFNAR	rotffnar	rolling on the floor for no apparent reason
ROTFL	rotfl	rolling on the floor laughing
ROTFLAVIAB	rotflaviab	rolling on the floor laughing and vomiting in a bucket
ROTFLMAO	rotflmao	rolling on the floor laughing my ass off
ROTFLMAOOL	rotflmaool	rolling on the floor laughing my ass off out loud
ROTFLMAOSTC	rotflmaostc	rolling on the floor laughing my ass off, scaring the cat
ROTFLMBO	rotflmbo	rolling on the floor laughing my butt off
ROTFLMFAO	rotflmfao	rolling on the floor laughing my fucking ass off
ROTFLMFAOPIMP	rotflmfaopimp	rolling on the floor laughing my fucking ass off, peeing in my pants
ROTFLMFAOPMP	rotflmfaopmp	rolling on the floor laughing my ass off, pissing my pants
ROTFLMFHO	rotflmfho	rolling on the floor laughing my fucking head off
ROTFLMHO	rotflmho	rolling on the floor laughing my head off
ROTFLMMFAO	rotflmmfao	rolling on the floor laughing my motherfucking ass off
ROTFLOL	rotflol	rolling on the floor laughing out loud
ROTFLUTS	rotfluts	rolling on the floor laughing unable to speak
ROTFPM	rotfpm	rolling on the floor pissing myself
ROTFWLMAO	rotfwlmao	rolling on the floor while laughing my ass off
ROTG	rotg	rolling on the ground
ROTGL	rotgl	roll/rolling on the ground laughing
ROTGLMAO	rotglmao	rolling on the ground laughing my ass off
ROTGLMFAO	rotglmfao	rolling on the ground laughing my fucking ass off
ROTK	rotk	*Return of the King* (Tolkien)
ROTM	rotm	run-of-the-mill
ROTW	rotw	rest of the world
ROW	row	rest of the world
ROWYCO	rowyco	rock out with your cock out
ROX	rox	rocks
ROXOR	roxor	rocks, awesome
ROXORZ	roxorz	rocks
ROXXOR	roxxor	rock
ROY	roy	Relative of yours?
ROZZERS	rozzers	police
RP	rp	role-play

UPPERCASE	LOWERCASE	MEANING
RPC	rpc	remote procedure call
RPC	rpc	role-playing chat
RPF	rpf	real-person fiction
RPG	rpg	rocket-propelled grenade
RPG	rpg	role-playing game
RPITA	rpita	royal pain in the ass
RPLBK	rplbk	reply back
RPM	rpm	revenue per 1,000 impressions
RPM	rpm	revolutions per minute
RPO	rpo	royally pissed off
RQ	rq	random questions (live journal community)
RQ	rq	real quick
RR	rr	restroom
RRB	rrb	restroom break
RRD	rrd	rickrolled
RRP	rrp	recommended retail price
RS	rs	*RuneScape* (MMORPG)
RSI	rsi	repetitive strain injury
RSKI	rski	Ruski (Russian - ethnic slur/derogatory)
RSN	rsn	real soon now
RSPCT	rspct	respect
RSPS	rsps	RuneScape Private Server
RSRSRS	rsrsrs	(same as "LOL")
RSS	rss	RDF Site Summary
RSS	rss	really simple syndication
RSS	rss	rich site summary
RSVP	rsvp	*répondez s'il vous plaît* (French for "please reply")
RT	rt	real-time
RT	rt	retweet
RT	rt	roger that
RTA	rta	read the article
RTARD	rtard	retard (disability slur/derogatory)
R-TARD	r-tard	retard (disability slur/derogatory)
RTBQ	rtbq	read the blinking question
RTBS	rtbs	reason to be single
RTD	rtd	ready to drink
RTE	rte	national broadcaster in Ireland
RTE	rte	runtime environment
RTF	rtf	return the favor
RTF	rtf	Rich Text Format
RTFA	rtfa	read the fucking article
RTFAQ	rtfaq	read the FAQ
RTFB	rtfb	read the fucking book
RTFF	rtff	read the fucking FAQ
RTFFP	rtffp	read the fucking front page
RTFI	rtfi	read the flipping instructions
RTFM	rtfm	read the fucking manual
RTFMFM	rtfmfm	read the fucking manual, fucking moron
RTFMM	rtfmm	read the fucking manual, moron
RTFN	rtfn	read the fucking newspaper
RTFP	rtfp	read the fucking post
RTFQ	rtfq	read the fucking question
RTFR	rtfr	read the fucking report
RTFS	rtfs	read the fucking summary

UPPERCASE	LOWERCASE	MEANING
RTFU	rtfu	ready the fuck up
RTG	rtg	ready to go
RTHX	rthx	thank you for the retweet
RTL	rtl	report the loss
RTM	rtm	read the manual
RTMS	rtms	read the manual, stupid
RTNTN	rtntn	retention
RTO	rto	radio telephone operator
RTR	rtr	read the rules
RTR	rtr	Roll Tide Roll
RTRCTV	rtrctv	retroactive
RTRMT	rtrmt	retirement
RTRY	rtry	retry
RTS	rts	real-time strategy
RTSM	rtsm	read the stupid manual
RTV	rtv	rock the vote
RTW	rtw	'round the world
RTW	rtw	ready to wear
RTWFB	rtwfb	read the whole fucking book
RTWFQ	rtwfq	read the whole fucking question
RU	ru	Are you?
RUA	rua	Are you alone?
RUABOG	ruabog	Are you a boy or girl?
RUAGOAB	ruagoab	Are you a girl or a boy?
RUBZ2NT	rubz2nt	Are you busy tonight?
RUDEBOY	rudeboy	gangster
RUFKM	rufkm	Are you fucking kidding me?
RUFS	rufs	Are you fucking serious?
RUGAY	rugay	Are you gay?
RUGTA	rugta	Are you going to answer?
RUH	ruh	Are your horny?
RUH ROH	ruh roh	uh-oh, Scooby Doo-style
RUK	ruk	Are you OK?
RUKM	rukm	Are you kidding me?
RUMBLE	rumble	brawl, fight
RUMF	rumf	Are you male or female?
RUO	ruo	weak (Chinese)
RUOK	ruok	Are you OK?
RUP	rup	rational unified process
RUR	rur	Are you ready?
RUS	rus	Are you serious?
RUT	rut	Are you there?
RUWM	ruwm	Are you watching me?
RV	rv	recreational vehicle
RVB	rvb	*Red versus Blue* (popular Web-series)
RVR	rvr	*Realm Versus Realm* (MMORPG)
RW	rw	real world
RWB	rwb	rich white bitch
RWL	rwl	roaring with laughter
RWNJ	rwnj	right-wing nut job
RWYS	rwys	reap what you sow
RX	rx	drugs or prescriptions
RX	rx	prescription
RX	rx	regards

UPPERCASE	LOWERCASE	MEANING
RYAF	ryaf	Are you a freak?
RYB	ryb	read your bible
RYC	ryc	Are you crazy?
RYC	ryc	regarding your comment
RYD	ryd	Are you divorced?
RYFC	ryfc	Are you fucking crazy?
RYG	ryg	Are you gay?
RYHN	ryhn	Are you happy now?
RYN	ryn	read your note
RYN	ryn	regarding your note
RYO	ryo	roll your own
RYS	rys	Are you single?
RYS	rys	Are you straight?
RYS	rys	read your screen
RYSS	ryss	Are you seeing someone?
RYT	ryt	Are you taken?
RYT	ryt	right, all right
RYTE	ryte	right
RYUA	ryua	Are you underage?
S&D	s&d	search and destroy
S&M	s&m	sadism and masochism
S&P	s&p	salt and pepper
S/	s/	substitute first word with second
S/B	s/b	should be
S/N	s/n	serial number
S/O	s/o	shout out
S/O	s/o	significant other
S/T	s/t	self-titled
S^	s^	What's up?
S'OK	s'ok	it's OK
S'UP	s'up	What is up?
S2	s2	love (heart shape)
S2A	s2a	sent to all
S2BU	s2bu	sucks to be you
S2G	s2g	swear to God
S2R	s2r	send to receive
S2S	s2s	safe to say
S2S	s2s	sorry to say
S2U	s2u	same to you
S2US	s2us	speak to you soon
S3X	s3x	sex
S4B	s4b	shit for brains
S4L	s4l	spam for life
S4S	s4s	support for support (Myspace)
S4SE	s4se	sight for sore eyes
S8TER	s8ter	skater
SA	sa	sibling alert
SaaS	saas	Software as a Service
SAB	sab	slap a bitch
SAB	sab	smoking a blunt
SAD	sad	pathetic
SAD	sad	seasonal affective disorder
SADAD	sadad	suck a dick and die
SAF	saf	single Asian female

UPPERCASE	LOWERCASE	MEANING
SAFE	safe	something or someone good
SAFM	safm	stay away from me
SAG	sag	wear trousers low around the waist
SAGE	sage	word added to a post to stop it getting bumped
SAGN	sagn	spelling and grammar Nazi
SAH	sah	sexy as hell
SAHM	sahm	stay-at-home mom
SAIA	saia	stupid ass in action
SAL	sal	such a laugh
SALA	sala	idiot, moron
SALAM	salam	peace (Arabic)
SALTS	salts	smiled a little then stopped
SALTY	salty	upset, annoyed, embarrassed
SALUT	salut	hi
SAM	sam	stop annoying me
SAMEFAG	samefag	person with multiple aliases on forums
SAN	san	storage area network
SAND NGGR	sand nggr	sand nigger (Middle Eastern person - ethnic slur/derogatory)
SANDNGGR	sandnggr	sandnigger (Middle Eastern person - ethnic slur/derogatory)
SANGA	sanga	sandwich
SANK	sank	something
SANS	sans	without (French)
SAP	sap	fool
SAP	sap	sad and pathetic
SARCY	sarcy	sarcastic
SARGE	sarge	chat up
SAS	sas	Special Air Service
SASE	sase	self-addressed stamped envelope
SAT	sat	Scholastic Assessment Test
SAT	sat	sorry about that
SATA	sata	serial advanced technology attachment
SATC	satc	*Sex and the City* (TV show)
SATS	sats	Standard Attainment Tests
SAUCE	sauce	misspelling of "source"
SAUCED	sauced	drunk
SAVAGE	savage	brutal but awesome
SAVVY	savvy	knowledgeable, well informed
SAYONARA	sayonara	good-bye (Japanese)
SB	sb	should be
SB	sb	smiling back
SB	sb	somebody
SBA	sba	stop bullshitting around
SBC	sbc	sorry 'bout caps
SBCG4AP	sbcg4ap	*Strong Bad's Cool Game for Attractive People* (game)
SBD	sbd	silent but deadly
SBF	sbf	single black female
SBFMA	sbfma	suck butter from my ass
SBI	sbi	surrounded by incompetence
SBIA	sbia	standing back in amazement
SBLAI	sblai	stop babbling like an idiot
SBM	sbm	single black male
SBRD	sbrd	so bored

UPPERCASE	LOWERCASE	MEANING
SBS	sbs	step by step
SBS	sbs	such bullshit
SBT	sbt	sorry 'bout that
SC	sc	silent chuckle
SC	sc	*StarCraft* (game)
SC	sc	stay cool
SC	sc	USC; University of Southern California
SCAM	scam	make out
SCAM	scam	rip off
SCART	scart	audio/video TV connector
SCH	sch	school
SCHEMIE	schemie	someone from a council estate
SCHWAG	schwag	low-grade marijuana
SCNR	scnr	sorry, could not resist/sorry, I couldn't resist
SCO	sco	San Francisco
SCOFF	scoff	eat fast
SCOFF	scoff	sneer
SCOOL	scool	school
SCOTUS	scotus	Supreme Court of the United States
SCOUSE	scouse	relating to Liverpool
SCOUSER	scouser	person from Liverpool
SCRAM	scram	go away
SCRAP	scrap	fight
SCREB	screb	dirty, scruffy person
SCRILLA	scrilla	money, cash
SCRIM	scrim	practice game
SCRT	scrt	secret
SCRTE	scrte	scrote (male genitalia)
SCRUB	scrub	loser who thinks he's something
SCSI	scsi	Small Computer System Interface
SCUBA	scuba	self-contained underwater breathing apparatus
SCURRED	scurred	scared
SD	sd	Secure Digital (memory card)
SD	sd	so drunk
SD	sd	suck dick
SD	sd	sweet dreams
SDF^	sdf^	shut da fuck up
SDK	sdk	software development kit
SDLC	sdlc	software development life cycle
SDMB	sdmb	sweet dreams, my baby
SDRAM	sdram	synchronous dynamic random access memory
SDSL	sdsl	symmetric digital subscriber line
SE	se	special edition
SEC	sec	second
SECKS	secks	sex
SECKSEA	secksea	sexy
SECKSY	secksy	sexy
SED	sed	said
SEEDS	seeds	children
SEEDS	seeds	marijuana seeds
SEEN	seen	I see, understand
SEG	seg	shit-eating grin
SEKKLE	sekkle	calm down
SEKS	seks	sex

UPPERCASE	LOWERCASE	MEANING
SELLIN	sellin	selling
SEO	seo	search engine optimization
SEP	sep	somebody else's problem
SERP	serp	search engine results page
SES	ses	marijuana
SESH	sesh	session (drinking, smoking, gaming, etc.)
SET	set	division of a gang
SETE	sete	smiling ear to ear
SEVIE	sevie	seventh grader
SEXC	sexc	sexy
SEXE	sexe	sexy
SEXI	sexi	sexy
SEXII	sexii	sexy
SEXILICIOUS	sexilicious	very sexy
SEXPOT	sexpot	sexy person
SEXXORZ	sexx0rz	sex
SEZ	sez	says
SF	sf	San Francisco
SF	sf	science fiction
SFAIK	sfaik	so far as I know
SFAM	sfam	sister from another mister
SFAM	sfam	sister from another mother
SFE	sfe	safe
SFH	sfh	so fucking hot
SFIPMP	sfipmp	so funny, I peed my pants
SFLR	sflr	sorry for late reply
SFM	sfm	so fucking much
SFR	sfr	so fucking random
SFS	sfs	so fucking stupid
SFSG	sfsg	so far so good
SFTBC	sftbc	sorry for the broadcast
SFTTM	sfttm	stop fucking talking to me
SFU	sfu	shut the fuck up
SFW	sfw	safe for work
SFWUZ	sfwuz	safe for work until zoomed
SFX	sfx	sound effects
SFY	sfy	speak for yourself
SG	sg	so good
SG2M	sg2m	sounds good to me
SGB	sgb	straight/gay/bisexual
SGBADQ	sgbadq	search Google before asking dumb questions
SGI	sgi	still got it
SGTM	sgtm	slightly giggling to myself
SGTM	sgtm	sounds good to me
SH	sh	same here
SH	sh	shit happens
SH	sh	shithead
SH!T :)	sh!t :)	shitface (pooface)
SH!T :)	sh!t :)	shithead (jerk)
SH!TA$$	sh!ta$$	shitass (idiot)
SH!TAZZ	sh!tazz	shitass (idiot)
SH!TBAG	sh!tbag	shitbag (idiot)
SH!TBAGGER	sh!tbagger	shitbagger (idiot)
SH!TBRAIN	sh!tbrain	shitbrains (idiot)

UPPERCASE	LOWERCASE	MEANING
SH!TBREATH	sh!tbreath	shitbreath (bad breath)
SH!TCANNED	sh!tcanned	shitcanned (fired)
SH!TCUNT	sh!tcunt	shitcunt (idiot)
SH!TDICK	sh!tdick	shitdick (idiot)
SH!TFACE	sh!tface	shitface (pooface)
SH!TFACED	sh!tfaced	shitfaced (drunk)
SH!THEAD	sh!thead	shithead (jerk)
SH!THOLE	sh!thole	shithole (idiot)
SH!THOUSE	sh!thouse	shithouse (bathroom)
SH!TSPITTER	sh!tspitter	shitspitter (butt)
SH!TTER	sh!tter	shitter (defecator)
SH!TTIEST	sh!ttiest	shittiest (worst)
SH!TTIEST	sh!ttiest	shitting (pooping)
SH!TTY	sh!tty	shitty (bad)
SH^	sh^	shut up
SHADDAP	shaddap	shut up
SHADE	shade	casual, disrespectful
SHADES	shades	sunglasses
SHADY	shady	shifty, sly, sneaky
SHAFT	shaft	screw, rip off
SHAG	shag	fuck
SHANK	shank	homemade knife
SHANK	shank	stab
SHAT :)	shat :)	shitface (pooface)/shithead (jerk)
SHATA$$	shata$$	shitass (idiot)
SHATAZZ	shatazz	shitass (idiot)
SHATBAG	shatbag	shitbag (idiot)
SHATBAGGER	shatbagger	shitbagger (idiot)
SHATBRAIN	shatbrain	shitbrains (idiot)
SHATBREATH	shatbreath	shitbreath (bad breath)
SHATCANNED	shatcanned	shitcanned (fired)
SHATCUNT	shatcunt	shitcunt (idiot)
SHATDICK	shatdick	shitdick (idiot)
SHATFACE	shatface	shitface (pooface)
SHATFACED	shatfaced	shitfaced (drunk)
SHATHEAD	shathead	shithead (jerk)
SHATHOLE	shathole	shithole (idiot)
SHATHOUSE	shathouse	shithouse (bathroom)
SHATSPITTER	shatspitter	shitspitter (butt)
SHATTER	shatter	shitter (defecator)
SHATTIEST	shattiest	shittiest (worst)
SHATTIEST	shattiest	shitting (pooping)
SHATTY	shatty	shitty (bad)
SHAWN	shawn	attractive man
SHAWTY	shawty	girl
SHAWTY	shawty	young girl/woman
SHD	shd	should
SHEILA	sheila	woman
SHERM	sherm	cigarette dipped in PCP
SHEXI	shexi	sexy
SHEXY	shexy	sexy
SHH	shh	be quiet, shut up
SHIAT	shiat	shit
SHID	shid	slapping head in disgust

UPPERCASE	LOWERCASE	MEANING
SHIET	shiet	shit
SHINNY	shinny	informal game of hockey
SHIOK	shiok	expression of happiness, pleasure
SHIP	ship	romantic relationship
SHITE	shite	shit
SHIZ	shiz	shit
SHIZIT	shizit	shit
SHIZNAT	shiznat	shit
SHIZNIT	shiznit	shit
SHIZZ	shizz	shit
SHIZZLE	shizzle	shit
SHIZZLE	shizzle	sure
SHK	shk	should have known
SHLD	shld	should
SHM	shm	simple harmonic motion
SHMEXY	shmexy	sexy
SHMILY	shmily	see how much I love you
SHO	sho	superhigh output
SHO	sho	sure
SHO'NUFF	sho'nuff	sure enough
SHOOK	shook	scared, frightened
SHOOP	shoop	Photoshop
SHOPPED	shopped	Photoshopped, manipulated
SHORTY	shorty	girlfriend, attractive girl
SHOTGUN	shotgun	front passenger seat
SHOTTA	shotta	drug dealer/thug/gangster
SHOULDA	shoulda	should have
SHOWIN	showin	showing
SHRN	shrn	so hot right now
SHT	sht	shit
SHT :)	sht :)	shitface (pooface)
SHTBGGR	shtbggr	shitbagger (idiot)
SHTBRAIN	shtbrain	shitbrains (idiot)
SHTBREATH	shtbreath	shitbreath (bad breath)
SHTCANNED	shtcanned	shitcanned (fired)
SHTCUNT	shtcunt	shitcunt (idiot)
SHTDICK	shtdick	shitdick (idiot)
SHTF	shtf	shit hits the fan
SHTFACE	shtface	shitface (pooface)
SHTFACED	shtfaced	shitfaced (drunk)
SHTHEAD	shthead	shithead (jerk)
SHTHOLE	shthole	shithole (idiot)
SHTHOUSE	shthouse	shithouse (bathroom)
SHTSPITTER	shtspitter	shitspitter (butt)
SHTTER	shtter	shitter (defecator)
SHTTIEST	shttiest	shittiest (worst)
SHTTIEST	shttiest	shitting (pooping)
SHTTY	shtty	shitty (bad)
SHU	shu	secure housing unit
SHUBZ	shubz	house party, rave
SHUCKS	shucks	expression of modesty or disappointment
SHUD	shud	should
SHUDDUP	shuddup	shut up
SHUG	shug	sugar

UPPERCASE	LOWERCASE	MEANING
SHUP	shup	shut up
SHURE	shure	sure
SHURUP	shurup	shut up
SHUSH	shush	shut up, be quiet
SHUT^	shut^	shut up
SHUX	shux	shucks, expression of modesty
SHWE	shwe	should we
SHWR	shwr	shower
SHYAT	shyat	shit
SHYT	shyt	shit
SI	si	stop it
SI	si	stupid idiot
SIA	sia	sorry I asked
SIAO	siao	school is almost over
SIAP	siap	sorry if already posted
SIAS	sias	say it ain't so
SIBIR	sibir	sibling in room
SIC	sic	*latin sicut* (just as), apparent mistake
SIC	sic	said in context
SICK	sick	awesome, cool
SICL	sicl	sitting in chair laughing
SICNR	sicnr	sorry, I could not resist
SICS	sics	sitting in chair snickering
SID	sid	acid, LSD
SIDK	sidk	sorry, I didn't know
SIF	sif	as if
SIFN'T	sifn't	as if not
SIFS	sifs	secret Internet fatties
SIG	sig	signature
SIG2R	sig2r	sorry, I got to run
SIGGY	siggy	signature
SIGH	sigh	exhale depressed
SIHTH	sihth	stupidity is hard to take
SIKE	sike	indicating the previous statement is false
SIKE	sike	psyche
SIKED	siked	psyched, excited about
SIL	sil	son-in-law
SILF	silf	sister I'd like to fuck
SIM	sim	subscriber identity module
SIM CARD	sim card	subscriber identity module for a mobile phone
SIMCL	simcl	sitting in my chair laughing
SIMCLMAO	simclmao	sitting in my chair laughing my ass off
SIMM	simm	Single In-Line Memory Module
SIMM	simm	Sorry, I'm married.
SIMMER	simmer	relax, chill
SIMT	simt	Sorry, I'm taken.
SINGLE	single	Stay intoxicated nightly, get laid every day.
SIO	sio	bye
SIOL	siol	shout it out loud
SIP	sip	"yep" in Spanish
SIR	sir	strike it rich
SIS	sis	sister
SIS	sis	snickering in silence
SISTA	sista	sister

UPPERCASE	LOWERCASE	MEANING
SIT	sit	stay in touch
SITB	sitb	sex in the butt
SITD	sitd	still in the dark
SITMF	sitmf	say it to my face
SITREP	sitrep	situation report
SITTING DUCK	sitting duck	vulnerable, helpless target
SIU	siu	suck it up
SIUP	siup	suck it up, pussy
SIUYA	siuya	shove it up your ass
SIV	siv	bad goalie in hockey
SIW	siw	someone is watching
SIWOTI	siwoti	someone is wrong on the Internet
SIZZLE	sizzle	drug oc, OxyContin
SJ	sj	San Jose
SJ	sj	society of Jesus
SK	sk	spawn kill
SK@NK	sk@nk	skank (dirty girl)
SK8	sk8	skate
SK8ER	sk8er	skater
SK8ING	sk8ing	skating
SK8R	sk8r	skater
SK8RBOI	sk8rboi	skater boy
SK8TR	sk8tr	skater
SKANKIN	skankin	form of dancing
SKED	sked	schedule
SKEED	skeed	high
SKEEN	skeen	I see, seen
SKEET	skeet	ejaculate
SKENG	skeng	knife
SKETCH	sketch	unusual, dubious
SKEWL	skewl	school
SKHOOL	skhool	school
SKI	ski	snort cocaine
SKI	ski	spend kids' inheritance
SKI INSTRUCTOR	ski instructor	cocaine dealer
SKIDADDLE	skidaddle	go away
SKILLZ	skillz	skills
SKINNY	skinny	information, gossip
SKINNY	skinny	thin
SKINS	skins	cigarette papers
SKINS	skins	TV teen drama
SKL	skl	school
SKN	skn	OK, cool, whatever
SKOOL	skool	school
SKOUL	skoul	school
SKTR	sktr	skater
SKU	sku	stock keeping unit
SKULLFCK	skullfck	skullfuck (sexual act)
SKULLFK	skullfk	skullfuck (sexual act)
SKUX	skux	a guy who's good with women
SKWL	skwl	school
SKYPE	skype	Internet telephone

UPPERCASE	LOWERCASE	MEANING
SL	sl	so lame
SL^T	sl^t	slut
SL4N	sl4n	so long for now
SLA	sla	service-level agreement
SLAB	slab	slow low/loud and banging, customized car
SLAP	slap	sounds like a plan
SLAPPED	slapped	drunk
SLEEPIN	sleepin	sleeping
SLEEPN	sleepn	sleeping
SLF	slf	sexy little fuck
SLF	slf	sounds like fun
SLFN	slfn	so long for now
SLGB	slgb	straight/lesbian/gay/bisexual
SLI	sli	Scalable Link Interface
SLICE	slice	eighth of an ounce (3.5 grams) of marijuana
SLICK	slick	sharp, cool, smooth
SLM	slm	*salaam* (Arabic for "hello")
SLNG	slng	slang
SLO	slo	slow
SLOL	slol	seriously laughing out loud
SLORE	slore	slutty whore
SLOS	slos	someone looking over shoulder
SLOSHED	sloshed	drunk
SLP	slp	sleep
SLR	slr	single-lens reflex (camera)
SLT	slt	*salut*, hello
SLT	slt	something like that
SLUF	sluf	short little ugly fucker (an asian male - ethnic slur/derogatory)
SLUGS	slugs	bullets
SLY	sly	still love you
SM	sm	social media
SM1	sm1	someone
SMACK	smack	heroin
SMACKED	smacked	high on marijuana
SMAD	smad	sad and mad
SMART	smart	self-monitoring analysis and reporting technology
SMB	smb	see my blog
SMB	smb	server message block
SMB	smb	suck my balls
SMBT	smbt	suck my big toe
SMC	smc	suck my cock
SMD	smd	suck my dick
SMDB	smdb	suck my dick, bitch
SMDH	smdh	shaking my damn head
SMDHE	smdhe	some mothers do have 'em
SMDVQ	smdvq	suck my dick quickly
SME	sme	small and medium enterprises
SMEG	smeg	all-purpose swearword
SMEG	smeg	fuck
SMEXI	smexi	smart and sexy
SMEXY	smexy	smart and sexy
SMF	smf	stupid motherfucker
SMFD	smfd	suck my fucking dick

UPPERCASE	LOWERCASE	MEANING
SMFPOS	smfpos	stupid motherfucking piece of shit
SMFT	smft	so much for that
SMG	smg	submachine gun
SMGDH	smgdh	shaking my goddamn head
SMH	smh	shaking my head
SMHB	smhb	suck my hairy balls
SMHID	smhid	scratching my head in disbelief
SMHID	smhid	shaking my head in despair
SMHO	smho	screaming my head off
SMIDSY	smidsy	Sorry, mate, I didn't see you.
SMITHWAWS	smithwaws	smack me in the head with a wooden spoon
SML	sml	screw my life
SMM	smm	social media marketing
SMOFO	smofo	stupid motherfucker
SMOOCH	smooch	kiss
SMOOSH	smoosh	hug, squeeze
SMS	sms	Short Message Service
SMST	smst	somebody missed snack time
SMT	smt	suck my tits
SMT	smt	sucking my teeth
SMTH	smth	something
SMTHIN	smthin	something
SMTHNG	smthng	something
SMTM	smtm	sometime
SMTO	smto	sticking my tongue out
SMTOAY	smtoay	sticking my tongue out at you
SMTP	smtp	Simple Mail Transfer Protocol
SMURF	smurf	experienced gamer posing as a newbie
SN	sn	screen name
SN	sn	side note
SN1	sn1	spare no one
SNAFU	snafu	situation normal, all fouled up
SNAFUBAR	snafubar	situation normal all fucked up beyond any recognition
SNAG	snag	sausage
SNAG	snag	sensitive New Age guy
SNAIL MAIL	snail mail	regular postal service
SNAKE	snake	snitch, backstabber
SNAKE OIL	snake oil	fake medicine
SNAKING	snaking	flirting
SNAP	snap	expression of dismay, surprise, joy, etc.
SNC	snc	social network check
SND	snd	search and destroy
SNERT	snert	snot-nosed egotistical rude teenager
SNES	snes	Super Nintendo Entertainment System
SNEW	snew	What's new?
SNF	snf	so not fair
SNF	snf	so not funny
SNIDE	snide	fake or counterfeit
SNIFF	sniff	cocaine
SNIPE	snipe	bid on eBay just before the auction ends
SNITCH	snitch	person who tells on someone
SNK	snk	video game company
SNL	snl	*Saturday Night Live*
SNM	snm	say no more

UPPERCASE	LOWERCASE	MEANING
SNMP	snmp	Simple Network Management Protocol
SNOG	snog	kiss
SNOGGED	snogged	kissed
SNOOKIE	snookie	pet name for bf or gf
SNOW	snow	cocaine
SNR	snr	signal-to-noise ratio
SNSD	snsd	*sho nyo shi dae* (girl's generation) Korean girl group
SNYK	snyk	so now you know
SO	so	shout out
SO	so	significant other
SO SO	so so	neither good nor bad, average
SOA	soa	Service-Oriented Architecture
SOA	soa	*State of Alert* (band)
SOAB	soab	son of a bitch
SOAD	soad	*System of a Down* (band)
SOAFB	soafb	son of a fucking bitch
SOAP	soap	Simple Object Access Protocol
SOAP	soap	a White person (ethnic slur/derogatory)
SOAW	soaw	son of a whore
SOB	sob	son of a bitch
SOBS	sobs	same old boring shit
SOC	soc	same old crap
SOCKPUPPET	sockpuppet	person using a false identity
SOCOM	socom	Special Operations Command
SO-DIMM	so-dimm	Small Outline Dual In-Line Memory Module
SOE	soe	service-oriented enterprise
SOE	soe	Sony Online Entertainment
SOF	sof	smile on face
SOF	sof	*Soldier of Fortune* (game)
SOFAS	sofas	stepping out for a smoke
SOFS	sofs	same old fucking shit
SOFT	soft	powdered cocaine
SOG	sog	sea of green (cannabis growing)
SOGOP	sogop	shit or get off the pot
SOH	soh	sense of humor
SOHF	sohf	sense of humor failure
SOI	soi	service-oriented infrastructure
SOI	soi	statement of intent
SOIDH	soidh	screenshot or it didn't happen
SOK	sok	it's OK/that's OK
S'OK	s'ok	it's OK
SOL	sol	shit out of luck/shit outta luck
SOL	sol	sooner or later
SOLID	solid	cool, awesome
SOM'M	som'm	something
SOM1	som1	someone
SOMADN	somadn	sitting on my ass doing nothing
SOME1	some1	someone
SOML	soml	story of my life
SOMSW	somsw	someone over my shoulder watching
SOMY	somy	Sick of me yet?
SON	son	close friend
SONAR	sonar	Sound Navigation and Ranging
SOO	soo	so

UPPERCASE	LOWERCASE	MEANING
SOOBS	soobs	saggy boobs
SOOC	sooc	straight out of camera (not Photoshopped)
SOOD	sood	cool
SOOL	sool	shit out of luck
SOOTB	sootb	straight out of the box
SOP	sop	same old place
SOP	sop	standard operating procedure
SORG	sorg	straight or gay
SORN	sorn	Statutory Off Road Notification
SORREH	sorreh	sorry
SORTA	sorta	sort of
SOS	sos	help
SOS	sos	same old shit
SOS	sos	save our souls (help!)
SOS	sos	son of Sam
SOSDD	sosdd	same old shit, different day
SOSG	sosg	spouse over shoulder gone
SOT	sot	short of time
SOT	sot	suck on this
SOTA	sota	state of the art
SOTC	sotc	stupid off-topic crap
SOTD	sotd	song of the day
SOTMG	sotmg	short of time, must go
SOTR	sotr	sex on the road
SOUND	sound	cool, awesome, good
SOW	sow	female police officer
SOWI	sowi	sorry
SOWM	sowm	someone with me
SOWWY	sowwy	sorry
SOX	sox	socks
SOZ	soz	sorry
SP@@K	sp@@k	spook (White person - ethnic slur/derogatory)
SP2	sp2	Service Pack 2
SPAM	spam	unsolicited e-mail
SPARK	spark	set light to (marijuana)
SPAT	spat	fight, argument, tiff
SPAZ	spaz	spastic
SPC	spc	Spic (Mexican person - ethnic slur/derogatory)
SPCK	spck	Spick (Mexican person - ethnic slur/derogatory)
SPECTRE	spectre	special executive for counter-intelligence, terrorism, revenge, and extortion
SPED	sped	someone who needs special education
SPENIS	spenis	small penis
SPEXY	spexy	sexy with glasses
SPF	spf	strictly platonic friend
SPIM	spim	instant messaging spam
SPINS	spins	effect of drinking too much
SPIT GAME	spit game	act of flirting
SPITAL	spital	hospital
SPK	spk	speak
SPLIF	splif	a cigarette of tobacco and cannabis
SPLIFF	spliff	(same as "SPLIF")
SPLOITS	sploits	exploits
SPM	spm	*South Park Mexican* (rapper)

UPPERCASE	LOWERCASE	MEANING
SPN	spn	*Supernatural* (TV show)
SPOC	spoc	single point of contact
SPOILER	spoiler	something you would've preferred to find out yourself
SPOOF	spoof	tube used to reduce smoking smells
SPOON	spoon	cuddle
SPOS	spos	stupid piece of shit
S'POSE	s'pose	suppose
SPOT	spot	lend money
SPOT ON	spot on	absolutely correct, perfect
SPRM	sprm	sperm
SPRUNG	sprung	obsessed with someone, in love
SPST	spst	same place, same time
SPTO	spto	spoke to
SPUN	spun	under the influence of methamphetamine
SPURS	spurs	UK football team (Tottenham Hotspur)
SPURS	spurs	US basketball team
SQ	sq	square
SQL	sql	Structured Query Language (for databases)
SQTM	sqtm	smiling quietly to myself
SQTM	sqtm	snickering quietly to myself
SQUARE	square	cigarette
SRAM	sram	static random access memory
SRCH	srch	search
sRGB	srgb	standard red green blue
SRH	srh	Supporting Radical Habits (clothing)
SRLY	srly	seriously
SRO	sro	standing room only
SROUCKS	sroucks	that's cool, but it still sucks
SRRY	srry	sorry
SRS	srs	serious
SRSLY	srsly	seriously
SRVIS	srvis	service
SRY	sry	sorry
SRYND2G	srynd2g	sorry, need to go
SRZLY	srzly	seriously
SS	ss	screenshot
SS	ss	so sorry
SS4L	ss4l	smoking sista for life
SSA	ssa	subject says all
SSATFM	ssatfm	Stop staring at the fucking monitor.
SSBB	ssbb	*Super Smash Brothers Brawl* (game)
SSBHM	ssbhm	supersized bum
SSC	ssc	safe, sane, consensual
SSC	ssc	super sexy cute
SSD	ssd	solid state drive
SSDD	ssdd	same shit, different day
SSDP	ssdp	same shit, different pile
SSH	ssh	Secure Shell
SSIA	ssia	subject says it all
SSID	ssid	service set identifier
SSIF	ssif	so stupid it's funny
SSINF	ssinf	so stupid it's not funny
SSL	ssl	Secure Sockets Layer
SSL	ssl	see subject line

UPPERCASE	LOWERCASE	MEANING
SSOB	ssob	stupid sons of bitches
SSRY	ssry	so sorry
SSSD	sssd	same shit, same day
SSWA	sswa	so say we all
ST	st	something
ST	st	stop that
ST&D	st&d	stop texting and drive
ST00F	st00f	stuff
ST1	st1	stoned
ST8	st8	state
STA	sta	Surveillance and Target Acquisition
STACK	stack	one thousand
STAMP	stamp	OK
STAN	stan	stalker fan
STANDARD	standard	of course, goes without saying
STAR	star	friend, buddy
STAT	stat	immediately (from Latin *statim*)
STATS	stats	statistics
STB	stb	soon-to-be
STBE	stbe	soon-to-be ex
STBX	stbx	soon-to-be ex
STBY	stby	sorry to bother you
STBY	stby	sucks to be you
STC	stc	subject to change
STD	std	sexually transmitted disease
STEAL	steal	punch
STEAMLOLLER	steamloller	laughing a lot
STEEZ	steez	style with ease
STEEZE	steeze	style with ease
STELLA	stella	flirty girl
STELLAR	stellar	awesome, excellent
STEM	stem	mix of stud and fem
STEXT	stext	sexy text message
STFD	stfd	sit the fuck down
STFF	stff	stuff
STFM	stfm	search the fucking manual
STFNG	stfng	search the fucking news group
STFU	stfu	shut the fuck up
STFUA	stfua	shut the fuck up already
STFUAH	stfuah	shut the fuck up, asshole
STFUB	stfub	shut the fuck up, bitch
STFUDA	stfuda	shut the fuck up, dumb ass
STFUGBTW	stfugbtw	shut the fuck up and get back to work
STFUN	stfun	shut the fuck up, nigger
STFUOGTFO	stfuogtfo	shut the fuck up or get the fuck out
STFUPPERCUT	stfuppercut	shut the fuck up
STFUYB	stfuyb	shut the fuck up, you bitch
STFUYSOAB	stfuysoab	shut the fuck up, you son of a bitch
STFW	stfw	search the fucking Web
STG	stg	swear to God
STH	sth	something
STHG	sthg	something
STHING	sthing	something
STHU	sthu	shut the hell up

UPPERCASE	LOWERCASE	MEANING
STK	stk	shoot to kill
STM	stm	short-term memory
STM	stm	smiling to myself
STMF	stmf	stay thirsty, my friends
STML	stml	short-term memory loss
STN	stn	spend the night
STOKED	stoked	very happy, excited
STOOPID	stoopid	stupid
STPD	stpd	stupid
STPPYNOZGTW	stppynozgtw	stop picking your nose, get to work
STR	str	short-term relationship
STR	str	strength
STR8	str8	straight
STR8UP	str8up	straight up
STRAP	strap	gun
STS	sts	smirk to self
STSP	stsp	same time same place
STT	stt	same time tomorrow
STUFU	stufu	stupid fucker
STUPD	stupd	stupid
STW	stw	search the Web
STW	stw	share the wealth
STY	sty	same to you
STYL	styl	speak to you later
STYLE	Style	see through your eyes
SU	su	shut up
SU2F	su2f	so used to flamers
SU2H	su2h	so used to haters
SUAC	suac	shit up a creek
SUAGOOML	suagooml	shut up and get out of my life
SUAKM	suakm	shut up and kiss me
SUC	suc	University of Southern California
SUCKA$$	sucka$$	suckass (idiot)
SUCKAZZ	suckazz	suckass (idiot)
SUCKS	sucks	is bad, is rubbish
SUFI	sufi	shut up, fucking imbecile
SUFI	sufi	super finger
SUFI	sufi	super finger-fucking imbecile
SUFID	sufid	screwing up face in disgust
SUH	suh	sir
SUIB	suib	shut up, I'm busy
SUIT	suit	businessman, boss
SUITM	suitm	see you in the morning
SUK	suk	suck
SUKA	suka	sucker
SUKZ	sukz	sucks
SUL	sul	see you later
SUL	sul	snooze, you lose
SUL8R	sul8r	see you later
SULA	sula	sweaty upper lip alert
SUM	sum	some
SUM1	sum1	someone
SUMFIN	sumfin	something
SUMMAT	summat	something

UPPERCASE	LOWERCASE	MEANING
SUMMIN	summin	something
SUMTHIN'	sumthin'	something
SUMTIN	sumtin	something
SUP	sup	What's up?
SUPA	supa	super
SUPER	super	very, really
SUPPOSABLY	supposably	supposedly
SURE	sure	yes (often sarcastic)
SUS	sus	see you soon
SUS	sus	suspect, suspicious
SUSFU	susfu	situation unchanged, still fucked up
SUSS	suss	suspicious
SUT	sut	see you tomorrow
SUTF	sutf	so used to flamers
SUTH	suth	so used to haters
SUTUCT	sutuct	So you think you can type?
SUV	suv	sport-utility vehicle
SUX	sux	sucks
SUX0RZ	sux0rz	sucks
SUX2BU	sux2bu	sucks to be you
SUXOR	suxor	sucks
SUXORS	suxors	sucks
SUXORZ	suxorz	sucks
SUXR	suxr	sucker
SUXX	suxx	sucks
SUXXOR	suxxor	sucks
SUYAH	suyah	Shut up, you asshole!
SUYF	suyf	Shut up, you fool!
SVN	svn	seven
SVP	svp	*s'il vous plait* (French for "please")
SVS	svs	someone very special
SVU	svu	special victims unit
SW	sw	So what?
SW	sw	*Star Wars*
SW	sw	street worker
SWAFK	swafk	sealed with a friendly kiss
SWAG	swag	scientific wild ass guess
SWAGG	swagg	style, coolness, confidence
SWAGGA	swagga	style or personality
SWAGGER	swagger	a person's style
SWAK	swak	sealed with a kiss
SWALK	swalk	sealed (or sealed) with a loving kiss
SWALK	swalk	sealed with a loving kiss
SWAMBO	swambo	she who always must be obeyed
SWANK	swank	cool, classy
SWANK	swank	second wife and no kids
SWANK	swank	single woman and no kids
SWAT	swat	scientific wild-ass guess
SWAT	swat	special weapons and tactics
SWEAT	sweat	like, love
SWED	swed	smoke weed every day
SWEET	sweet	awesome
SWEETIE	sweetie	pet name for bf or gf
SWEETY	sweety	(same as "sweetie")

UPPERCASE	LOWERCASE	MEANING
SWEXY	swexy	sweet and sexy
SWF	swf	single white female
SWIFT	swift	awesome
SWIM	swim	someone who isn't me
SWISHER	swisher	cheap cigar used for making blunts
SWIY	swiy	someone who isn't you
SWIZ	swiz	con, rip-off
SWIZZLE	swizzle	sweet
SWK	swk	*Star Wars* kid
SWL	swl	screaming with laughter
SWM	swm	single white male
SWMBO	swmbo	she who must be obeyed
SWMT	swmt	stop wasting my time
SWND	swnd	sound
SWOL	swol	well built, muscular
SWOLE	swole	muscular, in good shape
SWOT	swot	person who is always studying
SWP	swp	sorry, wrong person
SWPF	swpf	single white professional female
SWSW2B	swsw2b	single when she wants to be
SWT	swt	sweat
SWTF	swtf	Seriously, what the fuck?
SWY	swy	sowwy (sorry)
SX	sx	sex
SXC	sxc	sexy
SXCY	sxcy	sexy
SXE	sxe	straightedge (no drink, no drugs, no sex)
SXI	sxi	sexy
SXS	sxs	sex
SXY	sxy	sexy
SY	sy	sincerely yours
SYA	sya	see you
SYATP	syatp	see you at the party
SYDIM	sydim	stick your dick in me
SYDLM	sydlm	shut your dirty little mouth
SYF	syf	shut your face
SYFM	syfm	shut your fucking mouth
SYG	syg	shut your gob
SYIAB	syiab	see you in a bit
SYIAF	syiaf	see you in a few
SYITM	syitm	see you in the morning
SYK	syk	so you know
SYL	syl	see you later
SYL8R	syl8r	see you later
SYM	sym	shut your mouth
SYM	sym	So, you mad?
SYNC	sync	synchronize
SYOA	syoa	save your own ass
SYOTBF	syotbf	see you on the battlefield
SYOTOS	syotos	see you on the other side
SYRS	syrs	see you real soon
SYS	sys	see you soon
SYSOP	sysop	system operator
SYT	syt	see you there

UPPERCASE	LOWERCASE	MEANING
SYT	syt	see you tomorrow
SYTYCD	sytycd	*So You Think You Can Dance?*
SYU	syu	sex you up
SYWISY	sywisy	see you when I see you
SYY	syy	shut your yapper
SZ	sz	sorry
T!T	t!t	tit (breast)
T!TS	t!ts	tits
T!TZ	t!tz	tits
T#3	t#3	the
T&C	t&c	terms and conditions
T,FTFY	t,ftfy	there, fixed that for you
T.T	t.t	crying
T/A	t/a	try again
T:)T	t:)t	think happy thoughts
T@RD	t@rd	tard (mentally challenged - disability slur/derogatory)
T^T	t^t	crying
T_T	t_t	crying
T+	t+	think positive
T2B	t2b	time to blunt
T2M	t2m	talk to me
T2U	t2u	talking to you
T2UL	t2ul	talk to you later
T2UL8R	t2ul8r	talk to you later
T2YL	t2yl	talk to you later
T3H	t3h	the
T4A	t4a	thanks for asking
T4BU	t4bu	thanks for being you
T4M	t4m	transgender for male
T4P	t4p	thanks for posting
T4T	t4t	thanks for trade
T4T	t4t	tit for tat
T8ST	t8st	taste
TA	ta	thanks again
TAB	tab	acid, LSD
TAB	tab	cigarette
TABOO	taboo	forbidden, not talked about
TABOOMA	tabooma	take a bite out of my ass
TAC	tac	cannabis resin
TACI	taci	that's a crappy idea
TAD	tad	small amount
TADA	tada	exclamation when something is finished
TAE	tae	trial and error
TAF	taf	tell a friend
TAFN	tafn	that's all for now
TAG	tag	personal signature
TAGL	tagl	there's a good lad
TAH	tah	take a hike
TAHA	taha	take a hike, asshole
TAHB	tahb	take a hike, bitch
TAHT	taht	that
TAI	tai	think about it
TAIG	taig	that's all I got
TAKS	taks	Texas Assessment of Knowledge and Skills

UPPERCASE	LOWERCASE	MEANING
TAL	tal	thanks a lot
TAL	tal	try again later
TAM	tam	tomorrow morning
TANJ	tanj	there ain't no justice
TANK	tank	large person, heavily built
TANK	tank	really strong
TANKED	tanked	owned
TANKING	tanking	owning
TANQ	tanq	thank you
TANSTAAFL	tanstaafl	there ain't no such thing as a free lunch
TAPPED	tapped	crazy
TAR	tar	not very pure heroin
TARD	tard	retard (disability slur/derogatory)
TARD	tard	retarded person (disability slur/derogatory)
TARDIS	tardis	Time and Relative Dimensions in Space
TARFU	tarfu	things are really fucked up
TASTY	tasty	cool, awesome, good-looking
TAT	tat	rubbish, junk
TAT	tat	tattoo
TAT	tat	that
TAT2	tat2	tattoo
TATA	tata	good-bye
TATO	tato	all right, OK
TATT	tatt	tattoo
TAU	tau	thinking about you
TAUMUALU	taumualu	thinking about you, miss you, always love you
TAUNCH	taunch	*te amo un chingo*
TAV	tav	marijuana
TAW	taw	teachers are watching
TAY	tay	thinking about you
TB	tb	text back
TB	tb	titty bar
TB4U	tb4u	too bad for you
TBA	tba	to be announced
TBBH	tbbh	to be brutally honest
TBC	tbc	to be continued
TBCH	tbch	to be completely honest
TBD	tbd	to be decided
TBD	tbd	to be determined
TBE	tbe	to be edited
TBF	tbf	to be fair
TBFH	tbfh	to be fucking honest
TBFU	tbfu	too bad for you
TBH	tbh	to be honest
TBHIMO	tbhimo	to be honest, in my opinion
TBL	tbl	text back later
TBM	tbm	tactical boyfriend mention
TBMS	tbms	to be more specific
TBNT	tbnt	thanks, but no thanks
TBP	tbp	*The Pirate Bay*
TBPFH	tbpfh	to be perfectly fucking honest
TBPH	tbph	to be perfectly honest
TBQF	tbqf	to be quite frank
TBQH	tbqh	to be quite honest

UPPERCASE	LOWERCASE	MEANING
TBSS	tbss	too bad, so sad
TBT	tbt	truth be told
TBTP	tbtp	that's beside the point
TBU	tbu	to be updated
TBVH	tbvh	to be very honest
TBX	tbx	to be exact
TC	tc	take care
TCB	tcb	taking care of business
TCBY	tcby	the country's best yogurt
TCCIC	tccic	take care 'cause I care
TCFC	tcfc	too close for comfort
TCFM	tcfm	too cool for me
TCFN	tcfn	take care for now
TCG	tcg	trading card game
TCH	tch	sound of disagreement, frustration
TCHBO	tchbo	topic creator has been owned
TCK	tck	third culture kid
TCL	tcl	Tool Command Language
TCOB	tcob	taking care of business
TCOY	tcoy	take care of yourself
TCP	tcp	Transmission Control Protocol
TCP/IP	tcp/ip	Transmission Control Protocol/Internet Protocol
TD	td	touchdown
TD2M	td2m	talk dirty to me
TDD	tdd	Telecommunications Devices for the Deaf
TDDUP	tddup	'til death do us part
TDDWP	tddwp	'til death do we part
TDF	tdf	to die for
TDG	tdg	*Three Days Grace* (band)
TDG	tdg	too damn good
TDH	tdh	tall, dark, and handsome
TDI	tdi	Turbo Diesel Injection
TDI	tdi	Turbocharged Direct Injection
TDL	tdl	to-do list
TDL	tdl	too damn lazy
TDM	tdm	*Team Deathmatch* (game)
TDS	tds	technical difficulties
TDTM	tdtm	talk dirty to me
TDWDTG	tdwdtg	the devil went down to Georgia
TDWP	tdwp	*The Devil Wears Prada* (band)
TE	te	team effort
TE AMO	te amo	I love you (Spanish)
TEAL DEER	teal deer	(same as "TLDR")
TEC	tec	TEC-9 handgun
TECH	tech	technician
TECH	tech	technology
TEE	tee	T-shirt
TEEF	teef	steal
TEEF	teef	teeth
TEEN	teen	teenager, teenage
TEH	teh	the
TEH	teh	used to emphasize the next word
TEHO	teho	to each his/her own
TEK	tek	technique

UPPERCASE	LOWERCASE	MEANING
TEKKERS	tekkers	technique (in sport)
TEN	ten	person with a perfect body
TEOTWAWKI	teotwawki	the end of the world as we know it
TERD	terd	shit
TEVS	tevs	whatever
TEXT	text	an SMS message sent between cell phones
TF2	tf2	*Team Fortress 2* (game)
TFA	tfa	thanks for asking
TFA	tfa	the fucking article
TFB	tfb	that's fucking bullshit
TFB	tfb	time for bed
TFBUNDY	tfbundy	totally fucked but unfortunately not dead yet
TFC	tfc	*Team Fortress Classic* (game)
TFD	tfd	total fucking disaster
TFF	tff	that's fucking funny
TFFT	tfft	thank fuck for that
TFFW	tffw	too funny for words
TFIC	tfic	tongue firmly in cheek
TFIIK	tfiik	the fuck if I know
TFL	tfl	thanks for looking
TFL	tfl	tip for life
TFL	tfl	transport for London
TFLMK	tflmk	thanks for letting me know
TFLMS	tflms	thanks for letting me share
TFLN	tfln	texts from last night
TFLN	tfln	thanks for last night
TFM	tfm	too fucking much
TFM	tfm	total frat move
TFM2KAU2FO	tfm2kau2fo	That's for me to know, and you to find out.
TFMIU	tfmiu	The fucking manual is unreadable.
TFS	tfs	thanks for sharing
TFT	tft	*The Frozen Throne* (*Warcraft III*) (game)
TFT	tft	thin-film transistor
TFTA	tfta	thanks for the ad
TFTC	tftc	thanks for the (geo)cache
TFTF	tftf	thanks for the follow (Twitter slang)
TFTI	tfti	thanks for the information
TFTI	tfti	thanks for the invitation
TFU	tfu	that's fucked up
TFU2BAW	tfu2baw	time for you to buy a watch
TFYS	tfys	the fuck you say
TG	tg	thank God
TG	tg	thank goodness
TG	tg	too good
TG	tg	transgender
TGAL	tgal	think globally, act locally
TGFE	tgfe	together forever
TGFI	tgfi	thank God for the Internet
TGFITW	tgfitw	the greatest fans in the world
TGFT	tgft	thank God for that
TGFU	tgfu	too good for you
TGFUAP	tgfuap	thank God for unanswered prayers
TGHIG	tghig	thank God husband is gone
TGI	tgi	thank God, it's . . .

UPPERCASE	LOWERCASE	MEANING
TGIAF	tgiaf	thank God, it's almost Friday
TGIF	tgif	thank God, it's Friday
TGIFF	tgiff	thank God, it's fucking Friday
TGIM	tgim	thank God, it's Monday
TGIS	tgis	thank God, it's Saturday
TGIWJO	tgiwjo	thank God, it was just once
TGOD	tgod	Taylor gang or die
TGP	tgp	thumbnail gallery post
TGTBT	tgtbt	too good to be true
TGWIG	tgwig	thank God, wife is gone
TGWS	tgws	that goes without saying
TH@	th@	that
THA	tha	the
THANG	thang	thing
THANKIES	thankies	thank you
THANKX	thankx	thank you
THANQ	thanq	thank you
THANX	thanx	thank you
THANX	thanx	thanks
THAR	thar	there
THATZ	thatz	that's
THC	thc	tetrahydrocannabinol, active ingredient in marijuana
THE BOMB	the bomb	really cool
THE NICK	the nick	prison
THICK	thick	well proportioned, not fat or skinny
THIS	this	I agree
THIZZ	thizz	ecstasy
THIZZING	thizzing	tripping on ecstasy
THIZZLE	thizzle	ecstasy tablet
THKU	thku	thank you
THN	thn	then
THNK	thnk	think
THNQ	thnq	thank you
THNX	thnx	thanks
THO	tho	though
THOU	thou	you
THR	thr	there
THR4	thr4	therefore
THRASH	thrash	thrash metal (music style)
THRU	thru	through
THT	tht	that
THT	tht	think happy thoughts
THTH	thth	too hot to handle
THUG	thug	person struggling to make something of his/her life
THUG	thug	violent criminal
THUMBNAIL	thumbnail	small version of a picture
THUMBS DOWN	thumbs down	sign of disapproval
THURR	thurr	there
THWDI	thwdi	that's how we do it
THWU	thwu	to hell with you
THWY	thwy	the hell with you!
THX	thx	thanks
THXX	thxx	thanks, hugs

UPPERCASE	LOWERCASE	MEANING
THZ	thz	thank you
TI	ti	rapper from Atlanta
TI	ti	Texas Instruments
TI AMO	ti amo	*I love you* (Italian)
TI2O	ti2o	that is too obvious
TIA	tia	thanks in advance
TIAD	tiad	tomorrow is another day
TIAFAYH	tiafayh	Thanks in advance for all your help.
TIAI	tiai	take it all in
TIAS	tias	try it and see
TIATWTCC	tiatwtcc	This is a trap word to catch copiers.
TIC	tic	tongue in cheek
TIE	tie	take it easy
TIEM	tiem	misspelling of "time"
TIF	tif	that is funny/fun
TIF2M	tif2m	this is fucking too much
TIFF	tiff	argument, disagreement
TIFF	tiff	Tagged Image File Format
TIFS	tifs	this is funny shit
TIFU	tifu	that is fucked up
TIGAS	tigas	think I give a shit
TIGGER	tigger	tiger
TIGHT	tight	close
TIIC	tiic	the idiots in charge/control
TIL	til	today I learned
TIL	til	until
TILF	tilf	teenager I'd like to fuck
TILIS	tilis	tell it like it is
TIME	time	tears in my eyes
TINA	tina	crystal meth
TINALO	tinalo	this is not a legal opinion
TINAR	tinar	this is not a recommendation
TINF	tinf	this is not fair
TING	ting	thing
TINGTES	tingtes	there is no gravity, the earth sucks.
TINLA	tinla	this is not legal advice
TINSTAAFL	tinstaafl	There is no such thing as a free lunch.
TINWIS	tinwis	That is not what I said.
TIOLI	tioli	take it or leave it
TIPSY	tipsy	slightly drunk
TIR	tir	teacher in room
TIRF	tirf	that/this is really funny
TIS	tis	it is
TISA	tisa	that is so awesome
TISC	tisc	that is so cool
TISFU	tisfu	that is so fucked up
TISG	tisg	this is so gay
TISL	tisl	this is so lame
TISNF	tisnf	that is so not fair
TISS	tiss	this is some shit
TISW	tisw	that is so wrong
TITCH	titch	small person
TITCR	titcr	this is the credited response
TITF	titf	take it too far

UPPERCASE	LOWERCASE	MEANING
TITFCK	titfck	titfuck (sexual act)
TITFK	titfk	titfuck (sexual act)
TITT	titt	throw in the towel, give up
TITTYFCK	tittyfck	tittyfuck (sexual act)
TITTYFK	tittyfk	tittyfuck (sexual act)
TIW	tiw	teacher is watching
TIX	tix	tickets
TJA	tja	*hi* (Swedish)
TJB	tjb	that's just boring
TK	tk	team kill/killer
TK2UL	tk2ul	talk to you later
TKD	tkd	Tae Kwon Do
TKER	tker	team killer
TKM	tkm	*te quiero mucho* (Spanish for I love you)
TKO	tko	technical knockout
TKS	tks	thanks
TKT	tkt	don't worry (French)
TKU	tku	thank you
TL	tl	talk later
TL	tl	team leader
TL	tl	too long
TL	tl	tough luck
TL	tl	true love
TL,DR	tl,dr	too long, didn't read
TL:DR	tl:dr	too long: didn't read
TL; DR	tl; dr	too long; didn't read
TL8R	tl8r	talk later
TLA	tla	three-letter acronym
TLC	tlc	tender loving care
TLD	tld	told
TLD	tld	top-level domain
TLDNR	tldnr	too long; did not read
TLDR	tldr	too long, didn't read
TLGO	tlgo	the list goes on
TLI	tli	too little information
TLIWWV	tliwwv	this link is worthless without video
TLK	tlk	talk
TLK2ME	tlk2me	talk to me
TLK2UL8R	tlk2ul8r	talk to you later
TLKIN	tlkin	talking
TLKN	tlkn	talking
TLND	tlnd	true love never dies
TLOL	tlol	truly laughing out loud
TLTPR	tltpr	too long to proofread
TLYK	tlyk	to let you know
TM	tm	text me / text message
TM	tm	trademark
TMA	tma	take my advice
TMAAI	tmaai	tell me all about it
TMAI	tmai	tell me about it
TMB	tmb	text me back
TMB	tmb	tweet me back
TMBI	tmbi	tell me about it
TMD	tmd	"damn" in Chinese

UPPERCASE	LOWERCASE	MEANING
TMD	tmd	too much detail
TME	tme	too much effort
TMF	tmf	too much forehead
TMH	tmh	touch my hand
TMI	tmi	too much information
TMK	tmk	to my knowledge
TML	tml	tell me later
TML	tml	text me later
TML	tml	thank me later
TMM	tmm	tell me more
TMMRW	tmmrw	tomorrow
TMNT	tmnt	Teenage Mutant Ninja Turtles
TMO	tmo	take me out
TMO	tmo	tomorrow
TMORO	tmoro	tomorrow
TMOT	tmot	trust me on this
TMOZ	tmoz	tomorrow
TMP	tmp	Tactical Machine Pistol
TMR	tmr	tomorrow
TMR@IA	tmr@ia	the monkeys are at it again
TMRRW	tmrrw	tomorrow
TMRW	tmrw	tomorrow
TMRZ	tmrz	tomorrow
TMS	tms	that makes sense
TMS	tms	too much swag(ger)
TMSAISTI	tmsaisti	that's my story and I'm sticking to it
TMSG	tmsg	tell me something good
TMSGO	tmsgo	too much shit going on
TMSIDK	tmsidk	tell me something I don't know
TMTC	tmtc	too many to count
TMTH	tmth	too much to handle
TMTMO	tmtmo	text me tomorrow
TMTOWTDI	tmtowtdi	there's more than one way to do it
TMTOYH	tmtoyh	too much time on your hands
TMTT	tmtt	tell me the truth
TMW	tmw	tomorrow
TMW	tmw	too much work
TMWFI	tmwfi	take my word for it
TMY	tmy	tell me why
TMZ	tmz	celebrity news
TMZ	tmz	tomorrow
TN1	tn1	trust no one
TNA	tna	tits and ass
TNA	tna	Total Nonstop Action
TNB	tnb	typical nigger behavior (African American · ethnic slur/derogatory)
TNBM	tnbm	true Norwegian black metal
TNC	tnc	tongue in cheek
TNF	tnf	that's not funny
TNL	tnl	to next level
TNLNSL	tnlnsl	took nothing, left nothing, signed log
TNO	tno	trust no one
TNOT	tnot	take note of that
TNSTAAFL	tnstaafl	There's no such thing as a free lunch.

UPPERCASE	LOWERCASE	MEANING
TNT	tnt	'til next time
TNTM	tntm	that's news to me
TNX	tnx	thanks
TNXZ	tnxz	thanks
TO	to	time out
TO BOOT	to boot	as well, also
TOASTIE	toastie	toasted sandwich
TOB	tob	teacher over back
TOC	toc	table of contents
TOD	tod	time of day
TOD	tod	time of death
TOEFL	toefl	Test of English as a Foreign Language
TOFTT	toftt	take one for the team
TOFY	tofy	thinking of you
TOH	toh	the other half
TOH	toh	typing one-handed
TOJ	toj	tears of joy
TOK	tok	that's OK
TOK2UL8R	tok2ul8r	I'll talk to you later
TOKE	toke	inhale marijuana smoke
TOL	tol	thinking of laughing
TOL	tol	thinking out loud
TOLOL	tolol	thinking of laughing out loud
TOM	tom	time of month
TOMBOUT	tombout	talking about
TOMM	tomm	tomorrow
TOMO	tomo	tomorrow
TOMOZ	tomoz	tomorrow
TON	ton	one hundred
TONG	tong	Asian gangster
TONK	tonk	strong, muscular
TOOC	tooc	totally out of control
TOODLE	toodle	good-bye, toodlepip
TOOL	tool	person of low intelligence, a fool
TOON	toon	online character in RPG
TOOTSIES	tootsies	toes, feet
TOPPER	topper	person who always has a better story
TOPS	tops	wonderful, fantastic
TOS	tos	terms of service
TOT	tot	small child
TOTE	tote	carry
TOTES	totes	totally
TOTES PRESH	totes presh	totally precious
TOTL	totl	total
TOTM	totm	time of the month
TOTM	totm	top of the morning
TOTP	totp	talking on the phone
TOTPD	totpd	top of the page dance
TOTS	tots	totally
TOTT	tott	think on these things
TOTUS	totus	teleprompter of the United States
TOTZ	totz	totally
TOU	tou	thinking of you
TOUCH	touch	beat, kill, rob

UPPERCASE	LOWERCASE	MEANING
TOUCHE	touche	said when admitting opponent has made a good point
TOY	toy	thinking of you
TOYA	toya	thinking of you always
TP	tp	toilet paper
TP	tp	*Town Portal (Diablo 2)* (game)
TPAM	tpam	the person above me
TPB	tpb	*The Pirate Bay*
TPE	tpe	total power exchange
TPIWWP	tpiwwp	this post is worthless without pictures
TPM	tpm	tomorrow pm
TPS	tps	test procedure specification
TPS	tps	totally pointless stuff
TPT	tpt	trailer park trash
TPTB	tptb	the powers that be
TQ	tq	*te quiero*/I love you (Spanish)
TQ	tq	thank you
TQM	tqm	*te quiero mucho*/I like you a lot (Spanish)
TR00	tr00	true, loyal
TRA	tra	bye
TRANI	trani	transsexual
TRANNY	tranny	transsexual
TRBLE	trble	trouble
TRD	trd	tired
T'RD	t'rd	tard (mentally challenged - disability slur/derogatory)
TRDMC	trdmc	tears running down my cheeks
TRDMF	trdmf	tears running down my face
TREE	tree	marijuana
TRICKIN	trickin	spending money on a girl
TRIFE	trife	trifling, unimportant
TRILL	trill	true and real
TRIP	trip	experience when using a hallucinogenic drug
TRIPPING	tripping	under the influence of drugs
TRM	trm	that reminds me
TRNSL8	trnsl8	translate
TRNSLTR	trnsltr	translator
TROL	trol	police patrol
TROLL	troll	person who deliberately stirs up trouble
TROLLING	trolling	the act of being a troll
TROLOL	trolol	LOLing at somebody who is trolling
TROTW	trotw	the rest of the world
TROUT	trout	older man looking for a younger woman
TRU	tru	true
TRU DAT	tru dat	that is true, I agree
TRUFAX	trufax	true fact
TRYNA	tryna	trying to
TS	ts	talking shit
TS	ts	tough shit or totally stinks
TSA	tsa	Transportation Security Administration
TSC	tsc	that's so cool
TSFF	tsff	that's so fucking funny
TSH	tsh	tripping so hard
TSIA	tsia	title says it all
TSIG	tsig	that site is gay (homosexual slur/derogatory)
TSK	tsk	sound of annoyance

UPPERCASE	LOWERCASE	MEANING
TSM	tsm	thanks so much
TSNF	tsnf	that's so not fair
TSOB	tsob	tough son of a bitch
TSRA	tsra	two shakes of a rat's ass
TSS	tss	that's so sweet
TSTB	tstb	the sooner, the better
TSTCL	tstcl	testicle (male genitalia)
TSTL	tstl	too stupid to live
TSTOAC	tstoac	too stupid to own a computer
TSWC	tswc	tell someone who cares
TT	tt	telegraphic transfer
TT	tt	till tomorrow
T-T	t-t	crying
TT_TT	tt_tt	crying
TT4N	tt4n	ta ta for now
TTBC	ttbc	try to be cool
TTBOMK	ttbomk	to the best of my knowledge
TTC	ttc	text the cell
TTC	ttc	trying to conceive
TTD	ttd	textually transmitted disease
TTEOT	tteot	till the end of time
TTFAF	ttfaf	"Through the Fire and Flames" (song)
TTFL	ttfl	ta-ta for later
TTFN	ttfn	ta-ta for now
TTFW	ttfw	too tacky for words
TTG	ttg	time to go
TTGG	ttgg	time to go, girl
TTH	tth	trying too hard
TTHB	tthb	try to hurry back
TTIHLIC	ttihlic	try to imagine how little I care
TTIUWIOP	ttiuwiop	this thread is useless without pics
TTIUWOP	ttiuwop	this thread is useless without pics
TTIUWP	ttiuwp	this thread is useless without pictures
TTIWWOP	ttiwwop	this thread is worthless without pics
TTIWWP	ttiwwp	this thread is worthless without pictures
TTJASI	ttjasi	take this job and shove it
TTL	ttl	thank the Lord
TTL	ttl	time to live
TTL	ttl	time to live (network cache)
TTL	ttl	total
TTLLY	ttlly	totally
TTLY	ttly	totally
TTM	ttm	talk to me
TTMF	ttmf	ta-ta, mofo
TTML	ttml	talk to me later
TTMS	ttms	talking to myself
TTO	tto	time to own
TTP	ttp	to the point
TTR	ttr	time to relax
TTR	ttr	time to run
TTRF	ttrf	that's the rules, fucker
TTS	tts	text to speech
TTT	ttt	third-tier toilet (bad school)
TTT	ttt	to the top

UPPERCASE	LOWERCASE	MEANING
TTTH	ttth	talk to the hand
TTTKA	tttka	time to totally kick ass
TTTT	tttt	these things take time
TTTT	tttt	to tell the truth
TTTTY	tttty	time to talk to you
TTUL	ttul	talk to you later
TTUL8R	ttul8r	talk to you later
TTUS	ttus	talk to you soon
TTUTT	ttutt	to tell you the truth
TTY	tty	talk to you
TTY	tty	teletypewriter or teletype
TTYAB	ttyab	talk to you after breakfast
TTYAD	ttyad	talk to you after dinner
TTYAFN	ttyafn	talk to you a while from now
TTYAL	ttyal	talk to you after lunch
TTYAS	ttyas	talk to you at school
TTYF	ttyf	talk to you forever
TTYIAB	ttyiab	talk to you in a bit
TTYIAM	ttyiam	talk to you in a minute
TTYITM	ttyitm	talk to you in the morning
TTYL	ttyl	talk to you later
TTYL8R	ttyl8r	talk to you later
TTYLT	ttylt	talk to you later today
TTYM	ttym	talk to you mañana
TTYN	ttyn	talk to you never
TTYNA	ttyna	talk to you never again
TTYNL	ttynl	talk to you never, loser
TTYNW	ttynw	talk to you next week
TTYO	ttyo	talk to you online
TTYOTP	ttyotp	talk to you on the phone
TTYRS	ttyrs	talk to you really soon
TTYS	ttys	talk to you soon
TTYT	ttyt	talk to you tomorrow
TTYTM	ttytm	talk to you tomorrow
TTYTT	ttytt	to tell you the truth
TTYVS	ttyvs	talk to you very soon
TTYW	ttyw	talk to you whenever
TTYWL	ttywl	talk to you way later
TU	tu	thank you
TUDE	tude	bad attitude
TUFF	tuff	rugged
TUFF	tuff	tough
TUH	tuh	to
TUI	tui	turning you in
TUNE	tune	flirt
TURF	turf	area, part of the neighborhood
TUT	tut	take your time
TUVM	tuvm	thank you very much
TUX	tux	the penguin Linux mascot
TUX	tux	tuxedo
TV	tv	television
TVM	tvm	thanks very much
TW	tw	teacher watching
TW@T	tw@t	twat (female genitals)

UPPERCASE	LOWERCASE	MEANING
TW@TLIPS	tw@tlips	twatlips (idiot)
TW@TS	tw@ts	twats (vaginas)
TWAIN	twain	technology without an interesting name
TWAIN	twain	Toolkit Without An Informative Name
TWAJS	twajs	That was a joke, son.
TWAT	twat	vagina
TWBC	twbc	that would be cool
TWD	twd	texting while driving
TWDAH	twdah	that was dumb as hell
TWEAKED	tweaked	high on drugs
TWEAKING	tweaking	same as spun
TWEEKER	tweeker	a methamphetamine user
TWEET	tweet	a post on twitter
TWEETER	tweeter	person who posts on twitter
TWF	twf	that was funny
TWFAF	twfaf	that's what friends are for
TWG	twg	that was great
TWHS	twhs	that's what he said
TWI	twi	texting while intoxicated
TWIMC	twimc	to whom it may concern
TWIS	twis	that's what I said
TWISTED	twisted	high and drunk
TWIT	twit	foolish person
TWIT	twit	that's what I thought
TWITA	twita	that's what I'm talking about
TWITCON	twitcon	profile picture on twitter
TWITTER	twitter	a social networking site
TWITTER JAIL	twitter jail	having reached your tweeting limit
TWLOHA	twloha	to write love on her arms
TWOC	twoc	taken without owner's consent
TWOH	twoh	typing with one hand
TWOT	twot	total waste of time
TWS	tws	typical woman syndrome
TWS2WA	tws2wa	that was so two weeks ago
TWSS	twss	that's what she said
TWSY	twsy	that was so yesterday
TWT	twt	time will tell
TWTMC	twtmc	to whom this may concern
TWTTR	twttr	Twitter
TWU	twu	that's what's up
TWVSOY	twvsoy	that was very stupid of you
TX	tx	thanks
TXS	txs	thanks
TXT	txt	text
TXTING	txting	texting
TXTYL	txtyl	text you later
TY	ty	thank you
TYAFY	tyafy	thank you and fuck you
TYB	tyb	try your best
TYCLO	tyclo	turn your caps lock off
TYCLOS	tyclos	turn your caps lock off, stupid
TYFAYS	tyfays	thank you for all your support
TYFC	tyfc	thank you for charity
TYFI	tyfi	thank you for invite

UPPERCASE	LOWERCASE	MEANING
TYFN	tyfn	thank you for nothing
TYFYC	tyfyc	thank you for your comment
TYFYT	tyfyt	thank you for your time
TYG	tyg	there you go
TYL	tyl	text you later
TYM	tym	thank you much
TYM	tym	time
TYMBI	tymbi	thought you might be interested
TYP	typ	thank you, partner
TYPO	typo	typing mistake
TYRED	tyred	tired
TYS	tys	thank you, sir
TYS	tys	told you so
TYSFM	tysfm	thank you so fucking much
TYSM	tysm	thank you so much
TYSVM	tysvm	thank you so very much
TYT	tyt	take your time
TYTO	tyto	take your top off
TYTY	tyty	thank you, thank you
TYVM	tyvm	thank you very much
TYVVM	tyvvm	thank you very, very much
U	u	you
U IZ A 304	u iz a 304	you is a hoe
U$C	u$c	University of Southern California
U.U	u.u	expressing sympathy
U/L	u/l	upload
U/N	u/n	username
U'VE	u've	you've
U¢LA	u¢la	UCLA
U2	u2	you too
U2B	u2b	YouTube
U2U	u2u	up to you
U4I	u4i	up for it
UA	ua	user agreement
UA4I	ua4i	you asked for it
UAAAA	uaaaa	Universal Association against Acronym Abuse
UAE	uae	United Arab Emirates
UARK	Uark	you already know
UAT	uat	User Acceptance Testing
UAYOR	uayor	use at your own risk
UB2	ub2	you be too
UB3R	ub3r	super
UBD	ubd	user brain damage
UBER	uber	over
UBER	uber	ultimate, best (German for "above")
UBRS	ubrs	*Upper Blackrock Spire* (WOW)
UC&P	uc&p	up close and personal
UCMU	ucmu	you crack me up
UCTAODNT	uctaodnt	you can't teach an old dog new tricks
U'D	u'd	you would
UDC	udc	you don't care
UDDI	uddi	Universal Description Discovery and Integration
UDEK	udek	you don't even know
UDFS	udfs	you dumb fucking shit

UPPERCASE	LOWERCASE	MEANING
UDI	udi	unidentified drinking injury (bruise, scratch, ache, and so on)
UDK	udk	you don't know
UDM	udm	you da (the) man
UDP	udp	User Datagram Protocol
UDS	uds	ugly domestic scene
UDS	uds	you dumb shit
UDWK	udwk	you don't want to know
UDY	udy	You done yet?
UES	ues	Upper East Side (of Manhattan)
UFAB	ufab	ugly fat-ass bitch
UFB	ufb	un-fucking-believable
UFC	ufc	Ultimate Fighting Championship
UFIA	ufia	unsolicited finger in the anus
UFIC	ufic	unsolicited finger in chili
UFMF	ufmf	you funny motherfucker
UFN	ufn	until further notice
UFO	ufo	unidentified flying object
UG	ug	ugly
UG2BK	ug2bk	you've got to be kidding
UGBA	ugba	you gay bitch ass
UGC	ugc	user-generated content
UGG	ugg	ugly
UGGO	uggo	ugly person
UGGS	uggs	brand of boots
UGH	ugh	expression of disappointment or disgust
UGTBK	ugtbk	you've got to be kidding
UGTR	ugtr	you got that right
UH	uh	expression of hesitation
UHAB	uhab	You have a blog?
UHEMS	uhems	you hardly ever make sense
UHM	uhm	(same as "uh" or "um")
UHQ	uhq	ultra high quality
UHU	uhu	misspelling of "huh"
UI	ui	user interface
UJDS	ujds	you just did shit
UK	uk	Are you OK?
UK	uk	United Kingdom
UKR	ukr	You know, right?
UKTR	uktr	You know that's right.
UKWIM	ukwim	You know what I mean.
UKWUR	ukwur	You know who you are.
UL	ul	unlucky
UL	ul	upload
U·L	u·l	you will
ULBOM	ulbom	You looked better on Myspace.
U'LL	u'll	you will
UM	um	expression of hesitation
UMAD	umad	Are you mad?
UMBJ	umbj	You must be joking.
UMFRIEND	umfriend	sexual partner
UML	uml	Unified Modeling Language
UMML	umml	You make me laugh.
UMTWTM	umtwtm	You mean the world to me.

UPPERCASE	LOWERCASE	MEANING
UN	un	United Nations
UN2BO	un2bo	You need to back off.
UN4RTUN8LY	un4rtun8ly	unfortunately
UN4TUN8	un4tun8	unfortunate
UNA	una	use no acronyms
UNBLEFBLE	unblefble	unbelievable
UNC	unc	Universal Naming Convention
UNCE	unce	sound of club music
UNCLEFKR	unclefkr	unclefucker (homosexual slur/derogatory)
UNCRTN	uncrtn	uncertain
UNDIES	undies	underwear
UNESCO	unesco	United Nations Educational, Scientific and Cultural Organization
UNI	uni	university
UNICEF	unicef	United Nations Children's Fund
UNK	unk	crackhead
UNO	uno	you know
UNPC	unpc	unpolitically correct
UOK	uok	You OK?
UOM	uom	you owe me
UPCIA	upcia	unsolicited pool cue in anus
UPIA	upia	unsolicited pencil in anus
UPMO	upmo	you piss me off
UPnP	upnp	Universal Plug and Play
UPOS	upos	you piece of shit
UPPL	uppl	you people
UPS	ups	Uninterruptible Power Supply
UPS	ups	United Parcel Service
UPT	upt	uptown
UPW	upw	unidentified party wound
UR	ur	you are
UR	ur	your
U'R	u'r	you're
UR2G	ur2g	you are too good
UR2YS4ME	ur2ys4me	you are too wise for me
UR6C	ur6c	you're sexy
URA	ura	you are a
URA*	ura*	you are a star
URADRK	uradrk	you're a dork
URAFB	urafb	you are a fucking bitch
URAPITA	urapita	you are a pain in the ass
URAQT	uraqt	you are a cutie
URCRZY	urcrzy	you are crazy
URE	ure	you are
URG	urg	you are gay (homosexual slur/derogatory)
URGH	urgh	expression of annoyance, displeasure
URH	urh	you're hot
URHT	urht	you're hot
URI	uri	Uniform Resource Identifier
URL	url	Uniform Resource Locator, Internet address
URL8	url8	you are late
URM	urm	you are mad
URMS	urms	you rock my socks
URNC	urnc	you are not cool

UPPERCASE	LOWERCASE	MEANING
URP	urp	vomit, throw up
URS	urs	yours
URSAB	ursab	you are such a bitch
URSAI	ursai	you are such an idiot
URSDF	ursdf	you are so damn fine
URSG	ursg	you are so gay (homosexual slur/derogatory)
URSH	ursh	you are so hot
URSKTM	ursktm	you are so kind to me
URSMR	ursmr	You are shitting me, right?
URSSB	urssb	You are so sexy, baby.
URSTPID	urstpid	You are stupid.
URSTU	urstu	You are stupid.
URSW	ursw	You are so weird.
URTB	urtb	You are the best.
URTBITW	urtbitw	You are the best in the world!
URTM	urtm	You are the man.
URTRD	urtrd	you retard (mentally challenged - disability slur/derogatory)
URTW	urtw	You are the worst.
URVW	urvw	You are very weird.
URVW	urw	You are very welcome.
URW	urw	You are weird.
URW	urw	You are welcome.
URYYFM	uryyfm	You are too wise (two *y*s) for me.
US	us	United States
USAF	usaf	United States Air Force
USB	usb	Universal Serial Bus
USBCA	usbca	until something better comes along
USBM	usbm	United States Black Metal
USC	usc	University of Southern California
USCK	usck	you suck
USD	usd	United States dollar
USER	user	someone who uses other people to gain an advantage
USMC	usmc	United States Marine Corps
USP	usp	unique selling point
USPS	usps	United States Postal Service
USS	uss	United States ship
USSR	ussr	Union of Soviet Socialist Republics
USU	usu	usually
USUK	usuk	you suck
USUX	usux	you suck
USW	usw	*und so weiter* (German for "etc.")
UT	ut	unreal tournament
UT	ut	*Unreal Tournament* (online gaming)
UT	ut	You there?
UT2L	ut2l	you take too long
UTC	utc	Coordinated Universal Time
UTC	utc	under the counter
UTE	ute	utility vehicle, pickup truck
UTF	utf	Unicode Transformation Format
UTFS	utfs	use the fucking search
UTFSE	utfse	use the fucking search engine
UTH	uth	up the hoods
UTI	uti	urinary tract infection

UPPERCASE	LOWERCASE	MEANING
UTM	utm	you tell me
UTO	uto	unable to obtain
UTS	uts	under the skin
UTT	utt	under the table
UTTM	uttm	You talking to me?
UTUBE	utube	YouTube
UTY	uty	it's up to you
UV	uv	unpleasant visual
U'V	u'v	you have
UVE	uve	you've
UVGTBSM	uvgtbsm	you have got to be shitting me
UW	uw	you're welcome
UWC	uwc	you are welcome
UWS	uws	Upper West Side (of Manhattan)
UY	uy	up yours
UYA	uya	up your ass
UYAB	uyab	up your ass, bitch
V	v	very
V.V	v.v	sad, lonely
V/R	v/r	very respectfully
V@GIN@	v@gin@	vagina
V4G1N4	v4g1n4	vagina
V4V	v4v	vote for vote
V8	v8	engine type
V8	v8	vegetable drink
VA	va	various artists
VAC	vac	valve anti-cheat
VACA	vaca	vacation, holiday
VAG	vag	vagina
VAIR	vair	very
VAJAYJAY	vajayjay	vagina
VANILLA	vanilla	unexciting, conventional
VAT	vat	value-added tax
VATO	vato	dude (Mexican)
VB	vb	visual basic
VBEG	vbeg	very big evil grin
VBG	vbg	very big grin
VBL	vbl	visible bra line
VBR	vbr	variable bit rate
VBS	vbs	very big smile
VC	vc	venture capital
VC	vc	voice chat
VCD	vcd	video compact disc
VCDA	vcda	*vaya con dios, amigo*
VCI	vci	Virtual Channel Identifier
VCR	vcr	video cassette recorder
VDU	vdu	Visual Display Unit
VEETA	veeta	money
VEG	veg	sit around and do nothing
VEG	veg	vegetarian
VEG	veg	very evil grin
VENT	vent	Ventrilo (Internet chat program)
VERLAN	verlan	French reverse slang (from "*l'anvers*")
VERS	vers	versatile

UPPERCASE	LOWERCASE	MEANING
VET	vet	veteran
VEXED	vexed	angry, annoyed
VF	vf	vampire freaks
VF	vf	very funny
VFAT	vfat	Virtual File Allocation Table
VFE	vfe	virgins forever
VFF	vff	very fucking funny
VFM	vfm	value for money
VG	vg	very good
VG	vg	video game
VGA	vga	Video Graphics Array
VGC	vgc	very good condition
VGG	vgg	very good game
VGH	vgh	very good hand
VGL	vgl	very good-looking
VHS	vhs	Video Home System
VIBE	vibe	atmosphere, ambience
VID	vid	video
VIDS	vids	videos
VIG	vig	interest paid on a loan
VIP	vip	very important person
VIXEN	vixen	attractive woman
VIZ	viz	adult comic
VIZ	viz	namely ("*videlicet*" in Latin)
VJ	vj	video jockey (like DJ with lights and video)
VLB	vlb	VESA Local Bus
VLE	vle	Virtual Learning Environment
VLEO	vleo	very low earth orbit
VLOG	vlog	video log
VLOGGER	vlogger	video blogger
VM	vm	voice mail
VMI	vmi	Virginia Military Institute
VN	vn	very nice
VNC	vnc	Virtual Network Computing
VNH	vnh	very nice hand (in online card games, especially poker)
VNS	vns	very nice shot
VOD	vod	video on demand
VoIP	voip	voice over internet protocol
VOIP	voip	voice over IP, Internet telephony
VOM	vom	vomit
VP	vp	vice president
VP	vp	videophone
VP	vp	very pretty
VPI	vpi	virtual path identifier
VPL	vpl	visible panty line
VPN	vpn	virtual private network
VR	vr	virtual reality
VRAM	vram	video random-access memory
VRBS	vrbs	virtual reality bullshit
VRML	vrml	virtual reality modeling language
VRSTY	vrsty	varsity
VRY	vry	very
VS	vs	versus, against

UPPERCASE	LOWERCASE	MEANING
VS	vs	very stupid
VSC	vsc	very soft chuckle
VSF	vsf	very sad face
VTPR	vtpr	view to permanent relationship
VUB	vub	very ugly boy
VUG	vug	very ugly girl
VUM	vum	very ugly man
VUW	vuw	very ugly woman
VV	vv	very, very
VVV	vvv	referring to comment below
VW	vw	Volkswagen
VWD	vwd	very well done
VWEG	vweg	very wicked evil grin
VWP	vwp	very well played
VWP	vwp	very well put
VZIT	vzit	visit
VZN	vzn	Verizon
W	w	George W. Bush
W.B.S.	w.b.s.	write back soon
W.E	w.e	whatever
W.O.W	w.o.w	*World of Warcraft* (game)
W/	w/	with
W/B	w/b	welcome back
W/B	w/b	write back
W/DAY	w/day	weekday
W/E	w/e	whatever
W/E	w/e	whenever
W/E	w/e	whereever
W/END	w/end	weekend
W/EVA	w/eva	whatever
W/I	w/i	within
W/O	w/o	without
W/OUT	w/out	without
W/U	w/u	with you
W@	w@	What?
W@NK	w@nk	wank (sexual act)
W@NKJOB	w@nkjob	wankjob (sexual act)
W\E	w\e	whatever
W^	w^	What's up?
W'EVER	w'ever	whatever
W00T	w00t	hurrah
W00T	w00t	woo-hoo
W012D	w012d	word
W0P	w0p	Wop (Italian person · ethnic slur/derogatory)
W2D	w2d	What to do?
W2F	w2f	want to fuck
W2F	w2f	way too funny
W2G	w2g	way to go
W2HO	w2ho	want to hang out
W2M	w2m	want to meet
W3	w3	www (Web address)
W33D	w33d	weed
W3C	w3c	World Wide Web Consortium
W4M	w4m	woman looking for a man

UPPERCASE	LOWERCASE	MEANING
W4W	w4w	women for women
W8	w8	wait
W8AM	w8am	wait a minute
W8er	w8er	waiter
W8ING	w8ing	waiting
W8T4ME	w8t4me	wait for me
W8TER	w8ter	waiter
W911	w911	wife in room
WA	wa	wife agro
WA GWAN	wa gwan	what's going on
WAA	waa	crying
WAAM	waam	what's going on, what's up
WAAN	waan	want
WAB	wab	what a bitch
WACK	wack	low quality, lame
WAD	wad	without a doubt
WAD ^	wad ^	What's up?
WADR	wadr	with all due respect
WADZUP	wadzup	What's up?
WAEFRD	waefrd	when all else fails, read directions
WAF	waf	weird as fuck
WAFB	wafb	what a fucking bitch
WAFDA	wafda	what a fucking dumb ass
WAFFLE	waffle	pointless talk
WAFJ	wafj	what a fucking jerk
WAFL	wafl	what a fucking loser
WAFM	wafm	wait a fucking minute
WAFM	wafm	what a fucking mess
WAFN	wafn	what a fucking noob
WAFU	wafu	what a fuck up
WAG1	wag1	What's going on?
WAGWAN	wagwan	What's going on?
WAGWARN	wagwarn	What's going on?
WAGWUN	wagwun	What's going on?
WAH	wah	working at home
WAHM	wahm	work-at-home mom
WAI	wai	what an idiot
WAIS	wais	Wide Area Information Server
WAJ	waj	what a jerk
WAJ	waj	what a joke
WAL	wal	what a loser
WALAHI	walahi	I swear to God
WALE	wale	Rapper
WALLA	walla	*voila* (French for "here it is")
WALLAH	wallah	"I swear to God" in Arabic
WALLHAX	wallhax	wall hack (allows a player to walk through walls)
WALLY	wally	stupid person
WALOC	waloc	what a load of crap
WALSTIB	walstib	what a long strange trip it's been
WAM	wam	wait a minute
WAM	wam	what a mess
WAMH	wamh	with all my heart
WAMHAS	wamhas	with all my heart and soul
WAML	waml	with all my love

UPPERCASE	LOWERCASE	MEANING
WAN	wan	what a newbie
WAN	wan	Wide Area Network
WAN2	wan2	Want to?
WAN2TLK	wan2tlk	want to talk
WANA	wana	want to
WANAFUK	wanafuk	wanna fuck
WANKER	wanker	masturbate
WANKING	wanking	masturbating
WANNA	wanna	want to
WANNABE	wannabe	someone who wants to be what they are not
WANSTA	wansta	wanna be gangster
WAO	wao	wow
WAP	wap	wireless access point
WAPCE	wapce	women are pure concentrated evil
WAREZ	warez	pirated software (illegal)
WAS	was	wait a second
WAS	was	wait and see
WAS	was	wild ass guess
WAS^	was^	What's up?
WASH	wash	waste of time
WASP	wasp	white Anglo-Saxon protestant
WASSUP	wassup	What's up?
WASTE MAN	waste man	someone who is a waste of time and space
WASTED	wasted	drunk, stoned
WASTEMAN	wasteman	worthless person, waste of space
WASUP	wasup	What's up?
WAT	wat	what
WAT'S^	wat's^	What's up?
WATCHA	watcha	what are you
WATEV	watev	whatever
WATEVA	wateva	whatever
WATEVR	watevr	whatever
WATEVS	watevs	whatever
WATP	watp	we are the people
WATS	wats	what's
WATS ^	wats ^	What's up?
WATZ ^	watz ^	What's up?
WAU	wau	What about you?
WAU^2	wau^2	What are you up to?
WAUG	waug	Where are you going?
WAVEY	wavey	drunk, high
WAVY	wavy	very nice
WAVY	wavy	well dressed
WAW	waw	what a wanker
WAW	waw	what a waste
WAW	waw	what a whore
WAWA	wawa	Where are we at?
WAX	wax	without any experience
WAY	way	Where are you?
WAYCB	waycb	When are you coming back?
WAYD	wayd	What are you doing?
WAYDRN	waydrn	What are you doing right now?
WAYF	wayf	Where are you from?
WAYGOW	waygow	Who are you going out with?

UPPERCASE	LOWERCASE	MEANING
WAYH	wayh	Why are you here?
WAYLT	waylt	What are you listening to?
WAYN	wayn	Where are you now?
WAYOA	wayoa	What are you on about?
WAYSTTM	waysttm	Why are you still talking to me?
WAYSW	waysw	Why are you so weird?
WAYT	wayt	What are you thinking?
WAYTA	wayta	What are you talking about?
WAYUT	wayut	What are you up to?
WAZ	waz	what is
WAZ ^	waz ^	What's up?
WAZ UP	waz up	What's up?
WAZ^	waz^	What's up?
WAZZ	wazz	what's
WAZZA	wazza	What's up?
WB	wb	welcome back
WB	wb	write back
WBAGNFARB	wbagnfarb	would be a good name for a rock band
WBB	wbb	will be back
WBBS	wbbs	will be back soon
WBM	wbm	wannabe moderator
WBN	wbn	would be nice
WBP	wbp	welcome back, partner
WBR	wbr	with best regards
WBRB	wbrb	will be right back
WBS	wbs	write back soon
WBT	wbt	will be there
WBU	wbu	What (a)bout you?
WBY	wby	What (a)bout you?
WC	wc	water closet, toilet
WC	wc	welcome
WC	wc	Who cares?
WC3	wc3	*WarCraft III* (game)
WCA	wca	who cares anyway
WCB	wcb	will call back
WCD	wcd	What chu doing?
WCMTSU	wcmtsu	we can't make this shit up
WCS	wcs	worst-case scenario
WCUTM	wcutm	What can you tell me?
WCW	wcw	Webcam whore
WCW	wcw	World Championship Wrestling
WD	wd	well done
WD40	wd40	multipurpose lubricant
WDALYIC	wdalyic	Who died and left you in charge?
WDC	wdc	What's da craic?
WDF	wdf	worth dying for
WDHLM	wdhlm	Why doesn't he love me?
WDIC	wdic	What do I care?
WDIDN	wdidn	What do I do now?
WDIM	wdim	What did I miss?
WDITOT	wditot	Why didn't I think of that?
WDMB	wdmb	will do my best
WDOML	wdoml	worst day of my life
WDTM	wdtm	What does that mean?

UPPERCASE	LOWERCASE	MEANING
WDUC	wduc	What do you care?
WDUD	wdud	What do you do?
WDUM	wdum	What do you mean?
WDUS	wdus	What did you say?
WDUT	wdut	What do you think?
WDUTOM	wdutom	What do you think of me?
WDUW	wduw	What do you want?
WDUWTA	wduwta	What do you wanna talk about?
WDUWTTA	wduwtta	What do you want to talk about?
WDWDN	wdwdn	What do we do now?
WDWGW	wdwgw	Where did we go wrong?
WDYDT	wdydt	Why do you do that?
WDYE	wdye	What did you expect?
WDYG	wdyg	Where did you go?
WDYK	wdyk	What do you know?
WDYL	wdyl	Who do you like?
WDYM	wdym	What do you mean?
WDYMBT	wdymbt	What do you mean by that?
WDYS	wdys	What did you say?
WDYT	wdyt	What do you think?
WDYTIA	wdytia	Who do you think I am?
WDYW	wdyw	What do you want?
WDYWTD	wdywtd	What do you want to do?
WDYWTDT	wdywtdt	Why do you want to do that?
WDYWTTA	wdywtta	What do you want to talk about?
WE	we	whatever
WEB	web	World Wide Web, Internet
WEBBY	webby	Webcam
WEBINAR	webinar	Web-based seminar
WEE	wee	small
WEED	weed	marijuana
WEEE	weee	exclamation of excitement
WEF	wef	with effect from
WEG	weg	wicked evil grin
WEHT	weht	Whatever happened to?
WEL	wel	whatever, loser
WELC	welc	welcome
WELL	well	very, so
WELP	welp	well
WEML	weml	whatever, major loser
WEN	wen	when
WENG	weng	good-looking
WEP	wep	weapon
WEP	wep	wired equivalent privacy
WEPA	wepa	All right, cool, yeah!
WERD	werd	expression of agreement
WERK	werk	expression of approval, praise
WERKZ	werkz	works
WET BACK	wet back	illegal immigrant
WETSU	wetsu	we eat this shit up
WEV	wev	whatever
WEVA	weva	whatever
WEVE	weve	what ever
WEVR	wevr	whatever

UPPERCASE	LOWERCASE	MEANING
WEWT	wewt	alternative spelling of woot
WEY	wey	dude, buddy
WFH	wfh	working from home
WFHW	wfhw	what's for homework
WFM	wfm	works for me
WFYB	wfyb	whatever floats your boat
WG	wg	wicked girl
WGAC	wgac	Who gives a crap?
WGACA	wgaca	What do you think?
WGAF	wgaf	Who gives a fuck?
WGAFF	wgaff	Who gives a flying fuck?
WGAS	wgas	Who gives a shit?
WGASA	wgasa	Who gives a shit anyway?
WGAT	wgat	misspelling of "what"
WGO	wgo	What's going on?
WGPH2	wgph2	Want to go play *Halo 2*?
WH	wh	wall hack (allows a player to walk through walls)
WH0RE	wh0re	whore (hussy)
WH0RE :)	wh0re :)	whoreface (idiot)
WH0REBAG	wh0rebag	whorebag (idiot)
WH40K	wh40k	*Warhammer 40000* (game)
WH5	wh5	who, what, when, where, why
WHA	wha	What?
WHACK	whack	bad
WHADDYA	whaddya	What do you?
WHALE	whale	punch, beat
WHALETAIL	whaletail	thong
WHAT^	what^	What's up?
WHATCHA	whatcha	What are/do you...
WHATEV	whatev	whatever
WHATEVS	whatevs	whatever
WHATS ^	whats ^	What's up?
WHEEL	wheel	chat up, pick up (a girl)
WHEELING	wheeling	picking up women
WHEVAH	whevah	wherever
WHEVER	whever	whatever
WHEW	whew	expression of relief or amazement
WHF	whf	Wanna have fun?
WHIP	whip	expensive car
WHIPPED	whipped	controlled by girlfriend/wife
WHISKEY TANGO	whiskey tango	WT, white trash
WHIT	whit	with
WHITEWASH	whitewash	act like a white person
WHITY	whity	whitey (white person - ethnic slur/derogatory)
WHIZ	whiz	talented person
WHO	who	World Health Organization
WHOA	whoa	expression of surprise/slow down
WHODI	whodi	friend
WHR	whr	where
WHS	whs	wanna have sex
WHT	wht	what
WHT^	wht^	what up
WHTEVA	whteva	what ever

UPPERCASE	LOWERCASE	MEANING
WHTEVE	whteve	whatever
WHTEVER	whtever	whatever
WHTEVR	whtevr	whatever
WHTVR	whtvr	whatever
WHUBU2	whubu2	What have you been up to?
WHUBUT	whubut	What have you been up to?
WHUT	whut	what
WHYD	whyd	What have you done?
WIA	wia	wounded in action
WIBNI	wibni	wouldn't it be nice if . . .
WIC	wic	women, infants, and children
WIC	wic	*World in Conflict* (game)
WICKED	wicked	cool, great/very, extremely
WID	wid	with
WIDOUT	widout	without
WIDOW	widow	(same as "WW")
WIF	wif	with
WIFEY	wifey	serious girlfriend, wife material
WIFF	wiff	with
WIFI	wifi	wireless fidelity, wireless Internet
Wi-Fi	wi-fi	wireless fidelity, wireless Internet
WIGGER	wigger	white person pretending to be black
WII	wii	Nintendo game console
WIID	wiid	What if I did?
WIIFM	wiifm	What's in it for me?
WIKTT	wiktt	when I kissed the teacher
WILCO	wilco	will comply
WIMP	wimp	weak, cowardly person
WINNAR	winnar	winner
WIO	wio	without
WIP	wip	work in progress
WIR	wir	when it's ready
WIRED	wired	high on stimulants
WIRED	wired	online
WISP	wisp	winning is so pleasurable
WIT	wit	with
WITCHA	witcha	with you
WITFP	witfp	What is the fucking point?
WITH	with	where in the hell
WITP	witp	What is the point?
WITU	witu	with you
WITW	witw	What in the world?
WITWCT	witwct	What is the world coming to?
WITWU	witwu	Who is there with you?
WITWWYT	witwwyt	What in the world were you thinking?
WIU	wiu	What is up?
WIU	wiu	wrap it up
WIUWY	wiuwy	What is up with you?
WIV	wiv	with
WIW	wiw	wife is watching
WIWT	wiwt	wish I was there
WIWWU	wiwwu	wish I was with you
WIWWY	wiwwy	What is wrong with you?
WIYP	wiyp	What is your problem?

UPPERCASE	LOWERCASE	MEANING
WJD	wjd	what Jesus did
WJWD	wjwd	what Jesus would do
WK	wk	week
WKD	wkd	weekend
WKD	wkd	wicked
WKDAY	wkday	weekday
WKEND	wkend	weekend
WKND	wknd	weekend
WKS	wks	well-kept secret
WL	wl	whatta loser
WL	wl	will
WLC	wlc	welcome
WLCB	wlcb	welcome back
WLCM	wlcm	welcome
WLD	wld	would
WLKD	wlkd	walked
WLM	wlm	Windows Live Messenger
WLOS	wlos	wife looking over shoulder
WLTM	wltm	would like to meet
WLYK	wlyk	will let you know
WM	wm	woman marine
WMA	wma	Windows Media Audio
WMAO	wmao	working my ass off
WMD	wmd	weapons of mass destruction
WMF	wmf	wagging my finger
WMG	wmg	Warner Music Group
WMGL	wmgl	wish me good luck
WMJ	wmj	*Wat maak jy?* (Afrikaans for "What are you doing?")
WML	wml	wish me luck
WMMOWS	wmmows	Wash my mouth out with soap!
WMP	wmp	Windows Media Player
WMP	wmp	with much pleasure
WMPL	wmpl	wet my pants laughing
WN	wn	when
WNA	wna	want to
WNDITWB	wnditwb	We never did it this way before.
WNKR	wnkr	wanker
WNOHGB	wnohgb	where no one has gone before
WNRN	wnrn	why not right now
WNT	wnt	want
WNTD	wntd	what not to do
WNWY	wnwy	What's new with you?
WOA	woa	word of advice
WOAH	woah	misspelling of "whoa"
WOAT	woat	worst of all time
WOB	wob	waste of bandwidth
WOC	woc	welcome on cam
WOC	woc	women of color
WOCHIT	wochit	watch it
WOE	woe	what on earth
WOF	wof	while on fire
WOFT	woft	waste of fucking time
WOG	wog	a foreigner (ethnic slur/derogatory)

UPPERCASE	LOWERCASE	MEANING
WOG	wog	black person (African American - ethnic slur/derogatory)
WOGGE	wogge	What on God's green earth?
WOGS	wogs	waste of good sperm
WOLS	wols	slow
WOM	wom	women over mates
WOM	wom	word of mouse
WOM	wom	word of mouth
WOMBAT	wombat	waste of money, brains, and time
WONK	wonk	expert
WONKY	wonky	weird, not right
WOO HOO	woo hoo	expression of excitement
WOOK	wook	dirty hippie
WOOP	woop	woot
WOOT	woot	hurrah (wow, loot, woo-hoo)
WOOT	woot	want one of those
WOP	wop	offensive term for an Italian (ethnic slur/derogatory)
WOR	wor	our
WORD	word	OK, I agree, hey
WORD UP	word up	OK, I agree
WORDS	words	response to something you don't care about
WORM	worm	malicious computer program
WOS	wos	waste of space
WOS	wos	wife over shoulder
WOT	wot	what
WOTAM	wotam	waste of time and money
WOTCHER	wotcher	What are you up to? WU?
WOTEVS	wotevs	whatever
WOTLK	wotlk	*Wrath of the Lich King* (game)
WOTS	wots	word on the street
WOTV	wotv	What's on television?
WOTW	wotw	word of the week
WOUM	woum	What's on your mind?
WOW	wow	World of Warcraft
WOWZER	wowzer	exaggerated "wow"
WOWZERS	wowzers	wow
WOZ	woz	was
WP	wp	well played
WP	wp	wrong person
WPA	wpa	Wi-Fi Protected Access
WPE	wpe	worst president ever (Bush)
WPM	wpm	words per minute
WPWW	wpww	white pride worldwide
WR	wr	warm regards
WRDO	wrdo	weirdo
WRF	wrf	we're fucked
WRGAD	wrgad	Who really gives a damn?
WRGAF	wrgaf	Who really gives a fuck?
WRK	wrk	work
WRKR	wrkr	worker
WRM	wrm	which reminds me
WRNG	wrng	wrong
WRT	wrt	with regard to
WRT	wrt	with respect to

221

UPPERCASE	LOWERCASE	MEANING
WRTG	wrtg	writing
WRTHLS	wrthls	worthless
WRU	wru	Where are you?
WRU@	wru@	Where are you at?
WRUD	wrud	What are you doing?
WRUF	wruf	Where are you from?
WRUU2	wruu2	What are you up to?
WSA	wsa	wow, strong arms
WSB	wsb	Wanna cyber?
WSF	wsf	we should fuck
WSHTF	wshtf	when shit hits the fan
WSI	wsi	Why should I?
WSIBT	wsibt	When should I be there?
WSIC	wsic	Why should I care?
WSIDI	wsidi	Why should I do it?
WSM	wsm	woman seeking man
WSOP	wsop	World Series of Poker
WSP	wsp	What's up?
WSS	wss	Why so serious?
WST	wst	we're still friends
WSUL	wsul	will see you later
W'SUP	w'sup	What's up?
WSWTA	wswta	What shall we talk about?
WT	wt	what
WT?	wt?	"What the . . .?" or "Who the . . .?"
WTA	wta	winner takes all
WTB	wtb	want to buy
WTBACK	wtback	Wetback (Mexican person - ethnic slur/derogatory)
WTBD	wtbd	What's the big deal?
WTBH	wtbh	What the bloody hell?
WTC	wtc	What the crap?
WTC	wtc	World Trade Center
WTCF	wtcf	What the crazy fuck?
WTD	wtd	What the deuce?
WTDT	wtdt	what to do today
WTDTA	wtdta	Where they do that at?
WTF	wtf	What the fuck?
WTFAUD	wtfaud	What the fuck are you doing?
WTFAY	wtfay	Who the fuck are you?
WTFAYD	wtfayd	What the fuck are you doing?
WTFAYT	wtfayt	Why the fuck are you talking?
WTFAYTA	wtfayta	What the fuck are you talking about?
WTFB	wtfb	What the fuck, bitch?
WTFBS	wtfbs	What the fuck, bullshit?
WTFC	wtfc	Who the fuck cares?
WTFDIK	wtfdik	What the fuck do I know?
WTFDUM	wtfdum	What the fuck do you mean?
WTFDUW	wtfduw	What the fuck do you want?
WTFDYJS	wtfdyjs	What the fuck did you just say?
WTFDYM	wtfdym	What the fuck do you mean?
WTFDYW	wtfdyw	What the fuck do you want?
WTFE	wtfe	what the fuck ever
WTFEVER	wtfever	what the fuck ever
WTFG	wtfg	what the fucking god

UPPERCASE	LOWERCASE	MEANING
WTFGDA	wtfgda	way to fucking go, dumb ass
WTFH	wtfh	What the fucking heck?
WTFH	wtfh	What the fucking hell?
WTFHB	wtfhb	What the fucking hell, bitch?
WTFHWT	wtfhwt	What the fucking hell was that?
WTFIGO	wtfigo	What the fuck is going on?
WTFIGOH	wtfigoh	What the fuck is going on here?
WTFIT	wtfit	What the fuck is that?
WTFITS	wtfits	What the fuck is this shit?
WTFIU	wtfiu	What the fuck is up?
WTFIUP	wtfiup	What the fuck is your problem?
WTFIUWY	wtfiuwy	What the fuck is up with you?
WTFIWWU	wtfiwwu	What the fuck is wrong with you?
WTFIWWY	wtfiwwy	What the fuck is wrong with you?
WTFIYP	wtfiyp	What the fuck is your problem?
WTFM	wtfm	What the fuck, mate?
WTFMF	wtfmf	What the fuck, motherfucker?
WTFO	wtfo	What the fuck over?
WTFRU	wtfru	What the fuck are you?
WTFRU	wtfru	Where the fuck is you?
WTFRUD	wtfrud	What the fuck are you doing?
WTFRUDNG	wtfrudng	What the fuck are you doing?
WTFRUO	wtfruo	What the fuck are you on?
WTFRUTTD	wtfruttd	What the fuck are you trying to do?
WTFS	wtfs	What the fucking shit?
WTFT	wtft	What the french toast? (polite WTF)
WTFUAH	wtfuah	What the fuck, you asshole?
WTFUL	wtful	What the fuck, you loser?
WTFWJD	wtfwjd	What the fuck would Jesus do?
WTFWT	wtfwt	What the fuck was that?
WTFWTD	wtfwtd	What the fuck was that, dude?
WTFWTF	wtfwtf	What the fuck was that for?
WTFWY	wtfwy	Where the fuck was you?
WTFWYCM	wtfwycm	Why the fuck would you call me?
WTFYA	wtfya	What the fuck, you asshole?
WTFYB	wtfyb	What the fuck, you bitch?
WTG	wtg	way to go
WTGDS	wtgds	way to go, dumb shit
WTGP	wtgp	Want to go private?
WTGP	wtgp	way to go, partner
WTH	wth	What the heck? / What the hell?
WTH	wth	what/where/who the hell
WTHARUD	wtharud	What the heck are you doing?
WTHAU	wthau	Who the hell are you?
WTHAUWF	wthauwf	What the hell are you waiting for?
WTHAY	wthay	Who the hell are you?
WTHAYD	wthayd	What the heck are you doing?
WTHAYDWMGF	wthaydwmgf	What the hell are you doing with my girlfriend?
WTHC	wthc	Who the hell cares?
WTHDYDT	wthdydt	Why the hell did you do that?
WTHHYB	wthhyb	Where the hell have you been?
WTHIGO	wthigo	What the hell is going on?
WTHIWWU	wthiwwu	What the hell is wrong with you?

UPPERCASE	LOWERCASE	MEANING
WTHO	wtho	Want to hang out?
WTHRU	wthru	Who the heck are you?
WTHRUD	wthrud	What the hell are you doing?
WTHS	wths	Want to have sex?
WTHSWM	wthswm_N	Want to have sex with me?
WTHWT	wthwt	What the hell was that?
WTHWUT	wthwut	What the hell were you thinking?
WTHYI	wthyi	what the hell, you idiot
WTII	wtii	What time is it?
WTIIOT	wtiiot	What time is it over there?
WTITYB	wtityb	whatever, tell it to your blog
WTK	wtk	want to know
WTL	wtl	will talk later
WTM	wtm	What's the matter?
WTM	wtm	Who's the man?
WTMF	wtmf	What the motherfuck?
WTMFH	wtmfh	What the motherfucking hell?
WTMI	wtmi	way too much information
WTMTR	wtmtr	What's the matter?
WTMW	wtmw	Welcome to my world.
WTO	wto	World Trade Organization
WTP	wtp	What's the point?
WTP	wtp	Where's the party?
WTRUD	wtrud	What are you doing?
WTS	wts	want to sell
WTSHTF	wtshtf	when the shit hits the fan
WTT	wtt	want to trade
WTTC	wttc	Welcome to the club.
WTTIR	wttir	when the time is right
WTTM	wttm	without thinking too much
WTV	wtv	whatever
WTVA	wtva	whatever
WTVR	wtvr	whatever
WTWM	wtwm	What time are we meeting?
WTWR	wtwr	well, that was random
WTY	wty	why, thank you
WTYO	wtyo	whatever turns you on
WU	wu	What's up?
WU2KILU	wu2kilu	want you to know I love you
WUB	wub	love
WUBMBF	wubmbf	Will you be my boyfriend?
WUBMGF	wubmgf	Will you be my girlfriend?
WUBU	wubu	What have you been up to?
WUBU2	wubu2	What have you been up to?
WUBUT	wubut	What have you been up to?
WUCIWUG	wuciwug	what you see is what you get
WUD	wud	What are you doing?
WUD	wud	would
WUDEV	wudev	whatever
WUDN	wudn	What are you doing now?
WUF	wuf	Where are you from?
WUG	wug	What do you got?
WUG	wug	Where are you going?
WUGOWM	wugowm	Will you go out with me?

UPPERCASE	LOWERCASE	MEANING
WUH	wuh	What?
WUL	wul	watched user list
WULA	wula	What're you looking at?
WULD	wuld	would
WUM	wum	wind-up merchant
WUM	wum	woman
WUN	wun	bye
WUNY	wuny	wait until next year
WUP	wup	What's up?
WUS	wus	wimp
WUSSUP	wussup	What is up?
WUT	wut	what
WUTCHA	wutcha	What are you?
WUTEVA	wuteva	whatever
WUTEVR	wutevr	what ever
WUTS	wuts	what is
WUTUP	wutup	What's up?
WUU2	wuu2	What are you up to?
WUU22M	wuu22m	What you up to tomorrow?
WUUP2	wuup2	What are you up to?
WUUT	wuut	What are you up to?
WUV	wuv	love
WUW	wuw	What you want?
WUWCB	wuwcb	What do you want to chat about?
WUWH	wuwh	wish you were here
WUWT	wuwt	What's up with that?
WUWTA	wuwta	What you wanna talk about?
WUWTAB	wuwtab	What do you want to talk about?
WUWTB	wuwtb	What do you want to talk about?
WUWTB	wuwtb	What you wanna talk 'bout?
WUWU	wuwu	What's up with you?
WUZ	wuz	was
WUZ4DINA	wuz4dina	What's for dinner?
WUZA	wuza	What's up?
WUZUP	wuzup	What's up?
WW	ww	white widow (strong marijuana)
WW	ww	white woman
WW1	ww1	World War I
WW2	ww2	World War II
WWBD	wwbd	What would Batman do?
WWC	wwc	Who would care?
WWCND	wwcnd	What would Chuck Norris do?
WWDHD	wwdhd	What would David Hasselhoff do?
WWE	wwe	World Wrestling Entertainment
WWF	wwf	World Wildlife Fund
WWF	wwf	World Wrestling Federation (now WWE)
WWGF	wwgf	when we gonna fuck
WWHW	wwhw	when, where, how, why
WWIKT	wwikt	Why would I know that?
WWJBD	wwjbd	What would Jason Bourne do?
WWJD	wwjd	What would Jesus do?
WWJD	wwjd	What would Judd do?
WWNC	wwnc	will wonders never cease
WWOTW	wwotw	Wicked Witch of the West

UPPERCASE	LOWERCASE	MEANING
WWT	wwt	What was that?
WWTF	wwtf	What was that for?
WWUDTM	wwudtm	What would you do to me?
WWUT	wwut	What were you thinking?
WWW	www	World Wide Web
WWWY	wwwy	What's wrong with you?
WWY	wwy	Where were you?
WWYC	wwyc	write when you can
WWYCM	wwycm	When will you call me?
WWYD	wwyd	What would you do?
WWYDT	wwydt	Why would you do that?
WY	wy	Why?
WY	wy	Would you?
WYAS	wyas	Wow, you are stupid.
WYATB	wyatb	wish you all the best
WYAUIMG	wyauimg	Why you all up in my grill?
WYBMV	wybmv	Will you be my valentine?
WYBTS	wybts	Were you born this sexy?
WYC	wyc	Will you come?
WYCM	wycm	Will you call me?
WYD	wyd	What are you doing?
WYDN	wydn	What you doing now?
WYFM	wyfm	Would you fuck me?
WYFP	wyfp	What's your fucking problem?
WYG	wyg	Will you go?
WYGAC	wygac	when you get a chance
WYGAM	wygam	when you get a minute
WYGOWM	wygowm	Will you go out with me?
WYGWM	wygwm	Will you go with me?
WYHAM	wyham	when you have a minute
WYHI	wyhi	Would you hit it?
WYHSWM	wyhswm	Would you have sex with me?
WYK	wyk	would you kindly
WYL	wyl	whatever you like
WYLEI	wylei	when you least expect it
WYLSCWTW	wylscwtw	Would you like some cheese with that whine?
WYLTK	wyltk	Wouldn't you like to know?
WYLYM	wylym	Watch your language, young man.
WYM	wym	watch your mouth
WYM	wym	What you mean?
WYMM	wymm	Will you marry me?
WYMYN	wymyn	women
WYN	wyn	what's your name
WYP	wyp	What's your point?
WYP	wyp	What's your problem?
WYPSU	wypsu	Will you please shut up?
WYR	wyr	would you rather
WYS	wys	Wow, you're stupid.
WYSIAYG	wysiayg	What you see is all you get.
WYSITWIRL	wysitwirl	What you see is totally worthless in real life.
WYSIWYG	wysiwyg	What you see is what you get.
WYTA	wyta	What you talking about?
WYWH	wywh	wish you were here
WYWO	wywo	while you were out

UPPERCASE	LOWERCASE	MEANING
X	x	kiss
X TREME	x treme	extreme
X!	x!	a typical woman
X·(	X·(	angry
X)	x)	happy, mischievous
X.X	x.x	exasperated, irritated, annoyed
X]	x]	happy
X_X	x_x	dead
X~	x~	French kissing
X·1·10	x·1·10	exciting
X3	x3	cute face
XAXA	xaxa	ha ha
XB	xb	Xbox
XB36T	xb36t	Xbox 360
XBF	xbf	ex-boyfriend
XBL	xbl	Xbox live
XC	xc	cross-country
XCEPT	xcept	except
XCPT	xcpt	except
XD	xD	laughing, big grin
X·D	x·D	laughing, big grin
XELLENT	xellent	excellent
XFER	xfer	transfer
XGF	xgf	ex-girlfriend
XH	xh	ex-husband
XHTML	xhtml	Extensible Hypertext Markup Language
XING	xing	crossing
XIT	xit	exit
XL	xl	extra large
XLNT	xlnt	excellent
XLR8	xlr8	accelerate
XLS	xls	Microsoft Excel file extension
XM	xm	extreme
XMAS	xmas	Christmas
XME	xme	excuse me
XML	xml	Extensible Markup Language
XMPL	xmpl	example
XO	xo	hug and kisses
XOAC	xoac	Christ on a crutch
XOR	xor	hacker
XOVER	xover	crossover
XOXO	xoxo	hugs and kisses
XP	xp	experience
XP	xp	Windows operating system
X·p	x·p	joking
XPECT	xpect	expect
XPLANED	xplaned	explained
XPT	xpt	except
XROADS	xroads	crossroads
XS	xs	excess
XS	xs	extra small
XSLT	xslt	Extensible Style Sheet Language Transformation
XT	xt	cross-training
XTC	xtc	ecstasy

UPPERCASE	LOWERCASE	MEANING
XTRA	xtra	extra
XTREME	xtreme	extreme
XVID	xvid	video format
XW	xw	ex-wife
XX	xx	kisses
XYL	xyl	ex-young lady
XYZ	xyz	examine your zipper
XYZPDQ	xyzpdq	examine your zipper pretty darn quick
Y	y	Why?
Y	y	Yale University
Y	y	yawn
Y W	y w	you're welcome
Y!A	y!a	Yahoo! Answers
Y.Y	y.y	crying
Y/N	y/n	yes or no
Y/O	y/o	years old
Y/Y	y/y	yes/yes
Y?	y?	Why?
Y@NK	y@nk	Yank (American person - ethnic slur/derogatory)
Y_Y	y_y	crying
Y'ALL	y'all	you all
Y00	y00	you
Y2B	y2b	YouTube
Y2K	y2k	Year 2000
Y2K	y2k	you're too kind
YA	ya	yes, yeah
YA	ya	you
YA	ya	young adult
YA	ya	your
YAA	yaa	yet another acronym
YAAF	yaaf	you are a fag (homosexual slur/derogatory)
YAAFM	yaafm	you are a fucking moron
YAAGF	yaagf	you are a good friend
YAAI	yaai	you are an idiot
YAAR	yaar	dude, mate (Hindi)
YABA	yaba	yet another bloody acronym
YADA	yada	and so on, blah
YAF	yaf	you're a fag (homosexual slur/derogatory)
YAFI	yafi	you're a fucking idiot
YAG	yag	you are gay
YAGB	yagb	you ain't grizzly baby (cod)
YAHOO	yahoo	yob, lout
YAHWEH	yahweh	the name of God in Hebrew
YAK	yak	you already know
YAL	yal	*girl* (Hispanic)
YALL	yall	you all
YALLA	yalla	*hurry up* (Arabic)
YALLAH	yallah	*let's go* (Arabic)
YANK	yank	American
YANKEE	yankee	American
YANNO	yanno	you know
YANO	yano	you know
YAP	yap	steal, rob
YAPMO	yapmo	you are pissing me off

UPPERCASE	LOWERCASE	MEANING
YAQW	yaqw	you are quite welcome
YAR	yar	yes
YARD	yard	home
YARLY	yarly	yeah really
YAS	yas	emphatic "yes"
YAS	yas	you are sexy
YAS	yas	you are stupid
YASAN	yasan	you are such a nerd
YASF	yasf	you are so funny
YASFG	yasfg	you are so fucking gay
YASG	yasg	you are so gay
YASNY	yasny	you ain't seen nothing yet
YASW	yasw	you are so weird
YAT	yat	girl, woman
YAT	yat	Where you at?
YATB	yatb	You are the best.
YATFM	yatfm	You are too fucking much.
YATK	yatk	You are too kind.
YATWL	yatwl	You are the weakest link.
YAW	yaw	You are welcome.
YAWN	yawn	boring
YAY	yay	cocaine
YAY	yay	exclamation of approval
YAYO	yayo	cocaine
YBBG	ybbg	your brother by grace
YBF	ybf	You've been fucked.
YBFS	ybfs	You'll be fucking sorry.
YBIC	ybic	your brother in Christ
YBS	ybs	You'll be sorry.
YBW	ybw	You've been warned.
YBYA	ybya	You bet your ass.
YBYSA	ybysa	You bet your sweet ass.
YC	yc	you're cool/cute/crazy
YCDBWYCID	ycdbwycid	You can't do business when your computer is down.
YCHT	ycht	You can have them.
YCLIU	ycliu	You can look it up.
YCLIU	ycliu	You could look it up.
YCMIU	ycmiu	You couldn't make it up.
YCMTSU	ycmtsu	You can't make this shit up.
YCMU	ycmu	You crack me up.
YCNTU	ycntu	Why can't you?
YCT	yct	Your comment to?
YCTWUW	yctwuw	You can think what you want.
YD	yd	yesterday
YDEK	ydek	You don't even know.
YDG	ydg	You dig?
YDI	ydi	You deserve it.
YDK	ydk	You don't know.
YDL	ydl	Yellow Dog Linux
YDMS	ydms	You don't make sense.
YDPOS	ydpos	You dumb piece of shit.
YDS	yds	You dipshit.
YDTM	ydtm	You're dead to me.
YDUFC	ydufc	Why do you fucking care?

UPPERCASE	LOWERCASE	MEANING
YDUWTK	yduwtk	Why do you want to know?
YE	ye	yes, yeah
YE	ye	you
YEA	yea	yeah, yes
YEAP	yeap	yes
YEH	yeh	yes
YELLO	yello	hello
YELLOW BONE	yellow bone	light-skinned black woman
YEP	yep	yes
YER	yer	yes
YER	yer	you're
YER	yer	your
YERMOM	yermom	your mother
YERP	yerp	yes, what's up, OK
YESH	yesh	yes
YEW	yew	you
YEY	yey	same as yay
YEYO	yeyo	cocaine
YEZZER	yezzer	yes, sir
YF	yf	your friend
YFB	yfb	You fucking bastard.
YFG	yfg	You're fucking gay. (homosexual slur/derogatory)
YFI	yfi	You fucking idiot.
YFW	yfw	You're fucking welcome.
YFW	yfw	your face when...
YG	yg	young gangster
YG	yg	young gentleman
YGBK	ygbk	You gotta be kidding.
YGBSM	ygbsm	You gotta be shitting me.
YGG	ygg	You go, girl.
YGH	ygh	You go, honey.
YGI	ygi	You got it?
YGM	ygm	You get me?
YGM	ygm	You've got mail.
YGP	ygp	You got punked!
YGP	ygp	You got pwned!
YGPM	ygpm	You've got a private message.
YGPM	ygpm	You've got private message.
YGTBFKM	ygtbfkm	You've got to be fucking kidding me.
YGTBK	ygtbk	You've got to be kidding.
YGTBKM	ygtbkm	You got to be kidding me.
YGTBSM	ygtbsm	You've got to be shitting me.
YGTSR	ygtsr	You got that shit right.
YH	yh	yeah
YHBT	yhbt	You have been trolled.
YHBW	yhbw	You have been warned.
YHEW	yhew	you
YHF	yhf	You have failed.
YHGASP	yhgasp	You have got a serious problem.
YHGTBSM	yhgtbsm	You have got to be shitting me.
YHL	yhl	You have lost.
YHM	yhm	You have mail.
YHPM	yhpm	You have a private message.

UPPERCASE	LOWERCASE	MEANING
YHTBT	yhtbt	You had to be there.
YHU	yhu	you
YID	yid	yes, I do
YIKES	yikes	expression of shock or surprise
YIM	yim	Yahoo! Instant Messenger
YINS	yins	you guys, you all
YITB	yitb	yours in the bond
YIU	yiu	Yes, I understand
YIWTGO	yiwtgo	Yes, I want to go private.
YJLTG	yjltg	you just lost the game.
YK	yk	you kidding
YKI	yki	You know it.
YKIMS	ykims	You know it makes sense.
YKISA	ykisa	your knight in shining armor
YKM	ykm	You're kidding me.
YKM	ykm	You're killing me.
YKN	ykn	You know nothing.
YKW	ykw	You know who, you know what.
YKWIM	ykwim	You know what I mean.
YKWIS	ykwis	You know what I'm saying?
YKWYA	ykwya	You know who you are.
YKWYCD	ykwycd	You know what you can do.
YKYLM	ykylm	You know you love me.
YKYWYWM	ykywywm	You know you wish you were me.
YL	yl	young lady
YLB	ylb	You little bitch.
YLM	ylm	You love me?
YM	ym	Yahoo! Messenger
YM	ym	your mom
YMBJ	ymbj	you must be joking
YMBKM	ymbkm	you must be kidding me
YMCMB	ymcmb	Young Money and Cash Money Billionaires
YME	yme	Why me?
YMFP	ymfp	your most favorite person
YMG2C	ymg2c	Your mom goes to college.
YMGTC	ymgtc	Your mom goes to college.
YMIAW	ymiaw	Your mom is a whore.
YMISLIDI	ymislidi	You make it sound like I did it.
YMMD	ymmd	You made my day.
YMMS	ymms	You make me smile.
YMMV	ymmv	Your mileage may vary.
YMW	ymw	You're most welcome.
YN	yn	crossed fingers (MSN)
YN	yn	why not
YNG	yng	young
YNK	ynk	you never know
YNM	ynm	yes, no, maybe
YNT	ynt	Why not?
YNW	ynw	You know what?
YNWA	ynwa	You'll never walk alone.
YO	yo	hi
YO	yo	years old/year old
YO	yo	your
YOB	yob	hooligan, thug

UPPERCASE	LOWERCASE	MEANING
YOKED	yoked	well built, muscular, ripped
YOLO	yolo	you only live once.
YOMANK	yomank	You owe me a new keyboard.
YOMB	yomb	you owe me big.
YOO	yoo	you
YOOH	yooh	you
YOR	yor	your
YOUNGIN	youngin	young person
YOUNS	youns	you guys, you all
YOUS	yous	you, you guys
YOUSE	youse	you (plural)
YOY	yoy	why oh why
YOYO	yoyo	You're on your own.
YP	yp	yes, please
YP	yp	your problem
YPMF	ypmf	you pissed me off.
YPMO	ypmo	you piss me off.
YPOM	ypom	Your place or mine?
YQ	yq	I like you.
YQW	yqw	You're quite welcome.
YR	yr	yeah, right
YR	yr	year
YR	yr	your
YRBK	yrbk	yearbook
YRG	yrg	You are good!
YRMS	yrms	You rock my socks.
YRS	yrs	years
YRSAF	yrsaf	You are such a fool.
YRSM	yrsm	You really scare me.
YRSS	yrss	You are so sexy.
YRU	yru	Why are you?
YRUBM	yrubm	Why are you bugging me?
YRUSM	yrusm	Why are you so mean?
YRYOCC	yryocc	You're running your own cuckoo clock.
YS	ys	You suck.
YSA	ysa	You suck ass.
YSAL	ysal	You suck at life.
YSATI	ysati	You suck at the Internet.
YSF	ysf	You stupid fuck.
YSI	ysi	You stupid idiot.
YSIC	ysic	Why should I care?
YSIC	ysic	your sister in Christ
YSITM	ysitm	Your shirt is too small.
YSK	ysk	You should know.
YSL	ysl	Yves Saint Laurent
YSLS	ysls	You smell like shit.
YSM	ysm	You scare me.
YSMTU	ysmtu	You so made that up.
YSOAB	ysoab	You son of a bitch.
YSS	yss	You stupid shit.
YSS	yss	You suck severely.
YSWNT	yswnt	Why sleep when not tired?
YSYD	ysyd	yeah, sure you do
YT	yt	You there?

UPPERCASE	LOWERCASE	MEANING
YT	yt	You think?
YTB	ytb	You're the best.
YTB	ytb	youth talk back
YTD	ytd	year to date
YTF	ytf	Why the fuck?
YTFWUDT	ytfwudt	Why the fuck would you do that?
YTG	ytg	You're the greatest.
YTHWUDT	ythwudt	Why the hell would you do that?
YTIS	ytis	You think I'm special?
YTM	ytm	You tell me.
YTM	ytm	You're the man.
YTMND	ytmnd	*You're the Man Now, Dog* (website)
YTTL	yttl	You take too long.
YTTM	yttm	You talk too much.
YTY	yty	Why, thank you.
YU	yu	you
YUA	yua	you ugly ass
YUCK	yuck	expression of disgust
YUCKY	yucky	disgusting, gross
YUH	yuh	yes
YUH	yuh	you
YUM	yum	said when something tastes good or is attractive
YUMMY MUMMY	yummy mummy	attractive mother
YUO	yuo	you
YUP	yup	yes
YUPPERZ	yupperz	yes
YUPPIE	yuppie	young urban professional
YUR	yur	your
YUS	yus	yes
YUST	yust	Why you say that?
YVFW	yvfw	you're very fucking welcome
YVW	yvw	you're very welcome
YW	yw	you're welcome
YWAPOM	ywapom	You want a piece of me?
YWCA	ywca	Young Women's Christian Association
YWHNB	ywhnb	yes, we have no bananas
YWHOL	ywhol	yelling "woo-hoo" out loud
YWIA	ywia	you're welcome in advance
YWIC	ywic	Why would I care?
YWIMC	ywimc	Your wish is my command.
YWS	yws	you want sex
YWSYLS	ywsyls	You win some, you lose some.
YWU	ywu	Yo, waz up?
YWUD	ywud	Yo, what's up, dude?
YWVM	ywvm	You're welcome very much.
YWYWM	ywywm	You wish you were me.
YYSW	yysw	Yeah, yeah, sure, whatever.
Z	z	said
Z	z	zero
Z%	z%	zoo
Z'OMG	z'omg	oh my god
Z0MG	z0mg	oh my god
ZA	za	pizza

UPPERCASE	LOWERCASE	MEANING
ZAIN	zain	beautiful (Arabic)
ZECH	zech	energy, life
ZEX	zex	sex
ZH	zh	sleeping hour
ZH	zh	zero hour
ZIF	zif	Zero-Insertion Force
ZIG	zig	cigarette
ZIG ZAG	zig zag	cigarette paper
ZIMBO	zimbo	person from Zimbabwe (ethnic slur/derogatory)
ZING	zing	owned
ZIP	zip	ounce of marijuana
ZOMB	zomb	zombie
ZOMFG	zomfg	oh my fucking god
ZOMFG	zomfg	OMFG (hit z instead of Shift key)
ZOMG	zomg	(same as "omg")
ZOMGZORRZ	zomgzorrz	oh, my god
ZONKED	zonked	very tired or inebriated
ZOOT	zoot	spiff, joint
ZOOT	zoot	woo-hoo
ZOOTED	zooted	high on drugs
ZOT	zot	zero tolerance
ZPPRHEAD	zpprhead	zipperhead (Asian person · ethnic slur/derogatory)
ZT	zt	zoo tycoon
ZUP	zup	What's up?
ZUT	zut	damn it (French)
ZZZ	zzz	sleepy, bored, or tired